The B2B E-commerce Handbook

the B2B e-commerce handbook

How to transform your business-to-business global marketing strategy

Matt Haig

KOGAN PAGE

This book has been endorsed by the Institute of Directors.

The endorsement is given to selected Kogan Page books which the IoD recognises as being of specific interest to its members and providing them with up-to-date, informative and practical resources for creating business success. Kogan Page books endorsed by the IoD represent the most authoritative guidance available on a wide range of subjects including management, finance, marketing, training and HR.

The views expressed in this book are those of the author and are not necessarily the same as those of the Institute of Directors.

First published in 2001

Kogan Page Limited
120 Pentonville Road
London
N1 9JN
UK

Kogan US
22 Broad Street
Milford
CT 06460
USA

British Library Cataloguing in Publication Data

A CIP record for this book is available from the British Library.

ISBN 0 7494 3577 1

Typeset by Saxon Graphics Ltd, Derby
Printed and bound in Great Britain by Clays Ltd, St Ives plc

Contents

List of figures

Preface

The Internet's ability to reinvent and reorganize markets is most apparent in the business-to-business (B2B) sector. In fact, B2B is in many ways more in tune with the nature of the Web than any other area of online commerce.

In the light of this it is perhaps unsurprising that, when compared to the roller coaster ride experienced by many in the business-to-consumer (B2C) sector, B2B has emerged as the most solid and fertile area of e-marketing.

While consumer spending on the Internet remains unpredictable, business transactions are increasing at a constant rate. Furthermore, B2B e-marketplaces are highlighting the fact that the Internet is not just a new place to do business, but constitutes a whole new method and model for commerce. While this inevitably involves a process of relearning, the rewards for marketers willing to adapt to this radically new environment can make this task more than worthwhile.

About this book

This book is intended to provide anyone with an active interest in e-business with an insight into B2B e-marketing. By emphasizing the broad nature of B2B, it explains how almost any online company can incorporate a business-to-business component. While *the B2B e-commerce handbook* offers practical guidelines for success on the Web, these guidelines are placed in context and incorporated alongside real case studies. In particular, this book will help you to:

- learn from successful companies;
- understand why B2B is the most significant area of the new economy;
- market your business in a B2B e-marketplace;
- create a B2B Web site;
- participate in online business auctions;
- build a B2B brand;
- use search engines as a marketing tool;
- advertise your site to target business audiences;
- set up an affiliate scheme;
- find useful B2B Web sites in the B2B e-commerce handbook directory;

- share information via Intranets and Extranets;
- target prospects through e-mail marketing;
- evaluate developments influencing the future of B2B and e-business in general.

Ultimately, this book aims to provide a user-friendly introduction to the area of e-business and marketing, which, more than any other, really does seem built to last.

one

B2B basics

The aim of this first chapter is to provide an overview of B2B e-commerce as a whole, as well as to have a look at those factors most likely to shape its development. This is intended to place this book and its subject in a suitable context, and arm the e-marketer with an understanding, not only of what activities to pursue, but also the reasons why they should pursue them.

Defining B2B

B2B, or more specifically business-to-business e-commerce, is the umbrella term used to refer to transactions between businesses conducted online, and the business networks and supply chains that make these transactions possible. While business-to-business activity has always taken place, the Internet brings with it a new B2B framework. B2B companies no longer need to depend on the traditional one-to-one model for business transactions.

As well as enabling vendors (such as Dell Computers) to sell directly from their own e-commerce Web sites, the Internet has led to more sophisticated online marketplaces where a multitude of buyers and sellers are brought together in one place. These marketplaces, in theory at least, widen the spectrum of buyers *and* lower prices, as well as make the process of buying and selling much more convenient.

B2B marketplaces are referred to as either 'vertical' or 'horizontal'. Vertical B2B marketplaces aim to secure a large share of the transactions relating to a particular industry (eg automotive). Horizontal marketplaces on the other hand aim to serve a wide variety of transactions in order to function as a one-stop shop for small businesses. Both vertical and horizontal marketplaces work on a 'many-to-many' basis and create vast networks of buyers and sellers.

Between the one-to-one and many-to-many models there are, predictably, a number of other B2B frameworks such as catalogue sites (or 'distribution portals'),which write to suppliers and aggregate catalogues to attract a large audience, and auction sites where suppliers gather to bid on the business of a major buyer.

Typically, B2B sites are sustained via member subscription or transaction fees as well as other supplementary revenue channels such as advertising. The most active online B2B markets include automotive, computing and electronics, chemicals, paper and office products, transport and travel utilities and construction. Put simply, the benefits of B2B e-commerce are as follows:

- *Choice*. B2B technologies and marketplaces provide companies with a greater choice of trading partners, suppliers and transport logistics. This, in turn, leads to greater flexibility.
- *Speed*. B2B marketplaces help to reduce the time it takes to get a product or service to market, and help business decision-makers move faster. In addition, it enables businesses to make purchases quicker.
- *Streamlining*. The Internet helps business-to-business operators cut down their paperwork, eliminate bureaucratic systems and strengthen inventory control, leading to increased efficiency and productivity.
- *Response*. As Alan Haywood of Boston Consulting Group (BCG) Systems states, 'By changing the way the business process interacts with the other companies in the supply and production chain, B2B allows users to view and react to events as they unfold, responding instantly to unforeseen problems and unfolding opportunities.'

B2B statistics and estimates

- The B2B sector currently accounts for over half of total e-commerce spending, but will grow to 87 per cent of total e-commerce by 2004 (eMarketer Report 2001).
- Forrester Research predicts that the worldwide B2B market will reach $1.7 trillion in size by 2003 as both large and small companies shift to Web-based procurement of goods and services. They also predict that business-to-consumer (B2C) e-commerce revenues will reach only $108 billion.

- Covisint, the B2B automotive exchange created by Ford, General Motors and Daimler Chrysler, made $352 million in trade during the period October–December 2000.
- According to the Boston Consulting Group, the industries that stand to gain the most in B2B e-commerce over the next few years are retail, motor vehicles, shipping, industrial equipment, high tech and government.
- In 2000 B2B transactions over the Internet exceeded $433 billion, which constitutes an almost 200 per cent increase over 1999 sales.
- Savings to consumers (at the end of the chain), as a result of B2B e-commerce, are estimated to be $1 trillion by 2010.
- BCG predicts that by 2004, B2B e-commerce will bring about productivity gains equivalent to 1–2 per cent of sales. By 2010 that figure could grow to 6 per cent.
- Currently, 95 per cent of offline B2B purchases are made between buyers and sellers who have done business together before. Jupiter Research estimates that eventually 85 per cent of online B2B will be done within an established relationship.

B2B opinions

As it is one of the most hotly disputed areas of e-commerce, most Internet commentators have an opinion on B2B. Here is a selection of quotes from some of the leading e-commerce and e-marketing pundits on the Web, to give a flavour of the widely divergent attitudes towards the subject:

> Business-to-business is the stuff that makes everything run. . . business-to-business transactions will far surpass business-to-consumer deals and dwarf giants like eBay and Amazon.com in revenue and sales.
>
> *Varda Lief*, senior analyst, Forrester

> B2B is the iceberg waiting to emerge. Most people understand the business-to-consumer market because they are consumers themselves. . . With business-to-business, though, unless you are entrenched in that industry and really understand that market

segment, you are not going to appreciate how it's revolutionizing that business.

Steve Jurvetson, partner, Venture-Capital firm Draper Fisher Jurvetson

The true value in B2B is when it is i-to-i, that is, industry to industry.

Moses Ma, founder, BusinessBots

What you see today are a lot of technology companies or single-focused verticals that are declaring war on the old way of doing business. . . Each of these companies claims that it is going to change forever how purchases occur. From my point of view, that's like asking to be shot with the arrows – before they pour the hot oil on you.

Mark Walsh, CEO and president, VerticalNet

This business-to-consumer thing is kind of cute, but the real thing is going to be business-to-business.

Sergio Zyman, former head marketer of Coca-Cola and marketing author

B2B is grimy and dirty, but you can make a lot of money at it.

Walter Buckley, founder, Internet Capital Group

B2B is outside the scope of interest to most people.

Keith Regan, E-Commerce Times, March 2001

Most of the value created by B2B e-commerce will be captured by the buyers and sellers that particpate in e-marketplaces.

Paul Orlander, vice-president, Boston Consulting Group

In this tough economic climate, where it is more difficult to increase sales, we believe businesses will turn to cost-saving measures such as e-procurement to stretch their dollars as far as they can.

Lauren Shu, e-business research director, Gartner Research

The market for existing customers will be the bigger opportunity for B2B sellers because they have already established trust with buyers – many of whom are waiting for their favoured vendors to move online. The market for new customers is smaller but will grow over time, largely because Internet search capabilities will assist buyers in finding vendors.

Jean Gabriel Henry, analyst, Jupiter Media Matrix

Ultimately, the B2B market will be characterized by a handful of e-marketplace giants that serve the overall needs of an industry and scores of niche players serving a special segment within an industry or providing a specialized function across many industries.

Matt Holland, vice-president, Boston Consulting Group

General guidelines

Before examining the specifics of B2B e-marketing, it is important to emphasize the broad guidelines to follow when conducting your online marketing activity. These guidelines, explored below, need to be taken on board at the outset in order to achieve your long-term goals.

Know your customers

Needless to say, knowledge of who your customers are will help you to target them more effectively. By keeping track of their behaviour at your site and by finding out information via online order forms, you will be able to develop your Internet activity around your customers. However, it is essential for B2B companies not to abuse this knowledge. For instance, if customer e-mail addresses are sold to mailing list companies, your customers will not appreciate the increase in 'spam' messages they receive. Likewise, your company should not send marketing messages via e-mail to customers who haven't asked to receive them.

Think beyond the desktop

As the mobile Internet plays an ever more significant role within businesses, it is becoming increasingly important for B2B companies to accommodate m-business (mobile business) facilities. Indeed the mobile Internet is arguably of more relevance to B2B companies than it is to their B2C counterparts. In particular, the mobile Internet is helping to make auctions more effective, as it offers customers the chance of placing bids at any time and anywhere. Owing to the time-sensitive nature of B2B, auctions offering a mobile Internet option clearly make the auctioning process more convenient for everyone involved.

So-called third-generation or 3G wireless networks, offering high-speed mobile Internet connectivity, real-time video, and streaming audio, look set to provide even more mobile challenges and opportunities for B2B companies.

Embrace e-mail

Just as B2B e-marketers need to think beyond the desktop, they also need to think beyond the World Wide Web as e-mail remains the most popular Internet application. Furthermore, it has become more widely used than other communications methods on both sides of the Atlantic. By the year 2000 Roper Starch Worldwide could claim that e-mail was preferred by 48.5 per cent as the primary communications vehicle, compared with 39 per cent for the telephone and 3.5 per cent for traditional (or 'snail') mail. E-mail can help you build up long-term relations with customers as it enables you to make contact on a regular basis. By offering subscriptions to e-newsletters and other material relevant to your target audience, you will be able to build up a useful e-mailing list of companies. However, it is always important to abide by the rules of 'permission marketing'. In other words, you must always have companies' express permission before sending them any bulk e-mails.

As well as for mass mailings such as e-newsletters, e-mail should also be used for following up online enquiries and orders. For instance, if a company is ordering a product via your Web site it should receive an automated e-mail confirmation once its order has been placed. If there are any problems that occur prior to delivery, a personalized e-mail message should be sent to inform the customer of the problem as well as the action being taken to amend it.

Eliminate the weakest link

As B2B e-commerce and e-marketing generally depend on a network of businesses (distributors, resellers, service partners, retailers etc), it is vital for every business within the network to know exactly how the other businesses are performing. After all, the power of each network can only be as strong as its weakest link. As ClickZ columnist Philip Say advises, 'Pruning non-productive business relationships will improve the health of your organization and enable you to focus on your most profitable channels.'

Increase the 'lifetime value' of your customers

A few years ago the emphasis for most e-commerce companies was on getting as many customers as possible, by making sure as broad a range of people knew about their sites. However, this approach led to excessive over-spending and was one of the factors that contributed to the dot.com slump in 2000. The focus for both B2B and B2C companies is now on increasing the 'lifetime value' of existing customers, rather than on aggressively targeting new audiences. After all, it generally costs less to secure a consecutive sale than it does to win over a first-time customer. Furthermore, it is a lot easier to develop a product or service for an existing base of customers than it is to launch new services into a completely new market. Investing in fulfilment and the service offered to other businesses is therefore essential in order to ensure the long-term survival of any B2B operation.

Develop an e-CRM strategy

Following on from the last point, e-CRM refers to electronic customer relationship management, and is rapidly becoming one of the most significant areas of e-marketing. The reason for this is that while a lot of online marketing is concerned with promotional activity (ie generating awareness to win new customers), e-CRM is about customer retention.

As companies have started to realize that keeping hold of existing customers is a more cost-effective strategy than constantly trying to acquire new ones, a number of new e-CRM software products have appeared in order to meet this new demand. Indeed, according to Gartner Dataquest, the e-CRM market is one of the fastest developing areas in application software, with a growth rate of 26 per cent annually and worldwide expenditures expected to reach $15 billion by 2004.

However, e-CRM is about more than investing in software, it is about developing a customer-centric strategy, which ensures first-time buyers are more than happy to return.

Aim for dexterity

In an ever-shifting, unstable business environment B2B companies must constantly challenge their own thinking. Ultimately, companies wishing to stay in the 'comfort zone' are not going to be around for long. Stagnation is therefore the ultimate threat to a B2B business, while the ability to reinvent the organization has become the main goal. As Peter Solvik, senior vice-president and chief information officer of Cisco Systems, has put it, 'The new economy is about reinventing how business is conducted – in every single job, in every single corporation. There's a revolution going on, and we have to rethink every single relationship within the company and beyond.' Ultimately, companies need to focus less on particular products or specific markets, and more on organizational readiness. Instead of aiming solely for growth, the ability to adapt is now all-important.

Measure results

Evaluating results is one of the most complex, but also one of the most important, of all tasks facing B2B e-businesses. Increasingly B2B companies are having to quantify their own, and their product and service performance. According to Philip Say, improving a relevant set of performance metrics for your customers should be 'the central objective of your business'. He adds that 'incentive-based compensation or pricing can signal very clearly to customers that your company is willing to enter a true partnership and share risk mutually'.

Concentrate on service

Customer service isn't simply something business-to-consumer companies have to worry about. The Internet has raised customer-service expectations in every sector. Faced with a growing amount of choice, more information and 24-hour access to online companies, both business and consumer customers have higher expectations of service than they did in the pre-Internet era. One of the new demands on B2B companies is that of operating in 'real time'. In a book called *Real Time: Preparing for the Age of the Never Satisfied Customer*, Regis McKenna explains how companies need to compress time in order to meet the demands of the Internet. For instance, companies will need to be able to provide an immediate, relevant response to any online request. Furthermore, the Internet has blurred the line between products and services, with the rise in personalization and 'information products'. Even where companies are selling a uniform product, the Internet enables them to tailor the surrounding experience in line with customer requirements.

In an environment where search engine functions enable customers to locate the cheapest products in seconds and where intermediaries (the so-called infomediary services) allow buyers to determine prices, customer service becomes the key point of difference.

Exploit the power of networks

According to Metcalfe's Law (named after Robert Metcalfe, the founder of 3Com Corporation), the value of a network increases dramatically with each additional user. In fact, the network's value is the square of the number of its users. This 'network effect' means that companies can target networked communities on the Web and expect awareness of their product/service/site to increase exponentially. Furthermore, it also means that companies can get potential customers to market products and services among themselves, within networked business communities. Of course, the flipside of this is that if an individual or business within the network disagrees with your marketing message, they too have a wider platform from which to express their views.

A level playing field

Inma Martinez, founder of software development company Escape Velocity, is one of many commentators to note the levelling and inverting tendencies of the Internet: 'The Internet is a magical box that makes teeny companies look enormous. Your company could comprise just three guys and you could build a fantastic Web site that looks like it could kill the competition. On the other hand, your company could be an enormous corporation with a lot of muscle but a horrible Web site.'

However, while the Internet provides the appearance of a level playing field for the B2B sector, there are plenty of instances of excessive spending. Paul Allen's $100-million investment in

Oxygen Media, the $1.7 billion DoubleClick paid for Abacus Direct, and Jake Winebaum's decision to buy the Business.com domain name for $7.5 million are just some of the more extreme examples of the phenomenal sums spent in order to break into the B2B market.

Although there are companies willing to spend big money on consolidating their B2B activity, there is now a renewed focus on cost-saving strategies. The fact is that the major B2B players have stood back and watched B2C companies spend millions on carving out their market share, only to find themselves back where they started. The emphasis now, in both the B2C and B2B arenas, is on learning to do more with less.

The B2B future

Most e-business experts agree that the B2B e-commerce sector will continue to grow over the next few years as more and more B2C companies move into B2B markets. Although all the major e-market research companies disagree over exactly how fast the sector is going to develop, all agree that the long-term future looks bright.

Here are their predictions for the worldwide growth of B2B e-commerce for the 2001–2004 period (in billions):

Table 1.1 B2B e-commerce growth predictions for 2001–2004

	2001	2002	2003	2004
eMarketer	$449	$841	$1,542	$2,775
Forrester	$1,138	$2,061	$3,694	$6,335
Gartner	$953	$2,180	$3,950	$7,290
Goldman Sachs	$740	$1,304	$2,088	$3,201
Ovum	$345	$543	$858	$1,400

Web marketplaces

As well as Web sites selling their own products direct to other businesses there are online marketplaces that bring many business buyers and sellers together. Although their exact nature can vary considerably, there are essentially three types of Web-based B2B marketplaces – online catalogues, auctions and exchanges.

Online catalogues

Online catalogues simply collect the catalogue data of every supplier in a particular industry and place it on one central Web resource. Catalogues are important to companies for marketing purposes because they are one of the main ways to distribute product and service information to public marketplaces and private exchanges (see below). B2B catalogue sites are sometimes referred to as procurement portals.

Auctions

Auctions follow the catalogue format to an extent, but they enable more interactivity. Specifically, they provide a mechanism to negotiate prices and bid for products and services. Generally speaking, Web-based B2B auctions reverse the traditional auction formula where the aim is to help the seller get the best price. Instead, B2B Web auctions typically involve suppliers competing with each other by bidding down the price of their product/service. This inevitably benefits the buyer as, instead of having to bid higher for a particular service or product, they can wait till the suppliers have bid themselves down to a reasonable price. Typically, online auctions require companies to follow a registration process in order to take part. During this process, users have to provide their credit card information, shipping preferences, as well as agree to the site's code of conduct. Some sites (such as Business-Auctions.com) also manage secure auctions that restrict potential bidders to specific firms or individuals.

Exchanges

The B2B exchange enables suppliers, buyers and intermediaries to come together and offer products/services to each other according to set criteria. B2B Web exchanges provide constant price adjustments in line with fluctuations of supply and demand. The growing popularity of exchanges has led to a new buzz acronym – E2E – standing for exchange-to-exchange e-commerce, where buyers and sellers conduct transactions not only within exchanges, but also between them. Although exchange-to-exchange e-commerce initially seems to complicate the B2B environment, it does have some obvious advantages. The main benefit is that sellers can get higher prices for their products/services by putting them on various sites simultaneously.

According to Peter Henig in a *Red Herring* magazine article on the subject of B2B exchanges, the best ones are places 'where market participants can make spot purchases, auction off goods, obtain letters of credit, contract for logistics and distribution, monitor daily price and order flow, and even engage in the design and specification process peculiar to specific industry manufacturers'.

B2B exchanges operate according to criteria set either by the owner or by the users of the exchange. One of the most well known examples of a B2B exchange is Covisint, which has combined the electronic marketplaces of the world's largest vehicle makers. The online marketplace for components, suppliers, services and information has brought together Ford, General Motors, Daimler Chrysler and other automotive giants. GlobalNetXchange (GNX), a B2B exchange backed by Carrefour of France, Sears of the US and the UK's J Sainsbury (among others) is another high-profile, global example. Although B2B exchanges can be very effective they require industry support and considerable investment to survive in the long term.

It should be noted that these types of B2B marketplaces are not mutually exclusive. For instance, many B2B exchanges enable buyers and sellers to bid for and auction services/products.

Types of online exchange

It is becoming increasingly impossible to place B2B exchanges in one single category. Owing to this growing complexity, in 2000 eMarketer came up with new sub-categories to distinguish between exchanges that are run by third parties, industry consortia, and private companies.

Table 1.2 The three primary business models for online exchanges

	Description	**Example**
1. Third-party exchange	exchange is owned and operated by a third party that is not considered formally to be a trading partner, often a B2B startup	Chemdex
2. Consortia-led exchange	exchange ownership is shared between industry leaders and a technology partner	GM/Daimler Chrysler/ Ford exchange, Covisint
3. Private/proprietary exchange	Exchange is owned and operated by a single large firm	Wal-Mart's Retail Link

Source: eMarketer 2000

Industry marketplaces

Whichever industry you are in, there is likely to be an online B2B marketplace centred on it. One of the most famous industry marketplaces is Covisint, the automotive exchange created by Ford, General Motors and Daimler Chrysler.

Other major industry marketplaces include Chemdex online for the pharmaceutical industry (which includes SmithKline Beecham, and Bristol-Myers, Squibb) and Altrade, which offers wholesale energy trading of natural gas, crude oil, natural gas liquids and power.

B2B infomediaries

As well as sites enabling B2B companies to make monetary transactions with each other, there are also a number of sites serving to provide essential information. Their aim is to bring together as much customizable business information as possible, in order to facilitate B2B activity. Although they have a long way to go, infomediaries are already providing useful and wide-ranging services. For instance, VerticalNet.com provides relevant information relating to over 50 industries and uses customization tools to tailor its content.

It is also worth noting that many B2B e-commerce sites that traditionally concentrated on transactions online are now acting as portal or infomediary sites in order to attract a higher number of visitors.

Peer-to-peer

The development of peer-to-peer (P2P) technology (which so far has been mostly associated with music file-swapping and services such as Napster, Gnutella and MP3) will revolutionize the capabilities of B2B infomediaries, as it will enable virtually any piece of business information stored on a computer (word documents, e-mail messages etc) to form part of a searchable database. Obviously, companies will need to volunteer to put this sort of information within a peer-to-peer network, but as examples in the US already show, companies are more than willing to put information forward if it means they are able to gain significant data from other businesses.

The essence of peer-to-peer networking is the ability to share information or computer resources among all computers linked to a network without reference to a central server. As Louise Kehoe stated in a *Financial Times* article on the subject: 'Napster used the technology to enable users to share music files but file-sharing may be applicable to market reports, memos and other documents.'

Indeed, peer-to-peer has started to be recognized as a way to enable employees and even compatible businesses to access the multitude of files stored on computers throughout a company.

Groove Networks is possibly the most famous example of peer-to-peer B2B network. Established by Ray Ozzie, the software genius behind Lotus Notes, Groove Networks utilizes peer-to-peer in order to 'help businesses achieve a greater "return on connection" from relationships with customers, vendors and partners'. The Groove project has been funded by Intel Capital and has achieved weighty endorsement from Microsoft. Bill Gates has declared that Groove constitutes 'a deep and innovative software product that is a great indicator of where the Internet is going'. Furthermore, the Gartner Group, one of the leading US Internet market research firms, has predicted that 30 per cent of all US corporations (both B2B and B2C) will experiment with P2P by 2003.

B2B and increased productivity

Although the most famous Web names – Amazon, Yahoo!, AOL, ebay – are mainly (but not solely) focused on the consumer market, many analysts are predicting that B2B e-commerce will eventually eclipse its B2C counterpart. For instance, Deloitte predicts that B2B sales will be six times as large as the business-to-consumer market by 2004.

One of the main reasons for the rapid growth of B2B is the promise of increased productivity. In the US, New York's Federal Reserve Bank has anticipated that higher productivity and lower prices are going to be symptomatic of B2B growth. The joint head of global e-commerce at the Boston Consulting Group supports this view by claiming that B2B e-commerce will increase productivity by 9 per cent by 2005. A Goldman Sachs 2001 report went even further by concluding that B2B e-commerce could cut processing costs by over 20 per cent in certain industries, and that total business costs overall could fall by 12.5 per cent.

Whether these figures prove accurate or not, there can be no denying that in sectors where B2B e-commerce has well and truly taken off (such as the automotive industry), overheads have been lowered, profits have increased and prices have remained steady.

B2B2C (and back again)

Although they are often viewed as mutually exclusive, business and consumer markets are clearly interdependent and there is a manifest overlap between B2B and B2C. After all, the consumer is nearly always at the end of the chain no matter how much B2B activity occurs along the way.

It is also interesting to observe how many B2C companies are switching to or expanding into B2B. For instance, the consumer-focused auction site eBay now hosts the eBay Business Exchange aimed at the small business market. Not to be outdone, Yahoo! has launched its own B2B service, Yahoo! Industry Marketplaces, designed to be a one-stop business-to-business destination for information and services that enable industry professionals to research products, find the latest industry news and make purchasing decisions. The Industry Marketplaces are centred on three areas: electronics, IT software and IT hardware. That Yahoo! clearly believes that B2B is a natural component of its service is evidenced in the press release that announced the arrival of its Industry Marketplaces service. The release stated that 'Yahoo! is the number one destination site for at work users with 67.5 per cent work reach, and 18.4 million business purchase decision-makers visit Yahoo!.'

However, it is not just the Internet consumer giants who are venturing into business-to-business markets. Many successful, smaller-scale B2C online companies have crossed over into B2B. For instance, HotHotHot.com, the site that since 1994 has sold hot chilli sauce via the Internet, has successfully targeted the business market to remain on top of a now overcrowded niche market. HotHotHot.com's sales to other distributors, stores and restaurants now account for 60 per cent of total revenue, keeping the site's gross profit margins above the 40 per cent mark. Therefore, on every level, there are companies already proving that B2B and B2C activity can be compatible and even integrated within the same site.

Case study: Enron

Although it is not as internationally renowned as Yahoo! and other major e-commerce players, Enron boasts one of the largest e-commerce platforms in the world.

Enron trades commodities such as natural gas, electricity, and bandwidth to corporate customers. Unlike e-marketplaces that act as impartial intermediaries for buyers and vendors, Enron's e-marketplaces create a benchmark product at a set price. The company acts as a 'counterparty' in each trade, guaranteeing that commodities purchased on its site are delivered at the price and conditions agreed upon. It then makes money on the difference between what it pays for a commodity and what it sells it for.

Since it started in 1999 the company has carried out transactions totalling $1.5 billion per day over the Web (which now counts for over half of all the company's transactions). The Web has enabled Enron to tailor or 'structure' commodities around individual buyers' needs.

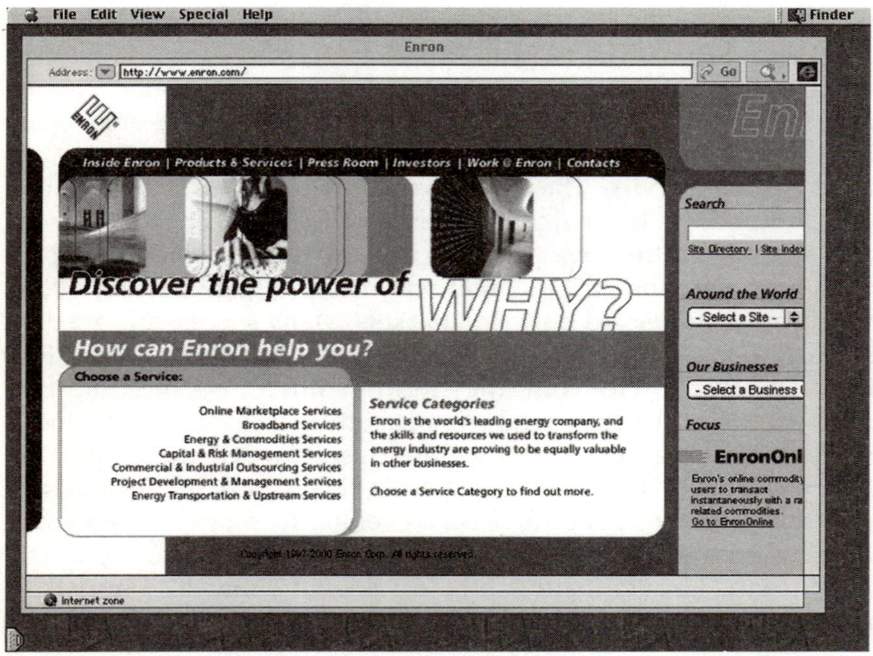

Figure 1.1 Enron: one of the largest players in the worldwide B2B arena

Summary

Although its exact future cannot be predicted, there is no doubt that B2B e-commerce is here to stay. Indeed, as many business-to-consumer operators start to worry about their long-term survival, more and more companies are 'crossing over' into the business market. However, as the rest of this book will show, marketing to a business audience is significantly different from targeting consumers. Certainly for those who believe marketing is solely about spending excessive amounts on advertising campaigns and consolidating a brand identity, there is a lot of rethinking that needs to be done.

two

Understanding the new economy

The Internet is more than just another sales channel or marketing medium, it is also an entirely new business model. In order for B2B e-marketing to be successful it is therefore essential to appreciate the sea-change the Internet is bringing about. By taking a closer look, it soon becomes apparent that, while the media hype has surrounded the dot.com disasters in the B2C arena, the real story concerns the way the Internet has changed the business and consumer markets almost beyond recognition. Indeed, B2B e-commerce itself represents an entirely new game plan for the e-marketer to consider.

Key characteristics

In order to maximize the chances of achieving your e-marketing objectives, it is important to highlight some of the key characteristics and emerging developments associated with the new economy. This will help you to understand what will and will not work, as well as to appreciate the new opportunities and threats B2B companies are faced with. Here are some of the main characteristics to consider:

- *Low barriers to entry*. The Internet has helped small companies enter long established markets that had previously been impossible to break into. In every online market agility has become as (if not more) important as size.
- *Customer power*. On the Internet the supply chain is transformed into a demand chain as the customer is able to wield all power.

Robert Baldock's prediction (made in his book *The Last Days of the Giants?)* that 'we are entering a buyer driven era, an era in which the customer will not just be a king, but a dictator', has already been proved accurate. It is also already clear that this applies equally to both B2B and B2C sectors. The time when companies could second-guess the demands of their customers is over.

- *Hyper time*. The Internet has accelerated the progression of market cycles and enables businesses to develop faster than they can offline.
- *Soft products*. As the new economy has progressed, we have witnessed a growth in 'soft' (ie intangible) products. Ideas, information and digitizable products are starting to replace hard (ie physical) goods.
- *Customization*. The interactive nature of the Internet enables products, services and content to be customized towards the interests of each particular business buyer or site visitor.
- *Information overload*. The fact that almost any individual or organization can establish a Web presence means that people are now faced with a deluge of online information. Companies that are able to act as 'infomediaries', helping users gather, filter and prioritize Web-based information, are going to have a head start within the B2B sector.
- *The 'death of distance'*. Frances Cairncross, a senior editor at the *Economist*, coined the phrase 'the death of distance' to describe the way in which the Internet can help to eliminate geographical restraints. In a 1995 article on telecommunications she famously predicted that 'the death of distance as a determinant of the cost of communications will probably be the single most important economic force shaping society in the first half of the next century'.
- *Connectivity*. In cyberspace individuals and organizations are more connected than they are offline. The rise in networked markets that facilitate the spread of word of mouth (or rather word of 'mouse') publicity clearly has a big impact for the B2B e-marketer.
- *Blurred boundaries*. In 1998 in the groundbreaking book *Blur: The Speed of Change*, Stan Davis and Chris Meyer highlighted the new economy's ability to merge and conflate previously separate groups or entities. For instance, they write of the 'blur of

desires' where 'products and services meld into one to become an offer, and where the roles of buyers and sellers merge into an exchange'.

Business in context

By becoming a part of the Web, businesses are placing themselves within a vast, contextual space beyond their immediate control. As a Web site's significance stems from its relationship to other places and people on the Web, companies must acknowledge their position within a broader business and economic context. Furthermore, as most Web users arrive at a site via somewhere else (search engines, Web directories, affiliate sites, link pages etc), companies must make sure their Web site fits within exactly the right 'hyperlink framework'. Other contextual issues include comparative pricing, increased competition and business Webs (see below).

The network effect

The Internet has increased our ability to build and exploit networks. It is evident that there are advantages and disadvantages in this situation.

The most obvious benefit is that people with special affinities can find one another around the world. As a result the Internet has the potential to alter fundamentally the relationships that we have with institutions and with other individuals. It empowers people by facilitating their access to information. The perceived disadvantage of the network effect is that businesses can no longer control their own fate single-handedly. Even Steve Ballmer, CEO of Microsoft, has conceded that 'There's no way we can succeed in isolation.'

However, while many choose to view this as a threat, many more are seeing it as an opportunity. The new necessity for business partnerships, alliances and affiliations broadens the wealth-making possibilities for those businesses willing to play their part within the network.

Business Webs

Just as the network effect has a big impact on the demand side of the market, so too can it revolutionize the supply side. Many Internet pundits, in order to explain the nature of this revolutionary change, have embraced the idea of the 'business Web'. A business Web (occasionally abbreviated to b-Web) is a cluster of businesses coming together over the Internet. While each company retains its identity, the companies function together, creating more wealth than they could ever hope to create individually while inevitably losing a degree of control. The rise in affiliate marketing (pioneered by B2C companies Amazon and CDNow) is the most obvious indicator of the rise in business Webs, as this book will show. As well as affiliate schemes, Extranets and other 'information exchanges' exclusive to the Internet can be used to help create business Webs.

It has been argued that in an era characterized by networked markets and 'business Webs' the corporate principles of defence and attack should be exchanged for a more open conciliatory approach. On the Internet, identifying complementary businesses to work with is now more important than combating perceived enemies.

Facing change

Change is now sudden, non-linear and constant. This means its amplitude and direction can never be forecast. As a result, companies need to focus less on specific products or specific markets, and more on organizational readiness. Similarly, instead of aiming for growth, the ability to adapt is now all important. Among the guidelines given in this chapter is the general advice to bring customers themselves inside the business entity.

The information product

There is already a move away from selling tangible (or hard) goods, towards information products. Even where physical goods are sold on the Web, they need to be presented as part of an 'information package'. For instance, Amazon is about much more than selling books or CDs at cheap prices. It is about supplying customers with the relevant information in order to make their purchase (customer reviews, editorial reviews, lists of products, what other customers bought in addition to this purchase, sales rankings, etc).

Information products destabilize the traditional economic view, as first articulated by Adam Smith, that with a small supply and a big demand, you have a business. In the information economy this rule is now belied by a contrary trend. As the supply of an information product increases, so too does demand for the product.

The rise in 'information products' complicates the market (from a business perspective) as it replaces the fixed and predictable determinants of a buying decision (price, location, function etc) with more subjective factors (such as the quality and relevance of the information for each individual user).

Pulling power

The Internet is primarily a 'pull' technology. That is to say, Internet users pull information towards them, rather than have it pushed in their direction. As well as sounding the death-knell for push marketing techniques (such as Web banners and spam), this also affects even more significant marketing areas. For instance, the Internet has helped to turn the business supply chain upside down, converting it into a demand chain. Customers, rather than suppliers, are now helping to determine factors such as how many units of a given product the market can absorb. Faced with near infinite choice, the customer really is the commander-in-chief of the new economy.

The marketing virus

The Internet has transformed marketing from an activity carried out by companies to one conducted by consumers themselves. As Seth Godin has put it, 'The idea is to create an environment where consumers will market to each other.'

The secret to successful e-marketing is being able to concede control to the market itself. In an attempt to explain the Internet's unique ability to accelerate interest in a product or service, Steve Jurveston coined the term 'viral marketing' in a 1997 Netscape newsletter. Jurveston, as one of the venture capitalists who helped to initially finance the free e-mail service Hotmail, had clearly witnessed the power of viral marketing at close range. By Christmas 1996, within a year of its launch, Hotmail had 10 million registered users. At that time, such phenomenal growth had not occurred anywhere else in media history.

Furthermore, this unprecedented performance had been achieved with a marketing budget of just $50,000 (needless to say, this was before Microsoft bought the company). Therefore Hotmail's fast-track success was not the result of an extensive advertising campaign, either online or offline. Instead, it has been attributed to a decision made by another Hotmail seed investor, Tim Draper.

Draper was adamant that every e-mail sent by a Hotmail user should incorporate the following message: 'Get your free Web-based e-mail at Hotmail.' By clicking on this line of text, the recipient would be transported to the Hotmail home page. While this message would not have had much effect at the foot of an e-mail sent by the company itself, when sent by a friend or relative it made an impact, confirming Marshall McLuhan's belief that the medium validates the message. The very act of sending a Hotmail message constituted an endorsement of the product and so the current customer was selling to future customers just by communicating with them. The recipients of a Hotmail message learnt not only that the product works, but also that their friend was a user.

Jurveston now believes that a viral marketing component must be built into the DNA of every Internet company in order for it to succeed. 'I can't think of any company that I'd consider that doesn't come with a viral marketing element,' he says.

Now, as we shall see, many B2B companies are using viral marketing techniques ('e-mail this to a colleague' buttons, affiliate schemes, community forums etc) in order to reach new audiences and increase their market share.

It is important to remember, however, that word of mouth can travel in two directions. Although many people find the term 'viral marketing' offensive, it not only suits the infectious nature of network-enhanced word of mouth, but also conjures up its negative potential.

By losing control of the marketing message, companies are at the mercy of online opinion. If customers have a bad experience of a certain product, word can spread at alarming speed. As *The Cluetrain Manifesto* states: 'The networked market knows more than companies do about their own products. And whether the news is good or bad, they tell everyone.'

This is not to say that viral marketing should be discouraged. Indeed, viral marketing occurs whether a company wants it to or not – via e-mail, Usenet discussion groups, consumer opinion sites such as E-pinions.com, and other interactive forums.

The only way companies can limit viral marketing's negative capacity is, paradoxically, by openly embracing it. By making it easy for conversations between customers to occur, companies will be satisfying the Internet user's primary objective: to interact with other people. As Seth Godin puts it, 'It's imperative to stop marketing *at* people. The idea is to create an environment where consumers will market to each other.'

This view is supported by John Owrid, a management partner at UK direct marketing agency Ogilvy One (which opened a virtual marketing unit last August). 'Traditional marketing strategies have never translated to the Web,' he believes. 'As the Net's infrastructure gets stronger, viral marketing gets easier and the rewards for those who can do it properly get bigger.'

Rebel voices

If hostile customers and aggrieved employees are ignored by a company, they can vent their disdain in online newsgroups and sites such as E-pinions.com. They can even set up an 'anti-site' such as Microsucks or Britishscareways (two real examples). Companies not only need to monitor the Web for negative (and positive) opinion, but they also need to be able to incorporate feedback directly into their own e-activity. The industrial age belief in the power and autonomy of the corporation must now be replaced with an equally strong belief in *incorporation*. The free-flow of information between customers and employees therefore should be encouraged, not prohibited, in order for businesses to flourish on the Web.

Summary

The command-and-control principles held by organizations in the era of mass production no longer apply in the information age. The Internet ensures that the external and internal forces that shape the development of a business are beyond its immediate control. This is due, in part at least, to the 'network effect', which facilitates the free-flow of information and ensures markets remain unpredictable.

Far from taking a pessimistic view, the B2B guidelines in the following chapters are founded on the belief that losing a degree of control can be positive as it forces companies to be more responsive to market trends and developments. Ultimately, an 'outside in' approach is advocated in order to help companies focus on their ability to adapt and change direction.

three

B2B Web design

There is no such thing as a perfect B2B Web site. It simply does not, and indeed cannot, exist. The Web itself is an inherently imperfect medium because, as its inventor Tim Berners Lee is more than happy to concede, it will always be 'a little broken'. Pursuing perfection on the Internet is therefore a self-defeating task. No matter how much a Web builder tries to control the fate of a site, it will always be vulnerable to external market (or other) factors.

Rather than ignoring this vulnerability, it should be acknowledged, even embraced, within the design of a site. Although there can be no single right way to design a Web site, there are general principles that can help focus your design efforts by making sure you take the Internet on its own, fundamentally imperfect, terms. As the information in this chapter attests, successful Web design has as much to do with understanding how people use the Net as it does with technological or artistic brilliance.

In-house or out-house?

The first question you will need to consider when designing and developing a B2B Web site is whether or not to hire an external company or use your own in-house resources. While there is no one right or wrong decision, it is important to consider very carefully the options. For small businesses, it may be appropriate to develop a Web site using a 'WYSIWYG' (What You See Is What You Get) Web design software. While this software costs money, it is significantly cheaper than the average Web design agency. Microsoft Front Page and Front Page Express remain among the most popular Web design software packages available. Macromedia's Dreamweaver and Adobe's GoLive are also well respected products.

For larger sites, investing in Web design software may not be enough. Developing and constantly updating content requires a serious investment in human resources, and not just for the IT department.

Owing to the sheer amount of effort involved in Web development, it is clear to see why many companies decide to outsource and use a Web agency. After all, the easiest way to build a Web site is to get someone else to do it for you. However, while Web design agencies are able to offer experience of programming and designing sites, they are not going to know your business as well as you do. If you do want to pursue the out-house route, you need to know exactly what you want your Web site to achieve.

The worst thing you can do is to go to a Web design firm and give them an open brief. Not only is this likely to be risky in terms of budget considerations, but it also means a Web designer may be tempted to exert his 'creative energy' on your site in a way you had not foreseen. Therefore, even if you are to outsource your entire Web development to an external party, it is important to get to grips with the essential principles of Web site design as outlined in this chapter.

A human approach

Web site design is, essentially, a human activity. Although some Web architects (particularly in the B2B sector) still shy away from the personal touch and prefer to create dehumanized sites full of corporate imagery and bland adspeak, most are now waking up to the Web's human nature. According to David Weinberger in *The Cluetrain Manifesto*, Web sites are built in a spirit of opportunism. Web designers cut and paste tried and tested images from each other, making the Web 'unpredictable, creative and always the result of human hands'. To treat a Web site as isolated is therefore a mistake. As a site's significance stems from its relationship to other places and people on the Web, B2B companies must acknowledge their role in the fundamentally human 'conversation' that is the Internet.

Good communication clearly helps businesses online to keep things on a human level. This is why effective B2B e-commerce sites, from Enron down, confirm transactions within minutes. If a customer is kept in the dark about what is happening they are unlikely to feel 100 per cent confident that what they have ordered will arrive on time and in the right condition.

A human approach can ultimately lead to an ongoing dialogue between a company and its business customers. The Web is an interactive medium dependent on two-way communication and has the potential to open up relations between firms and their clients and take them to a deeper level. As Kevin Roberts, Worldwide CEO for Saatchi and Saatchi, explains, 'On the Web, people tell you everything because there's no threat, no intimidation, no pressure.'

Setting objectives

The success of a B2B Web site depends entirely on the objectives it is meant to achieve. These objectives should be based on the requirements of the target audience, rather than the abstracted aims of the organization setting up the site. This 'outside in' approach is essential due to the fact that the Internet is a 'pull' rather than 'push' medium. In other words, Internet users pull information towards them after they have sought it out. It is impossible to push a Web site onto people unless it meets their needs. It is important to look at the four main reasons people use the Web: to find information, to interact, to shop or to be entertained. Depending on the business audience you are going after, you will need to find a way to design a site that satisfies at least one of these criteria.

As mentioned above, due to its vast, complex and decentralized nature, the Web will always be a little bit broken. The Web's frailty makes it more human and also renders the pursuit of perfection impossible. The politics of 'being right' must not therefore be transferred to a B2B Web site; rather, the objective should be to start a two-way conversation with your target audience, rather than to tell them 'this is how it is'.

Design etiquette

In the real world taste is a purely subjective issue. With regard to the Internet, however, there is a strong consensus of opinion regarding Web design etiquette. As a general rule, the more stripped down a

Web site's design is, the better. It is generally agreed, for instance, that the 'rainbow effect' caused by an over-abundance of colours should be avoided at all costs. (Two or three dominant colours are all that is needed to create a consistent brand identity.) As business decision-makers generally want to absorb information on a Web page in as short a time as possible, text and images should be used with strict restraint throughout a Web site.

Arguably the most important design principle is to keep it simple. As e-commerce expert Stephen Freeman points out, 'Simple isn't easy.' He reckons that, 'Sites that are overly confusing and filled with flashing gizmos that perform clever tricks without rhyme or reason are the ones which were created in an afternoon.' Simplicity of design is particularly important when it comes to e-commerce sites. Research shows that most online 'shopping carts' are ditched before reaching the checkout. One of the main reasons for this is the amount of effort required by the potential customer; extensive form filling can certainly complicate and lengthen the e-shopping experience. One solution is to store information so that visitors only have to fill in forms on their first visit. Other ways the e-commerce process can be simplified include isolating order buttons and enabling users to view their planned purchases as they progress through the site.

One reason for the paranoia about e-commerce security is the fact that the Internet is a new medium. E-commerce sites should be injected with a sense of familiarity and references to the 'real world' business experience. 'On the Internet, familiarity doesn't breed contempt,' says Sophie Burke of Shoeworld.co.uk, 'it builds brand loyalty. With the use of recognizable icons, browsers are easily transposed from a real world experience to one that is online.' (That's why most B2C e-commerce sites have adopted the shopping basket analogy so that visitors can wander the online aisles, pick up what they want and then head for the checkout.)

As Intel chairman Andy Grove has observed, e-businesses spend a lot of time thinking about what computers can do, but not much time thinking about what people can do with them. 'Fancy features may attract attention to a Web site,' he comments, 'but they're no substitute for understanding customers or for human relationships.' The emphasis on technology over psychology may be attributable to the fact that the Internet is still a relatively new media form. Problems occur when technology is seen as important for its own sake. However, many Web sites have failed because they have valued fancy graphics and technical features above human interaction.

Companies that have launched million-dollar Web sites, which have been bolstered by multi-million-dollar marketing campaigns, have failed to build repeat traffic because they have built a site from a technological rather than human perspective.

Usability

Usability is the buzzword most associated with Web design guru Jakob Nielsen, who became famous for highlighting the top mistakes in Web design. At a debate in London on the subject of usability (hosted by *Create Online* magazine), Nielsen, now widely regarded as the world's leading Web design expert, was asked what he understood by the term usability: 'To me, it's just a means of making sites easy to use,' he said. 'That's a pretty simple definition. People have different attitudes and opinions towards usability, but I don't know if people have different definitions.' He went on to explain that the word has two different meanings. There is an attribute meaning: 'in the sense that usability is an attribute of a system – ie can people use it?' It also has a process meaning: 'it's about the approach by which you achieve usability'.

Without adhering to the principles of usability, as advocated by Nielsen and his Web design disciples, it becomes more difficult for an e-commerce site to achieve its objectives. This is because usability involves, purely and simply, taking a user-centric approach to Web design.

If anything, the principles Nielsen has put forward on his Web site (www.useit.com) and in his book, *Designing Web Usability: The Practice of Simplicity*, are even more significant for the B2B sector than they are for companies targeting the consumer market. This is because business decision-makers generally have less time on their hands than users surfing the Web at home.

One of the main points of usability relates to download times. 'Fast response time is the most important criterion for Web pages,' Nielsen states. In other words, if Web pages don't load quickly, customers won't wait. (This is becoming less of an issue in the B2B sector where fast and constant connections are the norm.) According to Nielsen, the biggest 'crimes' in Web site design are as follows:

- *An emphasis on graphics*. Nielsen believes graphics (particularly graphics using Flash) get in the way of the user. One of his all-time pet hates is a corporate site that includes lots of gratuitous photos of smiling people.
- *Interstitials*. Interstitials, or pop-up windows that appear while a new Web page is being downloaded, should be avoided.
- *Advertising*. Nielsen claims that functional design elements that look like advertising will be ignored.
- *Motion*. Moving text and graphics are frowned upon.
- *Linkrot*. Links that lead to extinct or out-of-date Web pages make a Web site look unprofessional.
- *Focus groups*. According to Nielsen, 'You're not studying opinions, you're studying the system's design.'

The site that Nielsen holds up as the ultimate user-centric site is Yahoo! He believes it is 'consistently good in almost all elements you want to consider' and 'you know what to do when you're on different pages'. He also notes that although Yahoo! 'continues to tweak the design' it 'doesn't pull the rug out from experienced users'.

Here are some more words of wisdom, from the man *USA Today* called a 'true time machine' in his ability to predict Web trends, and who (at least according to the *Chicago Tribune*) 'knows more about what makes Web sites work than anyone else on the planet':

> On redesign:
> Nielsen believes 'users have only one reaction to a redesign: "I don't like change" '.
>
> On Web fashion:
> 'Fashion should be there in terms of the content, not the design. If you follow fashion too much, you will change all the time, and you will continuously categorize your users.'
>
> On good sites:
> 'What constitutes a good site relates to the core basis of human nature and not to the technology.'
>
> On bandwidth:
> 'Opening up for high bandwidth and opening up for multimedia in some ways just gives you more rope to hang yourself with.'

On Net virgins:
'It seems to be a law of nature that people have to fail on their first Web project.'

On flash intros:
'We all know users click the "Skip Intro" button right away because they want to get to the facts.'

On Web designers:
'Web designers are designing opportunities, but the users are the ones actually composing their own experiences in terms of mouse-clicks and interaction.'

On user experience:
'What we actually know from our studies is that the average user experience is a failure.'

On international sites:
'We always find great usability difficulties when overseas users have to use the sites. It's several things: the language, the culture, and the translation have been done poorly.'

Information, information, information

Unless a Web site is offering something of real value to potential clients or customers, it is unlikely to generate repeat visits. The Internet is, as mentioned above, according to marketing jargon, a 'pull' as opposed to a 'push' medium. This means that Internet users have to seek out information and pull it towards them. To do this they need to have a strong enough reason (a flashing company logo and fancy graphics are unlikely to prove sufficient incentives). Exclusive information and advice is one way to draw people to your site, especially if this information can be tailored to an individual user's specific needs. However, in order for information sites to really work, they should abide by the following guidelines:

- *Make the home page self-explanatory.* The first page a visitor arrives at is likely to be the one that makes the longest impression. Minimal text, simple (and not too many) links, as well as a speedy download time, are essential first page ingredients. When arriving at a site, visitors should immediately know what is on offer. The home page should include enough about the site and company to let people know they have come to the right place, but not so much that they are bewildered by an array of different options.

- *Keep navigation straightforward*. For information-heavy sites, the emphasis should be on straightforward navigation rather than fancy graphics. Think of how portal sites present their information. Indeed, simple, straightforward navigation is one of the most essential aspects in determining any B2B site's success. After all, if a trip to a site leaves people dazed and confused, they are unlikely to come back.
- *Obey the 'three click' rule*. Regarding navigation, the easiest way to make your site user-friendly is to obey what Web designers refer to as the 'three-click' rule. This states that no page of your site should be more than two clicks away from any other page.
- *Spread information over multiple pages*. While useful information is the backbone to practically all effective sites (especially for B2B companies), it is important to present this information in an accessible way. You should therefore spread information over a few pages rather than put a lot of text on a single page.
- *Use sub-headings*. Straightforward sub-headings should be used to create short and succinct 'text bites', which can then link to more in-depth material further into the site.
- *Make links clear*. Generally speaking, Net users like familiarity. They like to be able to recognize links in an instant, and become frustrated when presented with obscure icons and cryptic commands. Links with self-explanatory titles such as 'Home', 'Contact', and 'News' may seem boring, but they avoid confusion. If you want to exercise your linguistic or artistic ingenuity, link commands are not the place to do it.
- *Tell people where they are*. Try to give visitors some indication of their bearings. You can do this by providing a site map or by changing the colour of the current section in the navigation area.
- *Be unique*. As the Web is saturated with sites serving similar purposes, it is more important than ever to create a unique point of difference within a B2B site. This will help a site to stand out in the minds of seasoned Web users. When thinking of how to add unique information, it is important to make sure that it is relevant to the site's core target audience.
- *Think laterally*. If your Web site is designed to sell a product, you

should not limit the information to the product specifications alone. Think of what would interest your audience in relation to the product. This is what B2B software distributor GT has done with its Web site. Instead of solely providing information on the Web Detect product available from its site (software that can track stolen computers) they provide information and the latest on computer security issues in general.

- *Identify your audience*. Who are you creating content for? Are you designing for a clearly defined niche business audience or a broad cross-section of Internet users? Is it a domestic or international audience that you are targeting? The answers to these questions will help you dictate the design of your site. The more specific the target audience, the more you will be able to fine tune the information on your Web site.
- *Make it objective*. Information that is seen as biased will not be taken seriously. By referring to products and services that you don't provide (as well as those you do), you will lend a sense of authority to your site, and you will find it easier to build trust.
- *Keep it personal*. Tailored content is the secret to satisfying information hunger. The more interactive a site is, the more each site visit is a unique and personal experience. For really information-heavy sites, a search engine will provide the ultimate means of personalizing the visitor's journey through the site. On smaller sites, offering personal advice via e-mail is an effective, if rather time-intensive, solution.
- *Ask for contributions*. By asking visitors to contribute content to your site, you will be able to engage them at a deeper level, make your site more objective, *and* take the hard work out of your hands. Amazon makes good use of this approach by asking visitors to submit book reviews.

It may sound overly obvious but to succeed in the information age you need to provide information. If you can present this information in such an interactive and stimulating way then so much the better. As Stuart Melhuish, CEO for Amaze Ltd, has pointed out, B2B companies 'are coming to a more mature understanding of business transactions, instead of seeing them as solely taking place within the economic sphere'. The majority of people who go online, both B2B and B2C, are not looking to buy. They are, in general, looking for solutions to problems and answers to questions. They certainly do not want to click through screen after screen of fatuous self-praise. If a Web site is to cast a wider net and reach out to as many people as possible, it will have to integrate e-procurement into an informative online experience.

Syndicated content

If you do not have the time to supply a fresh stream of information, or it simply seems like too much hard work, you could always hire a company to supply you with suitable content. Syndicated content is becoming increasingly popular with e-commerce sites wanting to provide their visitors with a one-stop information shop. The way it works is simple: you pay a company (such as the US-based Screaming Media) for a news feed and they provide you with up-to-date stories relevant to your site. No matter how 'niche' your online business audience is, content providers will be able to supply the relevant information.

An 'outside in' approach

Ultimately, if businesses are to take the Internet on its own terms, the provision of relevant information is essential. In the past, B2B Web sites have often fallen into two equally unsatisfactory categories, which have taken as their inspiration outmoded real world templates. They have resembled either brochures or catalogues, and have therefore left consumers with little incentive to log on.

Increasingly, however, e-businesses are taking the cyber-bull by its horns and looking at things from the site user's perspective. This 'outside in' approach not only helps the online customer, but also instils them with the extra confidence needed to make a purchase.

By integrating your product or service details into something more informative, you will be able to join this new breed of e-business and realize your full online potential.

Designing on speed

Internet time is believed to move at seven times the speed of 'normal' time. Whether this is true or not, it cannot be disputed that in cyberspace we talk, shop and do business at an accelerated pace.

When a Web site is designed, it is therefore important to plan how often each area is to be updated. Information needs to be regularly refreshed in order to generate return traffic. Many people who *browse* (don't be fooled by this leisurely verb) the Internet return to the same sites every day. Information needs to be updated at regular intervals to keep a Web site fresh.

Moreover, visitors need to be made aware of the fact. Sites such as News Now (www.newsnow.com) make it clear not only when and how the site was last updated (in the case of News Now this is always within the last five minutes), but also when the next new content will appear. Another way in which hypertime should be acknowledged relates to download speeds. As patience is a virtue few Net users have time for, any design elements that will lengthen download times should be avoided. Spot graphics and images with minimal detail are preferable to large or intricate images for this reason.

Not only should you keep your content fresh and up-to-date, but you should also make sure your site makes an impact within a matter of seconds. If visitors are reaching your site via a search engine, they may have up to 10 other sites they want to visit before logging off. Your site must therefore be stimulating enough to satisfy 'itchy finger syndrome' while at the same time remaining simple and user-friendly. Lengthy site entries (10 seconds or over), excessive text and slow e-commerce processes must therefore be resisted.

Brochureware

By providing visitors with the opportunity to get actively involved with a Web site (as opposed to passively reading it), a site can build trust and strengthen loyalty. One of the revolutionary aspects of the Internet is its ability to provide people with open and direct access to companies. Companies that take advantage of this by using the Internet to enter into conversation with their clients, can make a lasting online impact.

Unfortunately however, a lot of company sites continue to ignore this fact, suffering as they do from an excessive amount of 'brochureware'. They present a glib and glossy picture of the company without acknowledging the audience they target. When designing or re-designing a site, forget the company brochure ever existed. Instead, think of how to interact on a human level with your audience.

The only way to make sure your site is more successful than your competitor's is to use it as a means of bringing potential clients closer to the heart of your business. The main way to do this is by facilitating interaction between your site and its business visitors.

Interactivity

Although most people and companies now appreciate the significance of the Internet, many still do not recognize the unique factors that separate it from more traditional media. One of the main differences between the Net and broadcast or print media is that it is interactive. Web sites should be viewed as two-way, not one-way communication tools, and be used to encourage productive dialogue. A lifeless company brochure or sales catalogue transferred to the Web simply will not work. Not only will interaction help keep visitors busy (and in turn make a site 'sticky'), but it can also enable you to understand a target audience in greater depth. Chat rooms, bulletin boards, guest books, B2B auctions, e-commerce options, search facilities and link pages are some of the most obvious ways to enhance interactivity.

The key to successful B2B e-marketing is building relations with a target audience. For mutually beneficial relations to be formed via a Web site, the site needs to be as interactive as possible.

Obviously some B2B Web sites are more geared towards interactivity than others. For instance, B2B e-marketplaces (and particularly online auctions) are by their very nature interactive as they are based around an Internet community. However, there are a number of ways other B2B sites can encourage interaction:

- *Use 'guest books'*. Guest books serve a similar purpose to bulletin boards although they are a lot easier to manage. Furthermore, they can be installed on a site for free using a service such as Freecode (www.freecode.com).
- *Provide e-mail links*. E-mail links throughout a Web site can be used to provide interactive customer support when it is required.
- *Incorporate feedback forms*. Online forms can be used effectively to give visitors a voice, providing they do not require too much effort on their part.

- *Encourage contributions.* Many successful B2B sites enable visitors to contribute to the content of a Web site either by participating in online forums or by sending articles of interest.

Text and the Web

A few years ago, Sun Microsystems (the US company that promoted the Internet hardest in the mid-nineties) conducted extensive research into how people read on the Web and came to the conclusion that, in actual fact, 'they don't'. Instead, Net users scan the screen, searching at speed for relevant text or images. People therefore do not want to be bombarded with screen after screen of unbroken text. Jakob Nielsen, the man behind the Sun research, proposed a series of guidelines for making text more in tune with the way people actually use the Internet and thereby avoiding information overload. This included: breaking text into bite-sized chunks (containing only one single idea), using frequent sub-headings, highlighting keywords and using bullet points. Where a lot of information needs to be conveyed, it is always best to spread it over a few pages than to put a lot of text on a single page.

The fact that people do not 'read' information on the Web, but rather scan, clearly affects both the way words are presented as well as the words themselves. When writing for the Web it is important to make text easy to read (black text on a light background is ideal) and keep it short and to the point. For instance, the most widely used offline font, Times Roman, does not transfer that well to the Web. Less fussy fonts such as Arial, Georgia and Helvetica are more effective, as is Verdana, which was specifically designed for the Web. The other point to mention with regard to Web writing relates to different language options. As only one in five people in the world speak English, a Web site cannot truly be considered 'worldwide' without catering for non-English speaking Net users.

HTML

HTML (HyperText Mark-up Language) is the computer programming code used to build and lay out Web pages. Its significance, however, extends beyond the IT department.

An understanding of the basics of HTML can help e-marketers to gain a deeper understanding of the way the Web is put together, and therefore get the most out of their online marketing activity. For instance, there are special instructions (called 'meta-tags') embedded within the HTML code behind a Web page that can affect the way a search engine indexes the site (even though these tags do not affect the visual design of the site in any way). At the very least, it is important to take on board the following facts about HTML:

- *HTML is invisible*. Although HTML tags are used to put the different components of a Web site together (text, images, links and so on) they remain 'behind the scenes' of Web pages. However, they can be viewed by clicking on a Web browser's 'Page Source' option. (It is often worthwhile visiting successful competitor sites and having a look at how their pages are put together and the keywords they use to achieve their ranking on the search engines.)
- *HTML tags are paired*. HTML tags work in pairs to indicate when each instruction begins and ends. For example, the tags <P> and </P>are used to indicate where a paragraph of text starts and finishes.
- *HTML tags cannot enable e-commerce*. HTML was invented as a means of presenting information on the World Wide Web in a coherent manner. Although they are used on e-commerce sites to put all the pieces together, they cannot actually manage transactions. For instance, while HTML is used to design online order forms, it cannot make these forms *do* anything. To enable a site to compute and process orders, it is necessary to use supplementary e-commerce software from companies such as Open Market (www.openmarket.com), Intershop (www.intershop.com) and Maestro Commerce (www.maestrocommerce.com).

The main HTML tags are as follows:

<HEAD> </HEAD>The head tags surround the title tags at the top of an HTML page.

<TITLE> </TITLE> The title tags enclose a brief description of the HTML document. This description is invisible on the Web site although it can be read by search engine 'robots'.

<BODY> </BODY> The tags surround the body of the document (ie everything that isn't enclosed within the head commands at the start of the document).

<H1> </H1> These tags surround the first heading of a Web page. (The next heading is surrounded by <H2> </H2> and so on.)

<HR> This horizontal rule is one of the few HTML tags that doesn't come in a pair. It is an instruction to place a horizontal line on a Web page.

<P> </P> These tags indicate the start and finish of a paragraph.

<B> </B> Bold text is placed within these tags.

<I> </I> These are the italics commands.

<A> </A> A hyperlink to another Web page or site is placed within these tags such as <A HREF = www.amazon.com" </A>. (HREF stands for hypertext reference.)

<FONTSIZE = 5> </FONT> This changes the text size.

At its most basic, a Web page HTML structure can look like this:

<HTML>

<HEAD>

<TITLE> My B2B Web page </TITLE>

</HEAD>

<BODY>

This is where you write the body text.

</BODY>

</HTML>

For more information on HTML, visit Mark Werbach's *Bare Bones Guide to HTML* at www.werbach.com/barebones. You can also try:

- *NCSA's Beginners Guide to HTML* (www.ncsa.uiuc.edu). This guide is intended to be an introduction to using HTML and creating files for the Web. Links are provided to additional information.
- *Web Monkey* (www.Webmonkey.com). Calling itself 'The Web Developer's Resource' this site provides a mine of information on HTML and other programming languages.

- *W3C's HTML guide* (www.w3.org). Co-written by World Wide Web inventor Tim Berners Lee, this is arguably the definitive guide to the subject.

Managing content

One of the biggest mistakes a company can make with regard to its Web strategy is to view Web creation as independent from content management. If a Web site is designed for the short term, with little thought for how it is going to be maintained, there will be considerable problems later on.

For information-heavy sites, content management systems are essential and should be incorporated within the initial design and development process. It is also important to decide not only which areas of the site are to be updated but also how often and by whom. For instance, the press area of a site would normally be the responsibility of the PR department and it would be updated every time a new press release was distributed. On the other hand, some areas of a site (such as the 'contact area') are unlikely to need updating at all, at least not on a regular basis.

Summary

Regardless of who is ultimately responsible for Web development, it is important that everyone actively involved in B2B e-marketing is aware of the essential principles of Web site design. After all, the Web site is viewed as the online 'face' of a company and is often a place of commerce in itself. By maintaining a user-centric approach, and by ensuring that form follows function, B2B Web sites can help build closer relations with key business decision-makers.

four

Intranets and Extranets

One of the main factors governing a B2B company's chances of marketing success is its capacity for knowledge management. By bringing together internal information, applications and resources within one coherent framework, organizations are able to improve business relations, save costs and ultimately attract more business. As this chapter will explain, organizations can choose whether this framework is internal (based on an *Intranet*), or whether some form of external access is allowed (via an *Extranet*).

Intranets

Intranets are 'micro-Internets' that enable companies to set up internal Web sites and e-mail systems accessible only to people within the organization. The technology they use is identical to that of the Internet – the significant difference is that Intranets only work within the confines of a private, localized network. Obviously, the main advantage of an Intranet is security. As access is password-protected it enables a level of privacy that is simply impossible on the Internet. However, companies are now able to place their Intranets on peer-to-peer networks in order to share information with other relevant companies. Many B2B operators over the last few years have discovered that Intranets can enhance the information flow (and hence productivity) of their internal system. The essential components of an Intranet are as follows:

- *A TCP/IP network.* TCP (Transmission Control Protocol) and IP (Internet Protocol) enable computers linked to the Intranet to connect and communicate with each other.

- *A Web server*. A Web server allows Web documents to be placed on the Intranet.
- *Browser/client software*. This enables members of the Intranet to browse through and download Intranet Web documents.
- *An e-mail server/software*. To send and receive internal e-mails via the Intranet, it is essential to have an e-mail server as well as client e-mail software.
- *FTP*. File Transfer Protocol is the method normally used to send files back and forth via an Intranet.
- *Chat systems*. Chat software systems facilitate real time online communication between employees.
- *Usenet*. Usenet can help to create newsgroup-style Intranet forums.

Conveniently, a lot of Intranet software is either free or very cheap. The freeware on offer includes Apache (one of the leading Web servers), Eudora Lite and Pegasus (e-mail client software applications). However, perhaps the most useful aspect of Intranets, at least from a B2B perspective, is the development of internal Web sites. Some organizations now have a multitude of internal Web sites providing information relating to specific departments and individuals. Also, owing to the scalable nature of TCP/IP protocols, an Intranet can expand and develop in line with an organization. Thousands of new users can join the Intranet and thousands of new documents can be added with minimal disruption to the network. Ultimately, Intranets help organizations to integrate their often-heterogeneous internal systems, applications, and information sources. For instance, Sun Microsystems' Sun Web Intranet serves as the primary index and retrieval system for approximately 4 million internal documents, as well as the test bed for implementing e-commerce and business applications.

Intranets and marketing

While Intranets are often viewed as little more than a way of grouping internal data together, they can also serve a genuine marketing function. Just as the World Wide Web is a media channel, so too is the Intranet a marketing medium. Many large companies allow external advertising on their Intranets, and many more use them to market themselves to their employees. For companies of the scale of Cisco Systems, Ford, Microsoft, or Pricewaterhouse-Coopers (see case study), this is a serious opportunity. These companies have all shown that Intranets can combine marketing functions with knowledge management in order to aid their B2B operations. For instance, 98 per cent of Cisco's 16,000 employees use the firm's Intranet on a regular basis. More than $300 million purchases have been made via the system, and more than 1,000 employees participate in 15 sales training classes every month.

Case study: PricewaterhouseCoopers: Knowledge Curve

The often-cited example of PricewaterhouseCoopers, with their award-winning Intranet site, illustrates just how effectively Intranets can serve marketing purposes, both within and outside the organization.

The PricewaterhouseCoopers' Intranet site, called Knowledge Curve, plays a critical role in the e-enablement of its business by giving people access to a personalized, online, virtual office 24 hours a day. It is also key to knowledge-sharing, continual learning and innovation within the professional services organization of more than 150,000 people in 150 countries. Clearly, when they amount to these sorts of numbers, employees themselves constitute a key marketing audience.

Susan O'Neill, a partner with the Global Knowledge Management of PricewaterhouseCoopers, says that the Intranet has now been 'expanded. . . to 55 countries, and we are always searching for new ways to serve the needs of our culturally diverse, multinational workforce'. The company also uses its Intranet to distribute a daily electronic newsletter (titled News Bytes), providing career information and details of training opportunities.

Not only does the Intranet regularly gain press attention by winning awards (for instance it has won the prestigious CIO Web Business Award every year since 1998), but also PricewaterhouseCoopers cites Knowledge Curve as a critical component in leveraging knowledge throughout the organization, furthering its ability to serve its global business clients.

In addition, Knowledge Curve has enabled Pricewaterhouse-Coopers to realize substantial cost savings. By consolidating various contracts with the external information vendors into one global contract, and placing the information on Knowledge Curve, the firm has saved millions of dollars.

Extranets

Put simply, an Extranet is a closed, or walled, network that (unlike an Intranet) is open to people outside as well as inside an organization. An Extranet therefore enables third party access to internal applications or information. This is useful for organizations who need to share internal systems and information with potential partners.

At the most basic level the term Extranet can be applied to a standard Web site that limits access to password holders only. These password holders usually include certain customers, partners, or suppliers outside the organization. This type, which originated in 1996, is becoming increasingly popular among sites aiming to build online business communities, as it creates an immediate barrier to entry (one of the prerequisites for any successful e-community).

When most people talk about Extranets, however, they are talking about external Intranets. As with Intranets, Extranets provide all the benefits of Internet technology with the added benefit of security. They use the same Internet technology (browsers, Web servers, HTML etc) and are confined to an isolated network. Unlike Intranets, however, Extranets have been extended so that some or all of its content is accessible to third parties. Some companies use Extranets as places where members share resources and conduct business with each other.

As Information Systems expert Mark Merkow puts it, 'The same technologies that work inside the company are just as effective between different companies too. Whether it's CAD files, purchase orders, design specs, payment instructions, or wherever information is present, Extranets can easily handle it.'

If your company has information that's locked away in an inaccessible database, you can convert the information into a Web-based format so that everyone allowed into the Extranet can access it. By using a program that can display database information as Web documents and that can enter information from Web page forms into the database, all the relevant people both inside and outside the organization can see, and (where applicable) update, selected information from the database by using only a Web browser. Obviously this type of Extranet would need to be tightly controlled so that access was limited to a select number of external parties.

Extra help

The most famous example of an Extranet is probably Federal Express's Tracking System (www.fedex.com). Its Extranet enables users in the US to access Fedex's public site, enter a tracking number and locate any package still in its system. It also allows users to prepare a shipping form, obtain a tracking number, print the form and schedule a pick-up. The Fedex type of Extranet therefore provides a win-win situation for both the customer and the host company. Customers have greater control over (and knowledge of) the whole process and the company benefits from getting the customer to do some of its work for it. If customers want to find out how something is coming along, it is clearly more cost-effective to let them see for themselves than to let them hear via an intermediary.

However, Extranets are not only used to add value to business–customer relations. They can also be used to improve the efficiency of relationships *between* companies. For instance, they can assist project management and control for companies that are part of a common work project. Basically, Extranets can be used for any area of business that involves sharing internal information with external parties.

The Intranet/Extranet difference

In most Intranets, a program called a Proxy Server is added to the network to provide one-way (outward) access to the Internet for users of the network. As well as providing Internet access for those within the Intranet, the Proxy Server creates a firewall to prevent external users (in other words, the Internet population at large) from accessing the private network.

With an Extranet, however, access is opened up to certain people outside the organization. Adequate security controls are ensured through Access Control Lists (ACLs) on the Web server, which can limit those who enter through the Internet to tightly controlled resources that can be defined as an organization requires. This means passwords can be distributed to as many or as few people as a company sees fit. There is an obvious market research opportunity here for those willing to take it. Extranets can help you gain more information about your target audience than a standard Web site, as getting past the barrier to entry provides people with an obvious incentive. Many companies require those businesses wishing to access the Extranet to complete a corporate profile and submit it for review. If this profile fits the criteria set by the company then Extranet access is given. If not, it still provides the company with useful audience information.

According to Matt Perry from e-marketing firm Net Marketeers, 'Building profiles of your visitors helps you to focus your promotional spending as well as the products or services you offer in ways no mass-marketing techniques can begin to match.' Furthermore, as the B2B market moves away from a concentration on hits and 'eyeball' counts, towards a new focus on increasing the 'lifetime value' of customers, Extranets provide companies with a way of concentrating exclusively on only those audiences that really matter.

Slimming supply costs

One of the main reasons companies decide to use an Extranet is to help streamline and cut costs in their supply chain. Heineken is one European company that uses Extranet technology to tighten the links with its regional suppliers. With its Extranet, which is given the apt acronym HOPS (Heineken Operational Planning System), resellers can log in, place their monthly forecasts for sales and place product orders. 'Now, beer from our brewery in Europe can make its way through the US retail channel in just about the same time it takes Anheuser-Busch to ship from its domestic breweries. We can react faster than ever before,' Heineken's vice-president Dan Tearno said in a press statement, when the system was implemented two years ago. By following Heineken's example, businesses can therefore use Extranets to save both time and money in the supply chain.

However, if suppliers are allowed access into the Extranet, considerable caution is required. Companies need to decide exactly how open their Extranet should be. For instance, when General Electric first implemented its Extranet, suppliers immediately called for it to be redesigned. The reason for this was the fact that its Extranet's open online bidding process caused (if not forced) the suppliers to chronically undercut each other's bids. The suppliers therefore felt isolated from a system that was intended to help them. As a result, GE reassessed its efforts and involved suppliers at every stage of the design process for the new and improved

Extranet. The GE Extranet now includes a blind bidding process with deadlines for bids posted well in advance.

The system now satisfies the needs of both the company and the suppliers, having halved the purchasing cycle down from a fortnight to a week. The lesson learnt from the pitfalls GE encountered is therefore to involve all suppliers (and other relevant parties) at every stage. After all, suppliers who aren't involved in the Extranet's design may accuse your business of a bias towards their competition. However, even if you take a completely inclusive approach, problems may occur. For instance, certain technologies used on the Extranet may exclude those businesses that are unable or unwilling to use them within their organization. It is wise to avoid those applications (such as Java applets) that are not universally acceptable on all Intranets.

A lowest common denominator approach is therefore essential when designing a B2B Extranet, as Extranets that are built with technologically sophisticated users in mind tend to exclude everyone else.

Extranet technology

The technology used for building an Extranet is essentially the same as with a standard Intranet. As with an Intranet and corporate Web site, the technology required depends on how the Extranet is intended to function. If it is just going to be used to give information, a remote access server and router will prove sufficient. If, on the other hand, the Extranet is going to *do* anything (such as process orders), database management applications will be required. Macromedia's Drumbeat and Allaire's Cold Fusion are two of the most widely used packages for building applications for databases. For order processing, the simplest solution is to use a shop-building package such as Maestro Commerce or Intershop to help you place order forms within the network. To build the database itself, you will need to use a tool such as Filemaker or Filemaker Pro. This will enable you to store relevant data relating to pricing, product specifications and so on.

As most Extranets connect the Internet to Intranets, secure 'firewall' technology is essential if you are to limit access to your internal information. A firewall can be simple or complex, depending on how specifically you want to control your Extranet traffic. A simple firewall might require only that you configure the software in the router that connects your Intranet to your ISP. A more complex firewall might be a computer running UNIX and specialized software (more firewall information is available at the Rotherwick Firewall Resource, www.zeuros.co.uk/firewall).

Test the water

Assess the possible value of an Extranet before you start developing it by gauging the opinion of your target audience. This could involve sending out a questionnaire via your e-mailing list asking about the sort of data they would like to access. Such research will help you to weigh up the financial (and other) rewards that could be brought about through an Extranet system. The aim, of course, is to try and balance your own objectives with those of the Extranet users. You will need to decide which information and applications need to be allocated to which business customers. Once all the technology is in place you could then test the Extranet with some of your customers (or other relevant third parties) prior to launch. This will help you to limit the potential for hiccups inherent in setting up each system.

Case study: Toshiba Information Systems: Internet FYI

The Electronic Imaging Division (EID) of Toshiba Information Systems has created a site that serves as both an Intranet and a dealer Extranet. The Internet FYI site is used by all internal employees and almost all external dealers, processing over 12,000 actual orders a month along with 70,000 enquiries.

The site enables sales representatives to interact more effectively with dealers and has provided dealers with the ability to manage their own information systems. The sales figures are updated five times an hour on the Internet FYI site.

Of particular relevance to marketing, according to Lew McCreary of CIO Web Business, is 'the ability to offer creative promotions and bundling deals that don't turn into transaction-processing nightmares when run through inflexible mainframe apps'. At roughly one-third the programming cost of what would have been needed to modify legacy systems, Internet FYI now handles the complex custom promotions relating to individual dealers.

Case study: Boeing: Genisys

The Boeing Extranet, Genisys, groups engineers and launch site employees in an online environment where information on the Delta rocket projects is distributed and kept up-to-date. Based in Boeing's Californian headquarters, the Genisys Extranet site facilitates programme management, engineering and some manufacturing for the Delta projects. The external parties involved in the Extranet are two vendors, Raytheon Corp. and Rocketdyre, as well as one customer, the United States Air Force. According to a company press release, 'putting accurate and consistent information into the hands of the 2,000 people with a stake in the Delta IV programme [the latest Delta project] would be impossible without Genisys, considering both the scope of the project and six dispensed locations where work on the project is done'.

Genisys has therefore enabled Boeing to overcome the constraints of time and physical location. For instance, engineers based in Europe can log on whenever they choose in order to locate fellow team members, check project developments, and even take a virtual (photographic) tour of launch sites and manufacturing facilities. Extranet members can also add and update information of their own.

Summary

Many companies already indicate the fact that Intranets and Extranets can be used to develop and support B2B activity. Their significance looks set to intensify once certain technological developments (particularly peer-to-peer networking and high-speed bandwidth) are fully realized within the B2B sector. These developments will ultimately revolutionize the way information is distributed inside and outside an organization, and extend B2B opportunities and possibilities even further.

five

B2B e-marketplaces

E-marketplaces have, on quite a few occasions, been described as online bazaars. They consist of many companies gathering together in Web-based exchanges or auctions in order to buy and sell products or services in a highly competitive environment. According to some estimates there will be 10,000 e-marketplaces by 2003, and as ClickZ columnist Claudia Bruemmer has warned, 'any business not planning to participate in an electronic trading network won't be around for long'. While this may be a bit extreme (giant corporations such as Cisco seem perfectly comfortable with the direct-selling B2B model), most B2B operators can no longer afford to ignore e-marketplaces.

As online marketplaces offer increased convenience for business buyers, they cannot be ignored by business vendors. This chapter will provide general information on this ever-evolving area of e-commerce, as well as look at the specific marketing issues related to it.

E-marketplace benefits

Although there are many different types of online marketplace, they all share one overriding characteristic: they facilitate the B2B buying and selling process. In particular, e-marketplaces provide business with the opportunity to easily find and compare products and prices and provide sellers with the ability to aggregate supply and demand.

While it is possible, in theory at least, to be a B2B operator without participating in an online marketplace or exchange, it is becoming increasingly difficult for businesses to survive by using an independent Web site as their one and only online sales channel.

By joining an e-marketplace, B2B operators are taking positive action and not waiting for customers to come and find them. Specifically, e-marketplaces can help companies to:

- *Generate awareness*. E-marketplaces enable companies to attract new audiences relevant to their industry.
- *Provide information*. The solution offered by e-marketplaces makes it easier for B2B operators to inform prospects with supplier catalogues and up-to-the-minute industry news.
- *Enable secure transactions*. E-marketplaces provide a secure environment for buyers and sellers to make transactions.
- *Network*. Essentially, e-marketplaces are online business communities that facilitate interaction between business colleagues and partners. Most e-marketplaces and exchanges include discussion areas.
- *Customize products and services*. The fact that online marketplaces enable companies to find more information on buyers means that products can be customized to a greater extent.

Case study: Hilton Hotels

In June 2000, Hilton Hotels launched a B2B exchange that combined the purchasing power of Hilton Hotels with that of other hospitality companies that will have the opportunity to participate. With Hilton as the 'anchor tenant', thousands of other hotels participate, making it (at least at the time of launch) the largest exchange in the hospitality industry.

The exchange links thousands of member buyers and suppliers in what Hilton refers to as 'the very fragmented hospitality industry' to create significant procurement and sales cost savings, as well as generate new sales opportunities for suppliers.

In line with many other industry-specific exchanges, the Hilton hospitality exchange facilitates bulk buying (and therefore lower prices) and leads to new sales opportunities for suppliers. Specifically, the hospitality exchange offers the following advantages:

- *Wide access*. The exchange provides access to more than 21,000 businesses offering the 'lowest possible' pricing from suppliers.

- *Usability*. Fully automated searching tools for identifying new suppliers enhances usability.
- *Bidding technology*. The exchange uses patented bidding technology allowing one-to-many and many-to-one bidding.

The exchange is a joint initiative with B2B e-commerce company Purch@se Pro.com, which already had a vast 'bid and purchase' network.

E-procurement

While most of this book is concerned with the seller side of B2B (promotion, distribution etc), it is useful to look briefly at the way B2B e-commerce affects the way companies *buy* products and services.

The rise in online marketplaces has brought with it a more convenient, timesaving and cost-effective means of purchasing products. Catalogues enable companies to conduct comparative surveys of trusted online vendors and online order forms enable both buyers and sellers to process transactions instantaneously. Also, because of the self-documenting nature of the Web, the paperwork involved is radically reduced.

B2B marketplaces are similar to consumer-based co-operative buying except that they involve the business procurement stage instead of the consumer buying stage. As ClickZ journalist Philip Say has commented in his B2B column, e-procurement systems eliminate the 'paper-approval bottlenecks and rogue purchasing practices that cost companies millions of dollars annually'.

Many e-marketplaces provide tailored services for business buyers, enabling them to type in information about their company and the products or services they want to purchase. The e-marketplace (be it a catalogue, exchange, auction or a combination of all three) can then notify customers of relevant product news via e-mail, and even get vendors to submit offers to fulfil an order.

Marketing via VerticalNet

VerticalNet (www.verticalnet.com) is the archetypal B2B e-marketplace (or in its own terminology 'e-commerce enabler') and is the Internet's leading creator and operator of vertical trade markets.

As its name indicates, VerticalNet is divided into vertical industry sectors through a variety of business portals such as Oil and Gas Online.com and Food Ingredients Online.com. In an interview with Internet Analyst, VerticalNet President and CEO Mark Walsh explained the vertical e-marketplace concept by stating that 'companies are part of an industry, not part of a group of other companies that are the same size. So we look at businesses that have a natural vertical orientation with their buyers, suppliers, distributors and value-added middlemen.'

Collectively VerticalNet forms a macro-marketplace comprising many distinct industry-focused communities that share online information resources, communication vehicles, and e-commerce channels and have access to technology-based companies. VerticalNet currently includes 58 industry-specific B2B marketplaces, all of which support 'commerce, content and community in a hosted environment'.

As many B2B e-marketplaces follow, to a greater or lesser extent, the VerticalNet model, it is worth looking at exactly how VerticalNet (and similar e-marketplaces) could assist your e-marketing activity. There are a number of ways e-marketplaces such as VerticalNet can help a B2B operator. These include:

- *Market research*. E-marketplaces often provide a mine of industry-specific information on companies, products, upcoming industry-related trade shows and events, industry and technical news. VerticalNet also incorporates Marketplace Discussion Forums centred on business sectors. These clearly provide valuable research and networking opportunities.
- *Storefronts*. E-marketplaces offer businesses the opportunity of setting up an online 'storefront' within the marketplace. This can help not only build brand awareness, but can also help generate leads and make sales. At VerticalNet the storefronts enable companies to create and maintain an online catalogue featuring up to 10 products. They also offer a direct link to the company Web site as well as real-time tracking and analysis of sales leads

Figure 5.1 VerticalNet: the leading operator of vertical trade markets on the Web

and orders. According to VerticalNet, storefronts help companies to 'leverage a powerful new channel to market and sell' products/services on the Web – without the costs of building and maintaining the technical infrastructure. To establish a storefront on the VerticalNet e-marketplace, you can apply online and take advantage of their one-year, pre-paid offer.

- *E-commerce centres*. VerticalNet's e-commerce centres provide another means of targeting new and existing customers in industry-specific marketplaces. As well as helping to build and publish a company's online catalogue, e-commerce centres simplify the customer's experience by providing multiple catalogue search methods and shopping-cart technology. VerticalNet also claims that these centres can lead to cost-savings: 'in most cases, customers using ECCs versus building a custom application realize significant cost reductions, including cost of customer acquisition, cost of sales, and overall order processing costs'. E-commerce centres also enable companies to tailor pricing for individual customers and provide a 'partner locator' enabling manufacturers, distributors, partners or suppliers who sell products under specific channel partner agreements to locate channel partners representing specific products within a certain geographical area.

The VerticalNet e-marketplaces are grouped around the following industry areas: communications, energy, environment/utilities, financial, food/packaging, food service/hospitality, healthcare, high-tech, industrial, manufacturing, public sector and science. It is also worth noting that VerticalNet now hosts direct and reverse auctions.

Case study: Yahoo! IT Software Marketplace (http://industrymarketplaces.yahoo.com/software)

Yahoo!'s IT Software Marketplace constitutes one-third of the company's Industry Marketplace launched in January 2001, which aims to provide industry-relevant services for businesses. As well as software, there are also marketplaces for electronics and IT hardware. Each marketplace offers business owners and professionals access to targeted, in-depth information and services, research capabilities from product databases, industry-specific news and a rich media Webcast centre.

According to Yahoo! the IT Software Marketplace is 'a focused destination for business users to research and compare software products and packages, find information on upcoming industry tradeshows and seminars and stay on top of the latest news from leading IT vendors and analysts'.

There are a number of lessons that can be learnt from Yahoo!'s software marketplace. Firstly, it is important to note that it is a collaborative project (Knowledge Storm, Bitpipe and IDG all help supply content). It also provides an excellent example of how a near infinite amount of B2B information can be made accessible to and tailored towards individual users. The IT Software Marketplace Resource Centre consists of:

- A directory of product and vendor information from Knowledge Storm. This constitutes an open directory of thousands of IT software and service solutions, connecting IT buyers and vendors via an online, searchable database listing information from over 3,500 business sellers.
- A site co-branded with Bitpipe, a leading syndicator of pro-

fessional literature on the Internet, which provides white papers and case studies from leading IT software industry vendors and analysts.

- Editorial content from computer magazine publisher IDG. As Yahoo! states, 'users can personalize and add news content to a My Yahoo! Page and have the latest industry-specific headlines at their fingertips'.
- A Webcast centre. If B2B companies are going to make the most of the opportunities high-speed, constant broadband access will bring, they will need to consider adding multimedia facilities. Yahoo!'s IT Software Marketplace includes a Webcast centre that features streamed video and audio programming of industry-specific information, including: video product releases, Internet-only shows, product training and instructional seminars.

Case study: Healthy Herbal Nutrients/Body2Mind.com

Healthy Herbal Nutrients, a company specializing in natural supplements and herbal remedies joined Body2Mind.com's B2B Natural Product Exchange. Healthy Herbal Nutrients adds to its marketing effort by using Body2Mind.com's promotional efforts, bringing potential buyers to its site inside the B2B exchange. Furthermore, by having a fully developed free site inside Body2Mind.com, Healthy Herbal Nutrients doubles the exposure of its own site (www.healthyherbalnutrients.com). Since Body2Mind is a vertical B2B exchange for the natural products industry, all businesses joining the exchange are potential partners and buyers, so Healthy Herbal Nutrients benefits from the highly targeted market inside the vertical portal (or 'vortal').

Body2Mind.com, a bricks and mortar company, was the first online marketplace devoted to direct business-to-business distribution of natural products. Retailers, wholesalers, distributors, brokers, raw material providers, organic farmers, and manufacturers worldwide are able to register for free membership and trade with each other in this neutral vertical exchange. Businesses are able to sign up and even receive a free Web site from the exchange. Significantly, members do not pay for this service and exposure until they actually receive an order risk-free proposition from another member.

Creating an online marketplace

For those companies wishing to set up an online marketplace – be it a catalogue, exchange or auction – there are a lot of serious issues that need to be considered. First and foremost, it is important to recognize that e-marketplaces are still in their infancy, and the volumes going through them remain relatively small. Even those marketplaces that are attracting vast numbers, VerticalNet for instance, have yet to make a profit (at the time of writing). Contenders therefore need enough initial funding to carry them through into the long term. Forrester Research predicts that low margin, commodity industries (cars, computers etc) are going to move quickly into the online B2B arena.

The second issue is deciding who your marketplace is going to serve. You will have to decide whether you are focusing on one specific sector or adopting a cross-industry 'jack of all trades' approach. For instance, Just2Clicks, which has decided to run five industry-specific marketplaces simultaneously, has come under criticism for taking too much on board. Sarah Skinner, Internet analyst at Durlacher (stockbrokers and investors in the Internet), claims that 'you have to ask "how are you going to manage five marketplaces, bring value to each of them and compete in each of them?" '. Even Just2Clicks' chief executive Karl Watkin conceded in *Business 2.0* that 'in a stable market it would seem to make sense to stay focused and concentrate on producing a great result in one area'. As most commentators acknowledge, however, this is *not* a stable market.

The other main issue is whether to build an online marketplace from scratch, or buy a software solution 'off the shelf'. There are certainly many supply chain packages from companies such as Ariba, Broadvision, Commerce One and Intershop. (Auction software is discussed in the next chapter.) Whether these products are suitable depends on the size and scale of the proposed marketplace. Larger companies may have a capable IT department willing to take the task on, smaller operators may not.

Perhaps the leading name, however, is Oracle. Oracle, the software company founded as Software Development Laboratories in 1977 by Larry Ellison, Bob Miner and Ed Oates, produces a wide range of B2B applications and tools that can fit most B2B requirements. Indeed, so large is the number of applications that Oracle provides a B2B Product Dashboard with links to each tool. Broadly speaking, these tools can be grouped under the headings of Exchange, Internet Procurement, Manufacturing, Supply Chain Management and Order Management software. Oracle is therefore able to provide the tools and services required to fulfil most B2B requirements. As indicated, Oracle software may be used to build e-marketplaces, specifically exchanges, which may be private or industry-based.

In the exchange arena Oracle offers tools including Exchange Marketplace and Oracle Supply Chain Exchange. Oracle also provides a comprehensive set of 'direct' B2B tools to link businesses together. In these instances software from the Internet Procurement, Order Management and Supply Chain Planning suites may be utilized.

Case study: Professional Contractors Group

The Professional Contractors Group (PCG) launched its free business-to-business contract matching service to put its members in touch with contracting companies, clients and agents. The online portal www.pcgroup.org.uk/portalpub/ allows companies to search for specifically skilled contractors from among PCG's highly-skilled membership and allows PCG's members to tender for specific contracts, which clients advertise on the site free of charge.

PCG's members create their own business profile, and clients and agents can visit the site to search for a specific criterion. From within the database of PCG members, the client is then provided with a list of available business profiles that fit their requirements. The opportunity to advertise is open to anyone wishing to register their details, although the opportunity to tender is available only to PCG members.

The portal's business-to-business contract matching service benefits clients and agents by providing direct access to thousands of the best contracting and consultancy companies, in IT, engineering, telecoms, aerospace and other disciplines. Clients and agents can publish their requirements free of charge on the portal, where they can be accessed by the 11,000 PCG members. The portal can be used by businesses to find 'high calibre individuals, full teams or experienced project managers who can put a team together on request'.

Case study: Spares Finder and GoIndustry

Spares Finder and GoIndustry, two business-to-business (B2B) companies that together help industry better manage, market, and dispose of its idle or used capital equipment and spares, formed a 'unique partnership' to cross-promote each other through their direct sales forces and on their Web sites (www.goindustry.com; www.sparesfinder.com). A Spares Finder client who wishes to buy or sell any surplus equipment can do so through GoIndustry's online marketplace or offline auctioneers and trading services. Likewise, GoIndustry customers are able to search for any spare parts they need in Spares Finder's database.

According to Spares Finder's operations director David Stroud, 'the clientele of Spares Finder very much corresponds with that of GoIndustry, so both companies can combine their efforts in order to offer their customers more comprehensive products and services, all from a single Internet point of contact'.

Survival of the fittest

In a 2001 report on European B2B e-marketplaces, Jupiter Communications predicted that the value of the online B2B market in Europe would increase from $185 million to $1.7 billion by 2004. However, in the same report Jupiter also predicted that many B2B e-marketplaces currently in existence would fail over the next few years. The report outlines the characteristics that the B2B marketplace survivors will have in common:

- *A high volume of transactions*. 'Unlikely to survive' was the verdict Jupiter passed on e-marketplaces without a high volume of business. The UK e-marketplace, BuildOnline.co.uk, a construction site that at the start of 2001 was managing projects worth in excess of £100 million, was cited as one of the most likely survivors.
- *Industry backing*. Support from industry leaders is deemed essential for long-term survival as this will lead to 'trustworthiness, financial support and a commitment to placing orders'.
- *Integrated offerings*. Jupiter's report is right to acknowledge that B2B companies need to 'integrate their online offering with offline services such as full telephone service and local cus-

> tomer support'. As Internet guru Esther Dyson prophesied, 'the future is multi-channel'. Marketplaces that offer callback services, local 24-hour customer service departments and links to real-world auctions were singled out for praise.

In addition, the Boston Consulting Group (which predicts that revenue from B2B e-marketplaces will approach $9 billion in 2005) has formulated a comprehensive report on the future of B2B, entitled 'The B2B Opportunity: Creating Advantage Through E-Marketplaces' (2001). The report, based on a three-month survey of nearly 500 executives of major business buyers, sellers and e-marketplaces, establishes the five factors that are essential for these B2B marketplaces to 'create the critical mass or liquidity required' to survive in the long-term as a viable business:

- *Room for differentiation*. 'Leave room for companies to differentiate themselves.'
- *Cost-effectiveness*. 'Stay cost-effective and focused on execution.'
- *Effective communication of benefits*. 'Clearly communicate to buyers and sellers the value that the e-marketplace creates.'
- *Welcome smaller businesses*. 'Extend the offering to small and mid-sized businesses.'
- *Flexibility*. 'Be flexible about changing the business model.'

In particular, this last point is significant. As the wildly divergent economic forecasts for the B2B sector indicate, the future for B2B e-marketplaces is uncertain.

In this ever-shifting, relatively unstable business environment every B2B company must be able to constantly challenge its own thinking. In the new economy, stagnation is the ultimate threat to business, while reinvention has emerged as the primary aim. B2B marketplaces wishing to stay in the 'comfort zone' are not going to be around for long. Change is now sudden, non-linear and constant, which means its amplitude and direction can never be forecast. As a result, marketplaces need to focus on organizational readiness and their ability to adapt. As Peter Solvik, senior vice-president and chief information officer of Cisco Systems, has put it: 'The new economy is about reinventing how business is conducted – in every single job, in every single corporation. There's a revolution going on, and we have to rethink every single relationship within the company and beyond.'

IronSpire, a private exchange founded in 1999 by technology and commercial construction experts to deliver real-time command, control and communication functionality to construction teams, differs from other e-marketplaces in that business managers, not technical staff, handle management of the site. The entire solution is delivered in an easily navigated project management 'dashboard', for more effective construction project management. The dashboard enables faster communication, minimizes mistakes and delays, and improves scheduling and financial reporting.

Furthermore, IronSpire's use of built-in workflow allows customers to handle existing business processes and create more flexible processes focused on improving efficiencies. As a result of this solution, IronSpire's decision cycle time has improved by as much as 2,400 per cent, overall communications improved by 40 per cent and the site is enabled to provide wireless notification to PDAs and mobile phones.

Case study: ICommerce

ICommerce, the first B2B marketplace hub to be developed in Ireland, incorporates a customizable trading platform and auction site in one of Europe's most ambitious online B2B environments. A joint venture between *Business & Finance Magazine*, Comit Gruppe and the Chambers of Commerce of Ireland, iCommerce aims to register 20,000 companies by the start of 2002. Strategic alliances with the Irish Exporters Association, the Institute of Purchasing and Materials Management and the Marketing Institute of Ireland look set to give ICommerce access to a further 100,000 companies. (Amarach Consulting states that 11 per cent of Irish companies are currently engaged in purchasing via B2B e-commerce platforms and at least 21 per cent expect to be doing so within 12 months.)

ICommerce clearly needed a B2B e-commerce solution provider that could cope with the immense scale of the project. Ian Hyland, CEO of ICommerce states that 'ICommerce has a mission to spread the benefits of online trading, so we need to partner with a specialist whose business model encourages, not penalizes, a high volume of transactions. After researching the best in the market, we found that Clarus eMarket had the most comprehensive understanding of the needs of market makers, buyers and sellers.'

Ultimately, ICommerce creates a unique business-to-business (B2B) marketplace where companies can service existing customers, find new ones and search and deal with suppliers for all business products and services.

Case study: ECeurope.com

ECeurope.com was launched in 1999 as a global business-to-business (B2B) eMarketplace. It manages a 'Trade Bulletin Board System' – a virtual business match-making service. ECeurope is currently one of the top 50 Trade BBS systems around the world and has a leading position within the European marketplace.

Rather than holding or selling physical stock, the 'Trade BBS' acts as an intermediary between international buyers and sellers and targets primarily small to medium-sized enterprises (SMEs) worldwide that wish to locate new business partners and generate new business via the Net.

It allows SMEs to 'post', 'search', 'view' and 'respond' to B2B trade lead messages (digital business ads) for any type of products or services categorized under 23 'vertical' industry categories and 166 sub-categories quickly, easily and cost-effectively.

Consolidate or die

An Arthur Andersen survey published in 2001 found that 50 per cent of e-commerce executives believe consolidation will increase the success of B2B online marketplaces. Indeed, many of the B2B success stories have been the result of 'strategic alliances' such as those formed between Ford, GM and Daimler Chrysler, and the joint B2B initiative by online computer e-tailors Compaq, Hewlett-Packard and Gateway. It is interesting to note that this triumvirate of computer manufacturers formed their collaborative exchange for supply chain management at around the same time Dell single-handedly set up its own B2B e-marketplace.

At the start of 2001, within four months Dell deserted its Dell Marketplace project, owing to what a Dell spokesperson referred to as 'a limited readiness of customers to make use of an electronic marketplace'. However, Jupiter Research senior analyst Tim Clark (who is infamous for collaborative projects) was quoted in

E-Commerce Times as saying that 'Dell's decision is not a sign that these industry marketplaces won't work. It's a sign that Dell had higher priorities.'

Case study: E-cement.com

E-cement.com, the first global B2B e-commerce marketplace for the cement industry, is an independent-based procurement and cement trading exchange. Providing an open, transparent market for the procurement and sales of plant, parts, bulk materials and related products, e-cement.com manages to deliver:

- reduced procurement process and transaction costs for customers and suppliers;
- increased buying power for independent purchasers by grouping orders;
- release of working capital through inventory reductions of all procured material;
- high value services, such as shipping and logistical support.

Furthermore, e-cement.com operates a global news and

Figure 5.2 E-cement.com: a vertical e-marketplace for the construction industry

information forum for the cement industry, offering a daily updated news service, alongside a suite of commercial and technical support services to the industry. Revenues are generated by service fees that vary according to the transaction method, as well as advertising.

The business is well placed to attract a significant share of the multi-billion pound global market for plant, spare parts and bulk commodities used in the cement industry and was contacted by several hundred cement manufacturers and suppliers worldwide who could benefit from this exchange.

Rick Haythornthwaite, Chief Executive Officer of Blue Circle, says that: 'Procurement and trading online makes huge sense for our industry. E-cement.com provides the first truly global marketplace for cement manufacturers and suppliers. Procurement alone offers a multi-billion pound market and substantial potential for savings. This venture gives further impetus to our cost reduction programme, and provides an efficient marketplace for us and other users.'

Case study: TexYard

The B2B online marketplace, TexYard, was launched to tackle inefficiencies in the $35 billion European fashion industry supply chain. TexYard addresses pricing and supply, the inefficiencies in the textiles sector that arise from the high degree of industry fragmentation, difficult cross-border market access, and the lack of supplier integration that characterizes the industry today. (According to ICG Europe, the European $35 billion fashion market is comparable in size with the US market but, with a few exceptions, it lags behind the US in the uptake of e-procurement.)

However, it cautions that the industry-wide benefits of e-procurement can only be enjoyed with the emergence of open, Internet-based standards, capable of supporting the ready exchange of data between retailers and manufacturers. The first retailers to use B2B e-commerce effectively will be able to leverage this opportunity to expand faster and more profitably than the rest of the market.

This is certainly the hope of TexYard, which uses the Internet to utilize multiple pricing mechanisms, including both forward and reverse auctions. In addition, financial services, logistics, inspection and sampling are also be supported online. According to co-founder of TexYard, Brent Dennison: 'There is an excellent opportunity to tackle key issues within the fragmented European textiles sector.' He claims that 'TexYard's solution addresses concerns such as leftovers and increasing seasonal swings in capacity, which are exacerbated by such trends as shorter product life-cycles in the fashion industry.'

As with similar industry-specific, vertical marketplaces, the TexYard.com site helps bring buyers and sellers together, by creating a simple and efficient process for purchasing online. The site helps buyers to find new suppliers, and to source, negotiate and track orders online, while helping suppliers to gain access to new business and simplify their selling process.

Summary

Basically, e-marketplaces work by cutting costs and inefficiencies in the supply chain and by creating new ways to buy and sell products and services. Although they are still in the early stages of their development, most analysts agree that e-marketplaces represent the future of the online B2B world. Whatever industry you are in – be it telecoms, automotive, energy, agriculture, finance or any other – there is, or soon will be, an online marketplace devoted to it. The fact is that this new means of doing business benefits both the buyer (who can search further and faster than ever before), the seller (who can reach new audiences and post an item for sale with minimal effort) and the middleman (the e-marketplace can make money on each transaction). In the next chapter we will look in more detail at one of the most radical forms of e-marketplace, the online B2B auction.

six

B2B auctions

The online auction is one of the fastest growing areas within the B2B sector. Although some of the most famous auction sites (eBay, Yahoo! Auctions, QXL, Go Network Auction etc) are mainly targeted towards the consumer, there are many newer auction sites that concentrate solely on B2B. Indeed, according to a Forrester Research report, B2B auctions and exchange-related transactions will total $746 billion by the end of 2004. This chapter looks at the various types of online B2B auctions as well as the manifold ways companies can benefit from them.

Dynamic pricing

One of the most obvious advantages of holding an auction, from both a buyer and vendor perspective, relates to pricing. The marketing effort (in terms of research) that normally goes into price is rendered unnecessary. In an online auction the guesswork is eliminated as the market sets the price (although the vendor retains the power to say no). Auction-based pricing is therefore referred to as dynamic pricing, to differentiate its pricing mechanism from those of static or fixed price vendors.

Online B2B auctions have successfully demonstrated that dynamic pricing is a critical component of B2B e-commerce. Indeed, research analysts have predicted that as much as one-third of B2B e-commerce over the next several years will involve dynamic pricing.

Of course, during the industrial age, fixed prices were essential in order to manage the sales of mass-produced goods. However, in the information age (and its emphasis on one-to-one marketing) fixed pricing is beginning to look fundamentally flawed. For instance, fixed prices, by their very nature, have proved slow to adjust to market conditions. This inevitably leads to a discrepancy between a product's actual market value and the price charged.

Although businesses have invested millions in trying to anticipate overall market demand, they have often achieved little success. Widespread Internet access and the ability to exchange large quantities of information in real time have also helped to bring about the shift from fixed to dynamic pricing.

According to Purnendu Ojhah, CEO of B2B exchange NexTag (www.nextag.net), 'the dynamic pricing model provides buyers and sellers with unprecedented control and flexibility, giving them the ability to get a great deal within seconds'. Forrester Research has predicted that more and more companies will come to share this view. 'Dynamic pricing is expected to grow twenty-five fold over the next five years,' said Forrester analyst Steven J Kafka at the beginning of 2001, with reference to a Forrester report on B2B auctions and exchanges. 'During this period of rapid expansion, today's rudimentary e-marketplaces will evolve to support matchmaking across multiple product attributes, automated matching of bids, and deeper integration with back-end systems. This new environment will enable broader participation of suppliers without the fear of price margins getting squeezed.'

Bidding in an online auction

There is no standard procedure for taking part and bidding in an online auction. Each B2B auction site has its own set of criteria depending on the type of auction service it provides. However, although the specific process varies between auction sites, the fundamentals remain essentially the same. Typically, the pattern for bidding on an auction site is as follows:

- First-time bidders log onto the auction site and register.
- The registration process normally involves submitting credit card details and agreeing to the site's rules for bidding for and purchasing products.
- Users are informed of any features specific to the site (such as automated facilities enabling a bid to progress even when the bidder is not logged on to the site).
- Auctions for certain products are promoted in advance, enabling potential bidders to plan ahead.
- As soon as an open auction is underway, users can begin to bid on products.

- Participants bid for goods by clicking a 'Bid' button and typing in a price (it is typical on auction sites for no bid to be valid unless a password has been registered).
- The auction ceases either at a set time or after a certain amount of time following a bid (if no further bids are made). These times are set either by the host site or participating vendors.
- The highest bidder is notified by e-mail with the relevant instructions and delivery details. The auction site then debits your account for the amount bid. Once the funds have cleared, the goods will be delivered.

Buyer guidelines

In the US the National Fraud Information Centre has formulated a set of guidelines for buyers participating in B2B auctions. These guidelines apply equally to UK businesses:

- *Know who you are dealing with*. Before placing a bid, buyers should check the seller's identifying information, such as address and e-mail.
- *Understand how the auction operates*. This is important because some B2B auction sites act solely as intermediaries and don't check the quality of the auctioned products.
- *Don't pay above market value*. Conduct a comparative survey of the bids on other auction sites and the price you would pay for the product from a 'real world' vendor.
- *Don't bid on items you don't intend to buy*. Even if you are placing a bid that is way under the market value, you cannot guarantee that you will not be the last bidder. Needless to say, the 'successful' bidder is obligated to complete the transaction.
- *Understand payment options*. Before you place a bid, make sure you understand the site's payment options. Credit card payment is usually preferable.

Selling via an online auction

If you want to sell via an online auction there are two choices: set up an auction at your own site or participate in an already established B2B auction site. Obviously, selling via an established site offers the advantage of being able to capitalize on an existing community of bidders, while selling via your own site provides you with greater control over the whole auction process. If a company chooses to become a vendor at an online auction site other than their own, the procedure will go something like this:

- The company makes contact with the auction site and provides the relevant details for the auction. (These details typically include logistics and storage arrangements, the lowest acceptable price for the auctioned product/service, digital photographs of the products etc.)
- The auction site in turn provides details regarding commission rates. These rates generally vary according to the type or volume of products/services.
- The auction site will then promote the auction to potential bidders.
- The products/services become part of a live auction where other businesses can view them and place bids if they are interested.
- The auction finishes at a set time agreed between the vendor and the auction site.
- If the products/services have been sold, the auction site either debits the company's account for the commission or sends an invoice.
- The products/services are sent to the successful bidder.

If you decide to become an auction vendor it is important to adhere to auction etiquette. For instance, you should always make sure that product descriptions are well written (and jargon-free) and policies are clearly outlined. While you must be sure to include relevant product information (manufacturer, condition, age, payment deadline etc), you must also avoid a hyperbolic sales spiel. Meaningless phrases such as 'incredible offer' and 'ultimate opportunity' are more likely to put business buyers off than generate interest. If you are selling a physical product (as opposed to an intangible service), you should also provide a digital photograph of the actual item. Furthermore, if you are putting a product up for auction you must also be prepared to answer questions from potential buyers (there may be many).

Setting up an auction at your site

The other way to benefit from B2B auctions is set up an auction facility at your site. Even if you only sell your own products and services, site auctions can prove very valuable in your own marketing activity. They can help you decide the best fixed price for new products as well as bring a new audience to your site.

You may decide, however, to open up your site to other vendors and charge a rate of commission for sales. This not only provides an extra revenue stream but is also likely to help you attract a greater number of visitors and build a community of bidders.

The ever-increasing popularity of online auctions has led to the development of a wide range of auction software applications from companies such as Auction Watch (www.auctionwatch.com), Open Site (www.opensite.com) and Instil (www.instil.com). For larger businesses, a total auction solution from companies such as Bid.com may be more appropriate.

Established in 1995, Bid.com is a global application provider of 'dynamic pricing solutions', helping organizations to buy and sell goods online. (The company specializes in a variety of B2B sectors including automotive, heavy machinery, capital markets, electronic media, travel and wireless communications.) Key features included in most auction software packages are:

- live bidding facilities;
- secure auction options;
- bulletin boards enabling vendor and buyer feedback;
- search engine functions;
- keyword profiling to help organize products placed for auction;
- live currency and exchange rate translators, enabling visitors to view prices in multiple currencies.

Even if an online auction is not the main way a company chooses to sell its products or services, it can be a very good complementary method.

Secure auctions

Some B2B auction sites host secure auctions that enable the vendor to restrict potential bidders to specific firms of individuals, who meet pre-set criteria (such as belonging to a certain industry or trade body). On most auction sites offering this service, you will not see these auctions on the auction index unless you are registered with the relevant vendor.

In a secure auction, the vendor, not the host site (unless they are one and the same), is in control of the registration process, and so they are able to remove or add companies to their registry as they see fit.

The reason vendors decide to host a secure auction, and therefore limit the number of potential bidders, is often related to preserving the integrity of a particular brand. For instance, software developers may not want to tarnish their name by passing their products on to unscrupulous distributors or retailers. Similarly, automotive companies looking to get rid of car brands at the end of their initial contracts often prefer to deal only with trusted dealers, who are able to provide excellent after-sales service. Owing to this 'trust factor', potential buyers are often able to bid at comparatively low prices.

As well as sites that host secure auctions alongside open auctions, there are also 'private auction sites' that only host secure auctions. Private auction sites enable business vendors to host online auctions where listings are only made available through a Web address that is not publicly searchable. Private auction sites therefore provide B2B companies with a highly secure method of pre-registering and validating users before they are able to view or bid for products on the auction site.

Reverse auctions

Many B2B auction sites include a 'reverse auction' facility. This enables users who cannot find what they are after to register the details of the required product or service. The auction site then stores these details on file and e-mails the user when the specified product or service is being auctioned. The main advantage of reverse auctions (as far as the buyer is concerned) is that they make it easier for the buyer to 'window shop' at various auctions before deciding to make a bid.

Mobile auctions

EBay is one of the dot.com big players to have embraced the idea of mobile auctions, providing mobile users with instant access to bids. EBay Anywhere enables users to access eBay auction services via Web-enabled mobile devices. The company has launched a 24-hour online trading service that enables sellers to post items for sale and potential buyers to bid on the available items.

Yahoo! now offers e-mail on its wireless service along with personal calendar and entertainment information. Interestingly, it also has plans for eBay-style mobile auctions. Meanwhile, European auctioneer site QXL.com has announced a deal with mobile Internet portal Iobox that will allow users to track auctions and receive bid alerts from their mobile phones.

Auctions work well on the mobile Internet because they overcome the constraints of time and place encountered on the 'fixed' or desktop Internet. As users carry their mobile phones with them, they are ideal for the time-sensitive nature of auctions. This also explains why news alerts, share price information, sporting results and travel and weather updates are also popular uses of the mobile Internet.

Jupiter Communications claims that mobile Web services need to 'complement the desktop Web but avoid replicating it, and online ventures should build offerings around the immediacy of mobile interactivity'. In other words, business cannot transfer its existing Web offerings to the mobile Internet if it wants to succeed at m-commerce. This explains why companies such as Amazon, eBay and QXL.com offer mobile users a stripped down version of its Web auction services, to convey only the most essential information. Furthermore, the fact that most mobile auction services enable users to receive bid alerts (for instance, to indicate when an auctioned product reaches a certain price) also means B2B companies are looking to add value to their existing Web offerings by embracing the instantaneous nature of the mobile Internet.

Case study: TekSell.com

US-based B2B auction site TekSell.com was one of the first sites to auction technology products between businesses. According to TekSell CEO Andy Cummins in an interview with ZDNet (in an article entitled *B2B Auction Sites Multiply)*, the main factor behind its success relates to pricing. 'The key was getting the price high enough to warrant touching it,' Cummins told ZDNet reporters Ed Sperling and John Moore. In the interview, Cummins also noted the average price of products sold on the company's Web site was $5,100.

TekSell targets both resellers and end-user businesses as customers. It auctions vendors' and distributors' excess inventory over the Web, first to authorized resellers and integrators, and then to the public at large.

Finding relevant auctions

There are a number of online auction sites that cater for a wide range of B2B sectors. For instance, Business-auctions.com and U-Bid-It.com both provide auction services for practically every type of B2B company. There are also many industry and geography-specific sites. To find these, it is best to use one of the major search engines (Google proves particularly helpful) and type in a combination of relevant keywords such as:

automotive+b2b+internet+auctions

or

b2b+auctions+uk

Some sites offer services enabling businesses to locate suitable online auctions. Auctionwatch.com and BidStream.com are just two of the sites that provide tailored auction services. For instance, they can arrange for companies to be listed on auction sites, and help track payments.

Learning from eBay

Although eBay (www.ebay.com) is not strictly a B2B auction site, it is worth looking at as it remains by far the most popular Web-based auction service in the world. Its success is also cited as the reason why many other popular consumer Web sites (such as Yahoo!) decided to conduct their own auctions.

Ebay's famous strapline – 'the world's personal trading community' – gets to the heart of two of the factors behind every successful auction, whether B2C, B2B or even C2C (consumer-to-consumer): community and personalization. Without the ability to create a loyal community of vendors and buyers, and personalize the auction experience around the specific requirements of each participant, an auction site will be unlikely to survive. The community feel at eBay is encouraged through interactive forums such as the eBay Café, while personalization is evidenced by the fact that participants can add their own personal interest pages.

Through the eBay Café bulletin boards, users (individual buyers and sellers) meet and get to know each other, discuss topics of mutual interest, and petition one another for information. Furthermore, these bulletin boards are public forums that encourage open communication between users. Significantly, the community also involves a self-policing element: members frequently form 'neighbourhood watch' groups to help guard against misuse of the eBay service. Another key to eBay's phenomenal success is simplicity. EBay strips the auction process down to the bare essentials. Vendors offer their products (or services) to potential buyers who then bid online. The vendor placing the highest bid wins the item. Each bid is then confirmed by e-mail and the bidders are notified every time they are outbid. This inevitably encourages ongoing activity.

Furthermore, it costs nothing for vendors and buyers to register at eBay and the cost incurred by the business or consumer vendor for placing an item up for auction is next to nothing. Also, with the recent acquisition of Half.com, eBay's community now benefits from a marketplace combining traditional auction-style trading and fixed-price trading.

It is worth noting that eBay now also incorporates a B2B component with the eBay Business Exchange, which aims to service the 'fast growing and fragmented small business marketplace'. It provides a destination on eBay for businesses to buy or sell new, used and refurbished business merchandise, such as industrial equipment, office equipment, computers and professional tools. At the time of writing, eBay listed over 3.5 million items for sale in over 2,500 categories.

Case study: DoveBid

Founded in 1937, DoveBid is an old-line industrial auction company, which has conducted thousands of industry-specific auctions on behalf of corporations, government agencies and financial institutions from around the world. It has now embraced the Web and has successfully managed to integrate 'real world' and online auctions.

Practically every one of its auctions is open to online bidders. In 2000, DoveBid launched a Webcast Network, which enables DoveBid and 18 affiliates to syndicate and broadcast DoveBid's auctions to over 5 million users each month. In that same year it also conducted the world's first tri-continent Webcast auction, broadcast live over the Internet from Melbourne and simulcast from Singapore and California.

In an interview with *eCompany Now* magazine (August 2000) DoveBid CEO Ross Dove explained that 'the cost of [bidding via a] Webcast is much lower for participants, and we are selling 50 per cent of our assets to remote bidders, so we know we are getting better pricing'.

DoveBid now claims that as many as 60 per cent of the capital assets purchased at its auctions come from buyers over the Web, rather than from the auction floor. According to a DoveBid spokesperson, 'This increased participation has driven greater competition amongst buyers for surplus assets, which in turn increases price premiums for up to 90 per cent – a benefit of DoveBid's Webcast technology for capital asset sellers.'

In addition to Webcast auctions, DoveBid has also crossed over into Featured Online Auctions, in which all bidding is purely online. DoveBid has conducted Featured Online Auctions for clients such as Daimler Chrysler and Boeing.

Figure 6.1 DoveBid: a real world auction house that has successfully transformed itself on the Web

Summary

Online auctions have become a fascinating new type of B2B exchange mechanism. As this chapter has shown, the dynamic pricing mechanism inherent in all Internet auctions can help reduce marketing costs and help streamline B2B activity. Furthermore, the database functionality of the Internet (which enables users to search through millions of items almost instantaneously) means that it is in many ways the perfect medium for hosting and participating in auctions. The Internet also enables far more people to participate in an auction than could offline, because restraints of time and place are all but removed.

Ultimately, as with other forms of B2B exchanges, auctions help to create market efficiency by linking interested vendors and buyers through a centralized online marketplace where transactions occur faster and selling prices are determined by market forces.

seven

B2B branding

Branding on the Internet is an altogether different practice from branding in the 'real world'. Whereas offline, a strong brand identity is often viewed as a luxury few companies can afford to invest in heavily, on the Internet branding is everything. Increased competition, lower barriers to entry, downward price pressure and enhanced interaction have all rendered a strategic approach to branding essential. As this chapter will explain, the key to e-marketing success (for B2B as much as B2C) is differentiation, the ultimate function of a brand.

Reasons for building a B2B brand

Branding is often considered to be the preserve of business-to-consumer companies who have to generate mass awareness of a product via extensive advertising campaigns. However, branding should not be ignored by B2B companies for a number of reasons.

The fact is that differentiation (the main purpose for any brand) is even more important for B2B companies than it is for those targeting the consumer market. As the majority of B2B e-commerce transactions occur in crowded online marketplaces, companies need to create a point of difference between themselves and their nearest rivals. It is hardly surprising that many of the strongest B2B brands (VerticalNet, McKinsey, Enron, B2Bnet, e-Cement.com etc) have been the first in their industry or have been the first to develop a new way of carrying out their business.

According to Pascal Burg, a consultant with management consultancy firm Edgar, Dunn and Company (www.edgardunn.com), B2B branding is important to customers because it simplifies their purchase decision and helps them 'cut through the clutter'. From the company's perspective, successful branding is important because not only does it mean more customers will arrive at its Web site, but it will also aid the transition into new marketplaces. Here are some more reasons why B2B cannot ignore branding:

- *Employees*. In addition to conveying a message to customers, brands can be used to align employees behind that message.
- *Recruitment*. Timothy Payne, CEO of Modis, believes that branding 'is absolutely critical to our recruiting efforts'.
- *B2C crossovers*. With more and more powerful consumer Web brands (Yahoo!, eBay, Ask Jeeves, AOL etc) moving into the B2B arena, B2B companies need to place a similarly high emphasis on creating clear and coherent brand identities.
- *Search engines*. Research has shown that search engine visitors are over three times more likely to click through to a site on a search engine listing if they recognize the name of the company.
- *Exponential growth*. As the Web continues to grow at an exponential rate, it becomes increasingly important to stand out.
- *Low risk for decision-makers*. According to Al Ries, chairman of marketing consulting firm Ries and Ries and author of *22 Immutable Laws of Branding*, 'People who buy products or services for companies don't want to get blamed if something fails. If the brand is powerful enough, then the person that makes the purchase won't get blamed. That's how the expression "No one ever got fired for buying IBM" got started.'
- *Price pressure*. Owing to the Internet's database functionality, consumers can conduct a comparative price study with relative ease. Furthermore, the Internet tends to increase the number of competitors within a sector, and this often puts even more downward pressure on the price of a product. The only way companies can prevent themselves competing on price alone is to establish a strong brand. Premium prices can remain because people automatically think that the strongest brand in an industry (be it Intel, Microsoft or Cisco Systems) is automatically better.

The B2B brand misconception

There are many who mistakenly believe that branding is not significant to B2B companies because business decision-makers are only influenced by tangible concepts such as pricing, and not by more abstract qualities. As Martin Lindstrom commented in his ClickZ column, 'It seems that B2B communications are governed by a "Why should I bother?" mentality. Businesses aren't emotionally driven, they're not brand-conscious, they buy on price.' Because of this erroneous assumption, most B2B Web sites look alike.

The fact is, however, that business decision-makers, think, feel, act and Web surf in a way very similar to consumers. The reason for this is that business decision-makers *are* consumers. The values consumers seek in a brand (value, trustworthiness, professionalism, consistency, convenience, reliability) are the very same values business decision-makers look for when making a purchase. Unfortunately, many B2B companies fail to recognize this fact and seem to believe that branding is about nothing more than a logo and a catchy strapline.

The other misconception about branding is that it is necessarily expensive. However, branding is not about costly advertising campaigns or hiring brand 'creatives' to work out an imaginative but largely irrelevant strategy. Instead, it is about uncovering your core values and expressing them in a way that makes sense to your online audience.

Brand-building guidelines

B2B e-branding is not rocket science. It simply involves looking at what your company stands for and communicating this to a target audience. Here are some of the ways you can bring out your brand:

- *Analyse your competitors.* A successful brand depends on difference. It is therefore important to analyse what your competitors are doing differently to you, and how you are (or could be) doing it better.
- *Be honest.* Trust is based on honesty. If you are making untenable claims about your company, your brand identity will be in trouble. This is especially the case on the Internet, where the true picture of a company is always brought into focus through online forums and message boards.
- *Concede control.* In the age of mass production and broadcast media, companies could retain control of their brand message.

On the Internet, however, companies have to accept that their brand identity is not formed solely by what they say about themselves, but also by what their customers and other interested parties are saying about them online.

- *Be consistent*. Strong brand identities depend on consistency. This does not mean that you should not change in response to market forces as they develop on the Internet. What it does mean is that you should be aware of your core values and be able to centre your marketing activity on them.
- *Form an association*. Branding is about forming a positive association or set of attributes when a brand name is mentioned. For instance, most people think of safety when they think of Volvo.
- *Be first*. Being the first company to get a product to market is an obvious advantage in the e-business arena, as it helps to form a positive association from the outset. This is especially important for B2B technology companies for whom branding is about providing new and innovative solutions.
- *Identify your audience*. Every aspect of brand building should stem from recognition of a knowledge of your audience. As Lee Traupel from Wolf Blast Interactive puts it, 'You can't conceptualize your creative, graphical imagery, content or what type of media you want to deploy until you know the size and characteristics of your target audience.' This argument is extended by B L Ochman on her Web Review site, where she states that above all else 'the user experience is your brand'. It therefore makes sense to bring customers inside the brand-building process by asking for their opinion.
- *Integrate online and offline methods*. It is important to unify your brand strategy by integrating your online and offline activity. After all, the Internet does not exist in a vacuum. Customers who hear about your company via the Web may also hear about you offline as well, and vice versa. As Laura Heinrich, vice-president of marketing for Digex has put it, 'A successful B2B campaign is like a soup. You need components from traditional PR, advertising, speaking opportunities. Everything plays a role.'

Case study: Hewlett Packard

In 1999 Hewlett Packard embarked on a $200 million B2B branding campaign in order to unify its identity. In an interview with *e-business* magazine, Carly Fiorina, CEO of Hewlett Packard, explained that prior to the campaign the company had 'been talking to the market with 100 different voices'. The aim of the B2B branding exercise, she claimed, was to 'speak to our customers with a single compelling voice about who we are and where we're going'.

According to Julia Mee, who headed the branding campaign, 'We're in a new economy in an Internet world where things are moving very quickly. Inventing the products isn't enough. It's more important that people understand our brand.'

The campaign involved co-ordinating a Web advertising strategy aimed solely at business decision-makers and emphasizing the reliability of the product. Hewlett Packard is now viewed as one of the biggest players in the B2B high-tech sector.

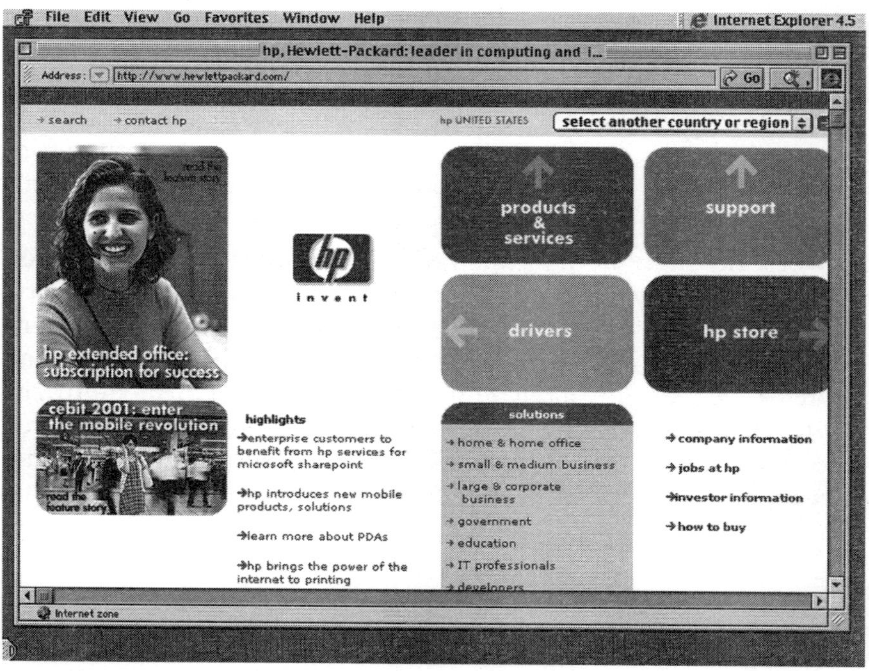

Figure 7.1 Hewlett Packard invested in a B2B branding campaign

Brand interaction

The Internet represents a new way of branding products and services as it has radically redefined the relationship between a company and its customers. Whereas in the Industrial Age branding was a one-way activity conducted by the company alone, it has now become a process in which the formerly passive target audience plays an active role. Customers themselves now have the opportunity to shape the brand message, whether a company wants them to or not. This is especially true when it comes to B2B branding owing to the rise of e-marketplaces, which by 2004 are predicted to account for 55 per cent of total B2B revenues. These online marketplaces facilitate an even greater level of interaction than has been so far witnessed in consumer markets. Companies must therefore not be afraid to actively involve their customers in the brand-building process, and should welcome online feedback.

The networked brand

It used to be the case that for a brand to survive it had to be autonomous and isolable from other companies. However, owing to the networked environment of the Internet this is not possible. Now, B2B brands need to forge connections in order to compete in the online space. As Philip Say commented in his ClickZ column, 'Brand value in B2B is determined by the quality of a company's network, the strength of its business relationships, and how closely it is tied to a market.'

This explains why many of the most successful online companies owe their success, in part at least, to affiliate marketing. However, affiliate schemes are not the only way to build a brand through connectivity. For instance, Sun Microsystems and Cisco Systems have managed to successfully establish their technology brands by offering training courses to Web developers.

Case study: Barnes and Noble.com

Barnes and Noble.com is one example of a consumer-focused organization that has used the power of its brand name to carve out its own niche in the B2B sector. It has set up a corporate book purchasing solution called Find It Now, which provides businesses with tailored, Intranet-based bookstores that enable employees to quickly and easily order books, training materials, and other resources specific to their needs.

According to the specifically branded Find It Now site, this service 'saves corporations time and money by streamlining the procurement process and integrating seamlessly within existing network infrastructures'. IBM, Oracle, Sun Microsystems, Microsoft, Hewlett Packard, Ford Motor Company, 3Com, Cisco Systems and Nortel Networks are just some of the companies that have subscribed to this new and unique branded service from the long-established and well-respected company. In the US, the Find It Now scheme, as part of the company's Business Solutions programme, has been recognized by the General Services Administration (GSA), adding further endorsement to its brand identity.

Brand protection

Once a B2B brand identity is established, it is important to preserve and protect that identity. The flip side to the Web's democratic nature is that anyone is able to publish or post material about your company on the Web, regardless of whether it happens to be true or not.

According to a study of 600 mid-size to large businesses conducted by Yankebrich Partners and Hill and Knowlton, over 60 per cent of CEOs are either 'concerned' or 'very concerned' about negative information about their company on the Internet. Furthermore, while it has often been B2C companies in the firing line, B2B operators are not immune. Owing to the interactive nature of B2B e-marketplaces, criticisms levelled against companies often emerge in online discussions or conversations. Furthermore, a B2B company is just as likely to have its brand tarnished online by an unscrupulous counterfeiter or a competitor looking to eat into its market share. There are, however, a number of tactics that can be deployed in order to protect an online brand. These include:

- *Monitoring discussion groups*. Disgruntled customers or competitors can use online discussion groups and often interactive forums to share their complaints with the e-business community. The fact is that word can spread very quickly on the Internet as markets are more connected. Furthermore, journalists are increasingly using online newsgroups to find inside information (or misinformation) about a company. For instance, when Intel ignored a story about their flawed Pentium chip (which originally was posted in a small academic newsgroup) it ended up gaining massive media coverage in the *Financial Times* and *The Wall Street Journal*. (If you are still in doubt about how much of a threat the Internet poses, it is worth remembering that some of the biggest scandals in recent history, such as the Monica Lewinsky affair, first came to light on the Internet.)

  While companies of Intel's size are able to recover from such knocks to their brand identity, smaller companies may find it more difficult. 'Large companies have the size and resources to withstand that kind of criticism, but a rumour can crater a small company,' says Harlan Teller, Hill and Knowlton's executive vice-president of worldwide corporate practice. The easiest way to monitor the discussion groups is to visit Google Groups (groups.google.com), formerly Deja News. This provides a searchable index of over 100,000 of the most popular groups. Type in your company (or product) name and wait for the Google Groups' search facility to return with articles featuring these words along with details of the discussion group within which they are posted. Other discussion group indexes are available at Liszt (www.liszt.com) and Newsguy (www.newsguy.com).
- *Respond to misinformation*. Once you have found misleading or inaccurate comments about your company you will need to correct it in as polite a way as possible. However, if a customer has a genuine complaint, it is important to acknowledge it and detail the actions you are going to take to amend the situation.
- *Use search engines*. Search engines are the most obvious place to start looking for mentions of your company online. However, search engines generally do not include brand new documents and there is no way of knowing which Web pages have been most recently indexed.

- *Check links*. One of the most effective ways to locate mentions of your company is to conduct a 'back link' search. This enables you to find out all the Web sites that contain a link to your site. AltaVista (www.altavista.com -.co.uk) is the main search site to offer this facility. To find links, simply type the word 'Link' into the AltaVista search box followed by your Web site address.
- *Use an e-media monitoring service*. As it is not always possible to monitor the Web in-house, many businesses hire e-media monitoring services to pick up references to their company site, products or services. One of the most popular services is Cyber Alert (www.cyberalert.com). This is a fully automated service that provides an 'effective, time-efficient and economical way to find and "clip" what is being said about a company'. The service automatically monitors over 3,500 Web publications, 63,000 Usenet discussion groups and 5 million other Web sites every day. Other services include Cyber Check (www.cybercheck.com), Durrants (www.durrants.co.uk) and E-Watch (www.eWatch.com).

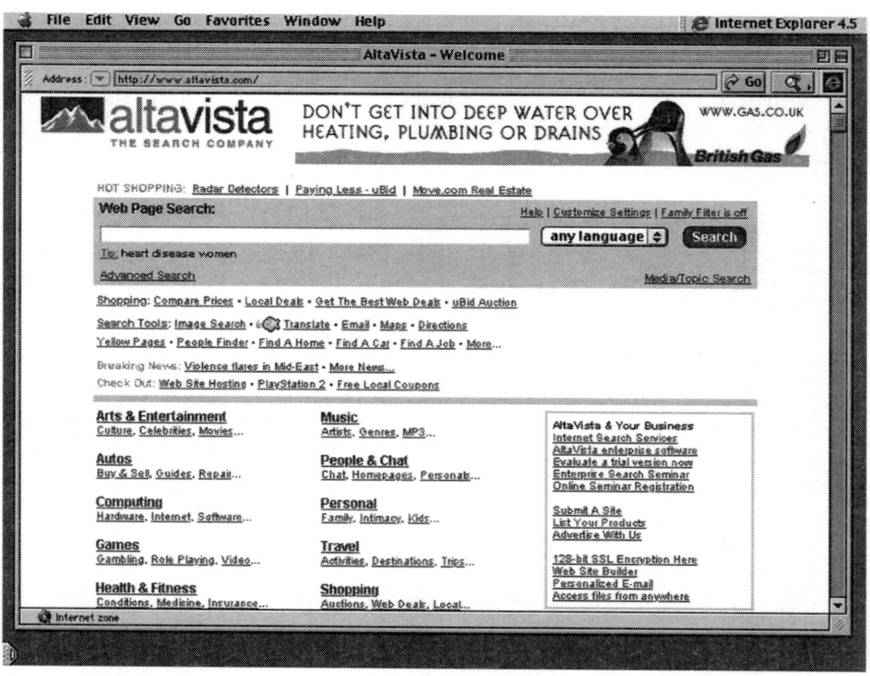

Figure 7.2 AltaVista enables you to conduct a 'back link' search

- *Look for anti-sites.* Another way a brand identity can be undermined online is by anti-sites – Web sites set up with the deliberate intent of damaging a company's reputation. Yahoo! lists over 300 'opinion' sites that criticize major corporations such as American Express, AOL, Bell Atlantic, British Airways, Chase Manhattan, Citibank, Ford, GM, Microsoft, Natwest Bank, Packard Bell and even Yahoo! itself. However, there is no denying the fact that anti-sites are more of an issue for business-to-consumer companies than those targeting a business market.
- *Hire a 'brand cop'.* Some large consumer companies, such as Coca-Cola, hire individuals whose job description solely involves monitoring and responding to online criticism and copyright infringement. This practice has yet to take off in the B2B sector.

The Web site as brand

The most important signifier of an online brand is, without any doubt, the company Web site. This is where you have the strongest opportunity to unify your corporate identity and speak directly to your target audience of business buyers. Here are some general points to consider when looking at a Web site from a B2B branding perspective:

- *Provide detailed product information.* As opposed to a consumer purchase, business decision-makers are unlikely to buy on impulse. They therefore tend to look through as much product information as they can on the company's Web site beforehand.
- *Build a community.* Web sites can be used to create a community of similar businesses. As Rory Sutherland, executive creative director of Ogilvy One, puts it, 'Once you have your loyal community, there are fabulous opportunities for cross-selling, personalized services and meeting the multiple needs of the same group.' A community helps to bring about loyalty and increase the 'lifetime value' of business customers.
- *Get your domain name right.* A Web site's domain name is a clear brand signifier. Good domain names are short, easy to spell, and

transfer well to different languages. As Al Ries has observed, 'Internet brands are invisible until you input the brand name into the keyboard. If you don't know the brand name and how to spell it, no sale can happen.' As a result many B2B operators consider a good domain name to be invaluable. This was certainly the reasoning behind business.com's reported payment of $7 million for its Web address.

- *Be consistent*. The design elements of your site should be consistent on every page in order to create an easily identifiable image.

Summary

B2B companies can no longer afford to ignore branding. In an ever more populated marketplace, successful branding becomes the key to differentiating your company's products or services. However, branding is not to be treated as isolated from your other e-marketing activities. In fact, branding constitutes the sum of these activities and develops in line with them. Ultimately, as a brand is the set of associations that a customer (or potential customer) has in his or her mind, it stems from the customer's own experience. By adopting an 'outside in' perspective, and by shaping a brand around customer expectations, companies can create an identity that can come to be valued by every member of their online target audience.

eight

Building business relations

A common misconception made by many companies is that the main purpose of marketing is to raise awareness and attract new customers. While this is undeniably important, the ultimate marketing objective should be to build long-term relations, not just short-term exposure. Furthermore, these relations should not just be with customers, but with complementary businesses, the media and other influential industry figures.

Building customer relations

Ninety-five per cent of offline B2B purchases are made between buyers and vendors who have done business together before. Jupiter Media Metrix predicts that over the next few years 85 per cent of *online* B2B transactions will be made between businesses with an established relationship. According to Jupiter analyst Jean Gabriel Henry in the *E-commerce Times*, 'The market for existing customers will be the bigger opportunity for sellers because they have already established trust with buyers – many of whom are waiting for their favoured vendors to move online.' After all, without establishing trust, both buyers and vendors are undertaking transactions with anonymous parties.

In the B2C sector, companies talk about the importance of the 'lifetime value' of their customers, having realized that constantly striving to win over first-time buyers is not a cost-effective marketing strategy. This is even truer for the B2B sector where, typically, the number of potential customers is smaller and the transactions made are larger.

The simple fact is that both business and consumer buyers prefer to purchase from a company they have 'tried and tested' than one they have never done business with before. Building customer loyalty should therefore be a priority for any B2B company. The aim is to ensure that first-time customers make a return visit. Here are some of the ways in which to win the trust and loyalty of site visitors and customers:

- *Create a community*. By creating an online community of users, a site can encourage repeat and regular traffic. This is where auction sites and other interactive B2B e-marketplaces have a natural advantage. Bulletin boards, live chat facilities and other online forums can all add to the community feel.
- *Gain external endorsement*. Third-party endorsement from customers, trade bodies and other relevant sources will help to secure trust.
- *Fulfilment*. According to research from Verdict, 'excellence in all aspects of fulfilment will separate the online winners from the losers over the next few years'. Successful fulfilment can be achieved in various ways. Sending out receipts, offering free delivery, showing exactly what products are and are not available and putting together a returns policy are just some of the things a B2B e-commerce site must do in order to fulfil the expectations of business customers. Perhaps the main thing to remember is to keep customers informed. For instance, if there are going to be delivery or other problems, ensure customers know about them straightaway.
- *Reveal full costs*. Make sure that full costs (including shipping, taxes and other charges) are made apparent, and not left for the small print.
- *Use e-mail for customer support*. Although a Web site is likely to be the starting point for relations with customers, e-mail helps keep these relations alive. It is always important to answer customer enquiries as soon as possible. This may involve using response systems such as Echo Mail (www.echomail.com) and Brightware (www.brightware.com), which allow you to preset criteria so that customers receive a more tailored response.
- *Privacy*. B2B operators must appreciate the significance of data privacy if they are to establish trust. Encryption standard and secure socket layer (SSL) technology must be deployed when passing on customer data and conducting transactions online.

- *Localization*. National, cultural and linguistic differences need to be recognized if a company is targeting a global audience. At the very least, automated currency converters and different language options are essential. It is also likely that different geographical areas are more receptive to certain products or services than others.

Reciprocal links

Reciprocal link partnerships can help you to forge healthy relations with similar businesses. Furthermore, after search engines, the main way people arrive at a B2B Web site is via a link from another site. It therefore makes sense to actively seek links from compatible business sites relating to your industry.

The other main reason to gain links to your site has to do with search engines. Most of the search engine agents (or 'robots') that trawl through the Web to compile their listings reach new sites via external links. Broadly speaking, the more links to a Web site, the higher the chance that it will be indexed and ranked high on a search engine or directory.

However, in order to attract links *to* your site it will probably be necessary to include links *from* your site. Reciprocal links help sites to increase their volume of traffic by providing an extra route for visitors and by generating awareness. It is certainly no coincidence that the most popular Web sites (MSN, Yahoo!, Amazon and so on) are the sites that have, either actively or passively, gained the most links.

Obviously, many links are acquired via affiliate marketing and banner advertising, but many more are gained through reciprocal deals. It is important to ensure that any links you include on your Web site are relevant to its target audience. However, the sites you form reciprocal link partnerships with don't have to be direct competitors, they just need to attract a similar target audience. Here are some guidelines to follow in order to find potential link sites:

- *Use search engines*. Use general and industry-specific search engines and directories to find suitable sites. Type in keywords that your target visitors would be likely to use to find a site like yours.

- *Visit trade sites*. Trade organizations often include a link section full of sites relating to a specific industry.
- *Make contact*. When you have found compatible sites, make available information about your site and explain why a reciprocal link partnership would be of benefit to them.

Web rings

A Web ring is a reciprocal link network that connects Web sites together relating to a common theme or specific industry. They increase the exposure of every site within the network by enabling visitors to move from one site to the next automatically, eventually ending up back where they started. Web rings are popular among business decision-makers, because unlike most search engines they ensure that the information they contain is relevant to one specific area of interest.

The largest Web ring organizer is Yahoo! Web Ring (dir.webring.yahoo.com), which includes over 2,000 Web rings in its Business and Finance section alone. One of the most popular of these rings is The Financial Directory Web Ring with over 100 sites.

Not only are Web rings a useful way of generating awareness for your site among new audiences, but also they can help develop online relations with other companies and create an online community working on the principle of mutual benefit.

The new media opportunity

The Internet has exploded the opportunities available for businesses seeking media coverage. One of the main reasons for this is that, through the act of establishing a presence on the Web, businesses are themselves becoming a part of the media. They no longer have to rely on intermediaries such as publishers, editors and journalists to get their message across.

However, media gatekeepers are still significant for companies seeking to consolidate their brand identity as they can provide useful third-party endorsement or approval. Furthermore, owing to the fact that there are more business publishers than ever before (with a more pressing need than ever to have a constant supply of new content), it is easier than ever before to target journalists.

While the Internet represents a new media opportunity, it also constitutes something of a threat. Whereas in the real world it remains possible to keep a distance from the media and to plan what to release and when, on the Internet such distance is denied. After all, competitors, investors, journalists and hostile business can all visit your site or read information about your company online. As I have argued in a previous book (*E-PR: The Essential Guide to Public Relations on the Internet*), on the Internet a company is permanently exposed to the outside world, and so everything it puts online can affect its reputation.

The problem with public relations

Ironically, PR has something of an image problem. Many companies, and even more journalists, view it as a rather superfluous and unnecessary activity. There are very good reasons for this. After all,

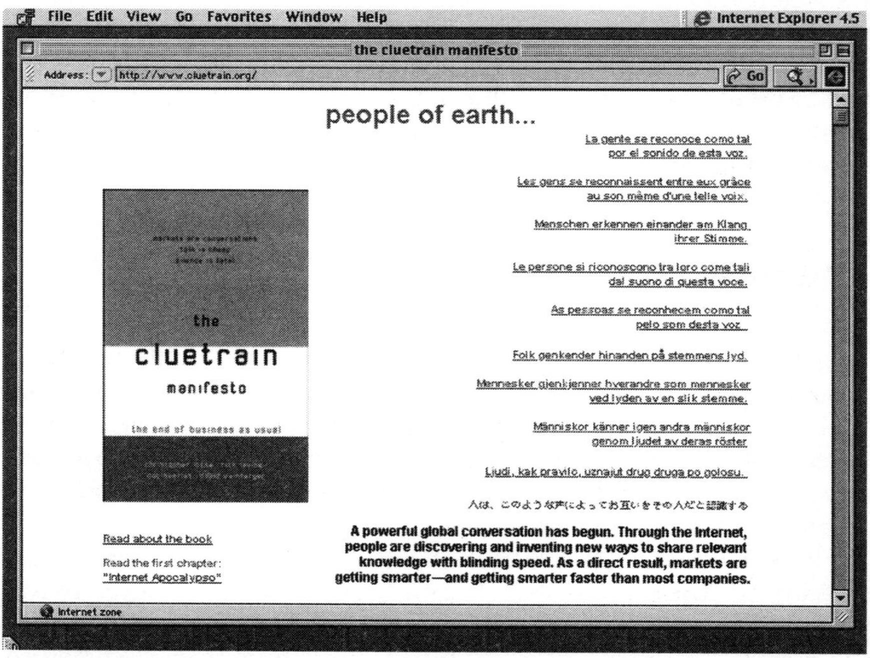

Figure 8.1 The Cluetrain Web site

some PR people have been very bad at adapting to the interactive nature of the Internet. This is because the one most important criterion for successful online communication is honesty, something that is all too often seen as irrelevant to the PR function.

Perhaps Christopher Locke, who writes in *The Cluetrain Manifesto*, provides the most articulate attack on the current state of PR:

> Everyone – including many PR people – senses that something is deeply phoney about the profession. And it's not hard to see what it is. Take the standard computer industry press release. With few exceptions, it describes an 'announcement' that was not made for a product that was not available, quoting people who never said anything, for distribution to a list of people who mostly consider it trash.

While the PR industry is often reluctant to embrace 'the whole truth and nothing but', the Internet acts as if it has been programmed to let the real picture emerge. However, for PR people willing to acknowledge this fact, there is a very important role to play. As Locke himself acknowledges, in the age of the Web where 'hype blows up in your face and spin gets taken as an insult, the real work of PR will be more important than ever'.

Therefore, if press releases and other PR tools are treated as an opportunity to honestly define a company's significance within an industry, rather than to provide a one-sided and untenable version of events, they can be of equal benefit to companies, journalists and customers alike.

The press release

Most PR campaigns revolve around press releases. Indeed, the press release remains the easiest and most popular method of distributing company information (of news value) to a wide media audience. Press releases are used by B2B companies to announce new products and services or any other news of significance to their industry (mergers, acquisition deals, fluctuations, staff cuts etc).

For B2B companies, which typically focus on a particular industry segment, the objectives of a press release are often different to those of a consumer-focused organization. For instance, the main target of a B2B press release is normally the online and offline trade press, as opposed to the consumer publications found on the local newsstand.

However, while the objectives may be different, the way a press release is put together and distributed via the Internet remains fundamentally the same. The main thing to consider is when a press release should be sent out. Here are some examples of good reasons to put together a B2B press release:

- *New company*. If you are a new company it makes sense to announce your arrival to the relevant media. However, you have to make sure that the significance of the company launch extends beyond your employees. For instance, if the CEO was formerly with a high profile company, this may provide a valid angle. If the launch of the company is unlikely to create a stir, it makes sense to wait a while until you have proved your significance.
- *Product/service launch*. New product launches usually warrant a press release, although journalists are unlikely to get excited if you are only announcing a product upgrade (such as a new, but hardly changed, version of a software package).
- *Company partnerships*. Partnerships and mergers make for a good press release as they combine the weight of your company with someone else's. They also often signify nascent industry development.
- *New appointment*. Obviously you should not send out a press release every time you gain a new member of staff, but when someone who is recognized in the industry is acquired, it often justifies an announcement.
- *Performance*. Press releases can be used to provide financial information and other performance statistics.
- *Legal news*. Court victories and settlements are definitely press release material.

Press release principles

While the Internet has enabled companies to distribute press releases faster and further than they ever could offline, the principles regarding what constitutes a good release remain intact:

- *Avoid sales language.* What many companies fail to grasp is that a press release is not an advert, but an informative document. It is therefore inappropriate to adopt a hyperbolic and over-the-top style. Exclamation marks, superfluous adjectives ('remarkable', 'amazing' etc) and exaggeration must therefore be avoided.
- *Follow the BLUF rule.* In press releases it is essential to give the Bottom Line Up Front.
- *Answer the Ws.* The 'W' questions (What? When? Who? Where? Why?) should be answered within the first paragraph.
- *Keep headlines short.* The press release headline should summarize the subject in as few words as possible.
- *Incorporate quotes.* Quotes can add life to a press release, providing they are real and not fabricated. Third party quotes from industry pundits or satisfied customers are valued higher than self-congratulatory statements from the CEO.
- *Make it obvious.* A press release should be clearly identified as such with the words 'PRESS RELEASE', 'MEDIA RELEASE' or 'FOR IMMEDIATE RELEASE' written across the top.
- *Place contact details at the foot of the release.* For press releases sent via the Internet, the contact details should be placed at the bottom. (While it has become standard practice to put contact information at the top of a press release, a survey of 1,000 journalists conducted by Mindset found that they prefer to see the headline announcement first, with the contact details at the end.)
- *Include an industry identifier.* If a B2B company is distributing a media release using an online newswire service such as Business Wire or PR Newswire, it needs to incorporate an industry identifier. An industry identifier is used to identify who exactly will be interested in the release. There are two ways of doing this. You can either state the industry it refers to (eg IT/software) or the journalists it is aimed at (eg business editors/IT journalists).
- *Include an 'about the company' paragraph.* At the foot of the release, before the contact details, you should include an 'about the company' paragraph. If there is more than one company mentioned in the release, each should have its own paragraph. Typically, an 'about the company' section includes the year the company was established and any significant milestones in its corporate history.

- *Remember that less is more*. The information in the release should be conveyed in as concise a manner as possible. The average length of a release (including 'contact' and 'about' information) is approximately 250 words. The maximum length should be 400–500 words. If you need to supply further information, do it via a company background. The great thing about sending press releases via the Internet is that unlike print releases (which only include as much information as the space allows), it is possible to provide hypertext links to more indepth information. Links to the company Web site should definitely be included within each release.
- *Make text accessible*. The press release text needs to be made as accessible as possible, as editors tend to scan them in a matter of seconds. Bulleted lists, charts, short paragraphs and subheadings can all help to make the text more digestible.
- *Place the release in context*. The biggest mistake B2B companies make in press releases is to ignore any information that places the news in a wider, industry context. By drawing in third-party opinion and mentioning other relevant industry developments, editors and journalists are more likely to see the release's newsworthy significance.
- *Include pricing information*. If the release is announcing a new product or service, the price is always the most important piece of information to include.
- *Be clear*. 'One of my pet peeves,' states David Guenette of the trade publication *CD-Rom Professional*, 'is receiving a press release that does not have a clear message.'
- *Be relevant*. The main thing to ensure is that the release is relevant to each recipient, otherwise you will only antagonize journalists. Andrew Kantor, the Senior Editor of *Internet World*, says that, 'I get a lot of releases that we never use (promotions, non-Internet products etc), and a look at an issue or two would make that obvious. Yes, I know you've simply pulled me from your database as "computer-magazine editor", but those databases are sophisticated enough nowadays that you can filter the type of release you want.'
- *Check the release*. Before sending out the release it is important to check it, using a regular text editor. It is also necessary to proof read *very* carefully for any spelling errors, misleading statements and inaccurate information.

While most of the above principles apply equally to online and offline press releases, there are separate factors to consider when sending a release via e-mail. For instance, always use the Blind Carbon Copy (Bcc:) function of your e-mail software in order to conceal each recipient's e-mail address.

The main criterion, as always with B2B e-marketing, is to adopt an 'outside in' perspective. In other words, instead of thinking about what you believe is significant, think from the publication's standpoint.

If you genuinely believe that the information you have to offer is likely to be viewed as interesting or important to the trade publications you are targeting, then it is worth distributing a release.

Online newswire services

If you have news of genuine industry-wide significance it will be a good idea to distribute your electronic press release via online newswire services. These are particularly well suited for B2B companies as they are most often used by trade publications. Although you have to pay for the services, they do not charge much and they enable you to reach many journalists in a very short time.

PR Newswire provides comprehensive communication ranging from press release distribution (for which it is best known) and market intelligence to the creation of online multimedia content and investor relations Web sites. To get an idea of the scale of this service, it's worth noting that PR Newswire distributes 1,200 press releases on a daily basis.

PR Newswire's main competitor, Business Wire, distributes about the same number of releases and, as its vice-president Phyllis Dantuono told the ClickZ magazine, this number is swelling. 'The growth in the past years has been exponential, mostly from dot.coms and the growth of online outlets. Plus business people are more interested in archiving news. The landscape has changed.'

Business Wire, which was the first newswire service to establish a Web site in 1995, delivers breaking business news and multimedia content to traditional and online newsrooms and targeted journalists. According to a statement by the company, 'The rise of global equity markets that churn at a 24/7 financial cycle requires a reciprocal global communications company that can meet this challenge.

No single company in the world has the reach of Business Wire. We provide a multi-channel distribution network on a 24/7 news cycle, which delivers important news to journalists and professional and individual investors around the world.'

Another fantastic service is provided by the Internet News Bureau (www.Internetnewsbureau.com), a newswire service provided by Internet.com. The INB has now become one of the most popular online press release services as it offers clients the ability to reach around 10,000 journalists and business professionals who have specifically subscribed to receive the service. According to INB, 'this subscription-only model assures that releases are distributed only to those who wish to receive them – which results in a high level of media coverage for INB clients'. In addition to its international distribution services, the company also offers a professional press release writing service. (Incidentally, the INB Web site writing service has a useful 'Media Relations Tips' section and enables visitors to subscribe to an Internet PR Discussion List.)

Electronic media packs

Media packs are used to provide members of the media and advertisers with a general company overview. Typically, they include a corporate history, contact details (including links to e-mail addresses), recent press releases, advertising rates (if applicable), biographies of key staff members and other significant information. The ultimate objective of a media pack is to give an insight into the past, present and future of a company.

The main benefit of Internet-based media packs is that they can be updated and distributed at minimal cost. They can also incorporate interactive elements and even multimedia material.

Summary

Relations with journalists, customers and other companies need to be strong in order for a B2B business to survive in the long term. Owing to the networked environment of the Web, a company must be willing to open itself up and provide honest and unfiltered information. It must also be prepared to work in concert with other businesses for mutual benefit. After all, in becoming a part of the Web, a company is automatically placing itself within a wider context beyond its autonomous control.

nine

Marketing via search engines

By far the most cost-effective way to promote any site, especially a B2B site, is via the major search engines. The fact is that way over 50 per cent of people seeking business information services online will make a search engine their first port of call. This fact is especially significant if you compare it to the wafer-thin 0.3 per cent of people who 'click through' banner adverts.

The most obvious way to get a search engine to notice you is to fill in its submission form at the site itself. To make sure you stand the best chance of getting indexed, however, you will also need to embed instructions into your site's HTML text for search engine 'robots' to pick up as they trawl through the Web.

HTML and meta-tags

HTML (HyperText Mark-up Language) is the computer programming code used to build Web pages. It is a series of instructions that tell Web servers and browsers how to display these pages on a user's computer screen.

Some HTML instructions, including 'meta-tags', help search engines to locate, index and categorize Web sites. (For more general information on HTML see the B2B Web Design chapter.)

Here are some guidelines to follow in order to make sure the HTML code of your Web site can help to maximize its chances of achieving a high ranking on the major search sites:

- *Place a site description in the title tag.* Search engines value the words in the title (<TITLE>) tag as more significant than any other words in your HTML text, excluding meta-tags. In fact, some search engines can narrow searches down to an index of just page titles. The title tag is what a Web browser (such as Microsoft Internet Explorer) will display in its title bar and is not simply the first line of HTML that is displayed on a Web page. Most search engines display the text between the <TITLE> and </TITLE> tags in their site indexes. Therefore, instead of using a string of keywords such as:

<TITLE> Club Car: B2B, auction, cars, automotive, industry </TITLE>

it is better to write in plain English, such as:

<TITLE> Club Car The leading B2B car auction site </TITLE>

It is also important to ensure every page has a title tag because (unlike meta-tags) title tags are visible to your visitors and so omitting a title tag is a mistake that will be noticed.

- *Place keywords and descriptions in meta-tags.* Meta-tags are instructions incorporated between the <HEAD> and </HEAD> commands at the top of a HTML page, in order to make the site easier for search engines to classify. Although meta-tags are not used by every search engine (for instance, they are ignored by Excite) they are vital to the indexing process of most of them. The syntax of the description meta-tag is as follows:

  <META name = "description" content = "A description of your Web site goes here">

  And the syntax of the keyword meta-tag is:

  <META name = "keywords" content = "a, list, of, keywords, and, relevant, phrases, goes, here">

The description tag allows companies to provide a brief word description of their site, which will appear on search engine displays. META descriptions should give a general flavour of what visitors can expect from your site or page without any superfluous information. The description tag will control what is displayed as a Web page summary, and will follow the title of your document in the search engine listing. The keywords tag provides companies with the opportunity to add relevant words that do not appear in the title or description tags. Search engines index both the description and keyword meta-tag contents as searchable words.

- *Use the image and link tags.* All images and links should have their own tags and ideally a keyword within them. Don't overdo this, though, as search engines may see it as 'spam indexing'.

Robots and spiders

Owing to the sheer size of the World Wide Web it is impossible for any search engine to index every site manually. Search engines therefore use indexing software agents referred to as 'robots' or 'spiders' to trawl the Web looking for relevant sites. Without the aid of human judgement, these agents rely on such criteria as keywords. Here are some of the ways to make your site more attractive to the search engine robots:

- *Take keywords seriously.* As mentioned elsewhere in this chapter, keywords are the most important criteria to consider when indexing a site.
- *Gain links.* The way search engine robots travel around the Web is by following external links. Therefore, the more links to a Web site, the more likely it is that the robots will find it.
- *Update your site.* Search engine robots regularly return to indexed sites so it is important to make sure that links are not left to go out of date.
- *Avoid graphics.* A graphic-heavy home page can put the search engine robots off.

- *Test browser compatibility.* Checking your site from different browsers will help you make sure it looks good to visitors and search engines alike.
- *Keep frames to a minimum.* Avoid frames because search engine robots cannot read them.

However, while robots are still relied upon for the bulk of an index, more and more search engines are supplementing technology by employing panels of experts to rank sites on the basis of quality. At Lycos, for instance, its team of human experts is responsible for choosing the first 10 results in a search. (The next three results are determined by the popularity of sites, and the remainder are based on keywords in a site found by Lycos's robot.)

Site submissions

Instead of waiting for the search engine robots to pay your site a visit, it is advisable to submit your site, normally using search engine submission forms. You can visit each search engine individually and complete the registration form on each one. The advantage of manual registration is that you can tailor the information to each individual search engine.

Obviously, if you choose to register your site by hand, you will have to decide which sites are worth the effort. It is impractical to register your site with a thousand search engines so you should stick to those that your target audience is most likely to use. For most B2B companies there will be industry-specific search engines that attract a relevant audience. A lot of visitors, however, will arrive via the main general search engines (the five top search sites account for 60–75 per cent of the total engine traffic). Therefore, the search engines that are absolutely crucial to be indexed on are:

Google – www.google.com
Yahoo! – www.yahoo!.com
AltaVista – www.altavista.com
HotBot – www.hotbot.com
Excite – www.excite.com
GoTo – www.goto.com
Looksmart – www.looksmart.com
Lycos – www.lycos.com

Industry search engines

While business-to-consumer companies can limit their search engine submission efforts to the major search engines, B2B companies may also need to concentrate on speciality search engines relating to their industry (or the industries they are targeting). Many e-marketplaces and B2B vertical portals incorporate search engines and directories within them. A list of speciality search engines can be found at Search Engine Watch (www.searchenginewatch.com) and Submit It! (www.submit-it.com).

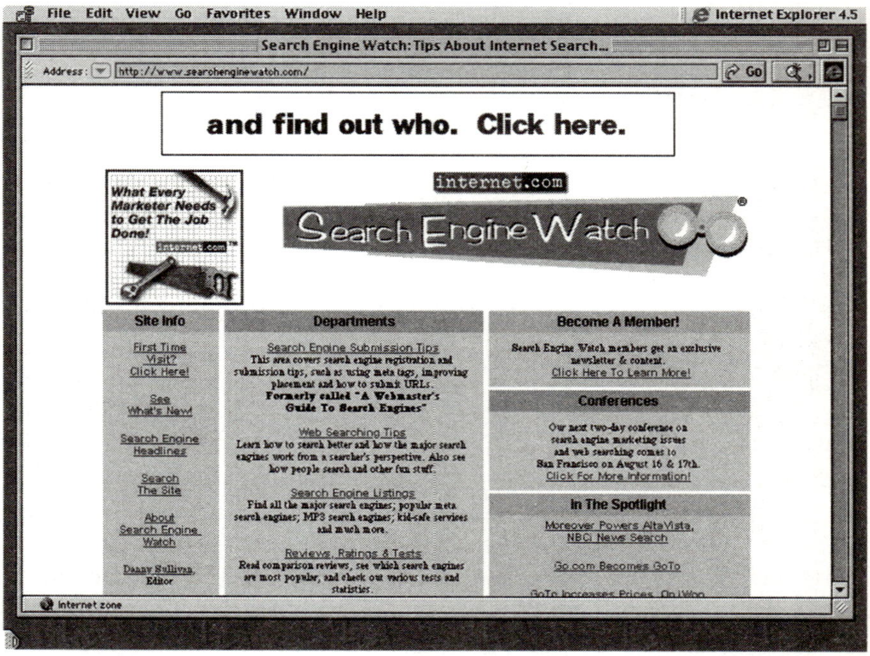

Figure 9.1 Search Engine Watch: overseen by Webmaster Danny Sullivan, this site is the ultimate resource for search engine information

Keyword guidelines

Keywords are the words used by search engine users to find Web sites. Search engines therefore index sites according to the keywords that are incorporated within, or provided by, the Web sites they include in their listings. Relevant keywords should be used not only in search engine submission forms, but also in the relevant HTML tags and the main text of a Web site. Here are some general guidelines for formulating keywords:

- *Use singular and plural forms.* When individual users type keywords into a search engine they type either the singular or plural of a word, they rarely type both. It is therefore important for sites to incorporate both the singular and plural forms of relevant words in order to attract all of their target search engine visitors. For instance, for an automotive site, the words 'car' and 'cars' should both be included.
- *Use active and passive verbs.* Again, search engine visitors may either use the active or passive form of a verb, so both should be included in keyword lists.
- *Don't stack keywords.* Keyword stacking (repeating keywords in meta-tags) is a dirty trick used by some sites to achieve a higher ranking when that particular keyword is typed into a search engine. However, the search engines have wised up to this practice and many (including Lycos and Infoseek) penalize sites found guilty of stacking keywords. According to Submit It!, some users have reported being dropped from a search engine's database owing to keyword repetition.
- *Use phrases.* Use two or three word phrases alongside keywords (research has shown that 80 per cent of searches are done via phrases and not individual words).
- *Be relevant.* Make sure the keywords you use are directly relevant to your target audience. To do this, think about what your visitors want from your site, as opposed to what your site wants out of them.
- *Get help.* There are a number of sites that help you refine your keyword selections. Good Keywords (www.goodkeywords.com) will help you find all the relevant keywords related to a primary keyword.

- *Don't be vague.* Vague and generic keywords such as 'business' or 'Internet' should be avoided as they apply to an infinite number of companies. For instance, when the keyword 'B2B' is typed into the Google search engine it returns 1,230,000 results. Instead of using a vague phrase like 'software solutions' you should use something more specific such as 'traffic analysis software'.

The keywords are the most important thing to get right, as they relate to the words and phrases people type in to the search engine to find information. You will need to think long and hard about what exactly your site offers visitors and which terms people are most likely to use when looking for a site like yours. IFA.co.uk, the financial site that has the highest ranking on Yahoo! (still the largest search site), uses a total of 50 keywords in its tags. This comprehensive list includes 'finance', 'financial', 'advice', 'advisor', 'adviser', 'equity', 'equities', 'save' and 'savings'.

The other thing to note about meta-tags is that although they can increase the chance of a high ranking by 1,000 per cent, very few sites actually use them. Those that do therefore have an automatic headstart.

Search engine directories

One of the most important things to remember is that no two search engines work in the same way. This is perhaps most evident in the length of time each search site takes to index a site. At AltaVista and Infoseek it's between one and two weeks; at Excite, HotBot, Lycos and Webcrawler it's two to four weeks; while at Yahoo! it takes anything up to eight weeks.

There are a number of other things particular to each search engine that you need to watch out for. For instance, the Lycos search engine creates Web site titles and descriptions from the text of a Web page rather than from those provided via HTML tags or site submission forms. Its search agent selects a portion of the site that it deems to be representative and then displays this section as the site's description.

Google, on the other hand, takes brief extracts of text that surround the keywords (as typed in by the search engine user) and strings them together in its site listings. It is also worth bearing in mind that some search engines (such as Excite) ignore keywords altogether. However, with the case of Infoseek (which supports both the keywords and description meta-tags), the description meta-tag must be used in order to prevent the first 200 characters of the Web page's main text becoming the Web page description.

AltaVista now implements a system designed to prevent organizations and individuals from using automated submission tools to get pages into its index. If a user visits AltaVista and clicks its 'Submit' link they will be taken to a page containing a unique submission code. They then have to enter this code in a box before they can submit a page. According to SearchEngines.com, 'the new system may mean a little more work for some, but by blocking those who attempt to spam AltaVista with hundreds of submissions, it can also give all honest Webmasters a better chance of attaining higher rankings'.

Ultimately, it is a good idea to visit all the main search engines individually in order to ensure that their specific criteria are acknowledged and adhered to.

Search engine advertising

Search engine advertising is a relatively new phenomenon. 'The idea of paid placements would have never been entertained in years prior,' says Danny Sullivan, who writes the Search Engine Watch Newsletter. 'But now we're having more and more paid placements and other paid programmes on search engines.'

Having lost faith in standard banner advertising (which now yields click-through rates of less than 1 per cent), advertisers have turned to search engines to attract visitors to their sites. Indeed, in many ways, the major search engines are the obvious place to advertise a company's Web presence. After all, Internet users only choose to go to a search engine when they are looking for new sites to visit.

Some search engines are clearly more receptive towards advertisers than others. For instance, Look Smart (www.looksmart.com), which is one of the technologies behind Microsoft MSN search site (www.msn.co.uk), enables advertisers to affect the search process itself. It has human editors searching the Web for suitable sites, but looks in closer depth at sites (such as Amazon.com) that have paid to have more pages reviewed by the editors.

Inktomi (the index that supplies data to HotBot, AOL, MSN and certain areas of Yahoo!), has a system that guarantees site owners inclusion on its database if they pay a fee. Payment ensures inclusion on its database within two days and confirms a Web site listing for a period of 12 months. While payment ensures sites are listed, your ranking is not. Inktomi is using the same process as before to rank sites. The company is phasing out the free 'Add URL' pages that are listed on its site, although it still sends out its robots and sites can be listed free this way.

However, there is a law of diminishing returns to watch out for here. As the main reason visitors go to search engines is for objective search results, advertising is often frowned upon by search engine users. In their opinion, the more advertising, the more the search site is devalued. They therefore tend to avoid the more commercial search engines such as GoTo.com and FindWhat.com, where companies bid against one another for top billing.

Nevertheless, in a B2B MarketingBiz.com special report entitled 'Top 10 B2B Internet Marketing Tactics That Worked Best in 2000', search engine advertising emerged as a successful B2B promotional tactic. During 2000, B2B MarketingBiz.com interviewed over 100 B2B marketers from famous companies such as IBM, VerticalNet and UPS, as well as smaller innovative firms such as SilverStream and Wanted Technologies. They also spoke with leading B2B nteractive agencies including Folio Z and Passaic Park. The report discovered the following findings about B2B search engine advertising:

- *Search term ads work well.* Although general ads on search engines such as Yahoo! don't work for most B2B e-marketers, ads linked to specific search terms often proved more successful.
- *Text beats graphics.* According to the report, 'most marketers found text ads, such as those that can appear on Google (www.google.com) or Northern Light (www.northernlight.com), did substantially better than graphical banner ads'. This is probably because the prospect is actively looking for text to read to learn where they should click next on their search for information.
- *Facts work better than jargon.* B2B MarketingBiz.com found that ads based on facts work a lot better than glaringly obvious ads based on sales jargon.

- *Careful copywriting is essential.* Owing to the inevitable limitations of space on search engine ads, careful copywriting is essential in order to get a good response rate from visitors.

Here is some information on the ways in which advertisers can consolidate their presence on other major search engines:

- *AltaVista (www.altavista.com).* AltaVista includes a paid placement service where advertisers can be incorporated within the 'Sponsored Links' section at the foot of each page (these placements are arranged with GoTo.com).
- *Ask Jeeves (www.askjeeves.com).* Advertisers can appear among the results at the bottom of the page.
- *Google (www.google.com).* Google's 'Sponsored Link' ads appear at the top of the page, although they are presented on a shaded background (unlike the other listings).
- *Lycos (www.lycos.com).*Advertisers can appear on the 'Featured Listings' section at the top and in the middle of its pages (as with AltaVista, these are paid links from GoTo.com).
- *Yahoo! (www.yahoo.com).* The sponsored listings in the commercial Yahoo! categories are paid links.

Search position software

Many companies use search position software in order to improve their search engine rankings. The main reason people use positioning software is to save time. It can often take over 30 hours a week for companies to make the necessary adjustments to maintain a high indexing on search engines and Web directories.

As *Publish* magazine has reported, 'If you're managing a large site, or a number of sites, or you simply intend to win this war with your competitors now and forever, then you'd be well-advised to invest in software that can significantly reduce the tedium of the process when it's done on a large scale.'

Furthermore, search engine software can help sites to go beyond meta-tags in their efforts to achieve high rankings. As First Place Software's president Brent Winters has put it, 'The big myth is that simply updating your meta-tags and submitting your site will make you visible on the search engines. That's just not true anymore.'

One of the leaders in the search position software market is the inexpensive Web Position Gold (www.webpositiongold.com) product from First Place. Among other things, this software product can help to:

- create HTML Web pages designed to rank near the top of search indexes;
- compare a site's HTML code to that of any already top-ranked Web page and then suggest improvements to boost that site's ranking ahead of those it was compared against;
- use a 'Page Editor' to facilitate easy changes;
- automate the uploading of pages to a Web site;
- submit and register Web sites with the main search engines;
- measure a Web site's search rankings in the major search engines for any keywords selected by the user;
- facilitate the schedule of daily, weekly, or monthly search engine rank checking and site registrations;
- track unique visitors or hits and even identify the keywords typed into each search engine to find the Web site.

Among the believers in this type of software is Danny Sullivan from Search Engine Watch (arguably *the* authority on search engines). He claims that 'the real genius to Web Position is that it walks you through the process of building doorway pages from scratch'.

Web Position Gold's main competitor is Microsoft Central's Submit It! (www.submit-it.com) although it is quite a different product. While Web Position Gold offers the ability to create doorway pages, Submit It! concentrates mainly on submission services. Specifically, Submit It! enables companies to:

- fill in a submission form for every Web page;
- submit these pages to over 400 search engines and directories;
- re-submit their sites automatically to make sure they remain listed;
- check where they are listed with the main search engines and directories with a Submit It! monthly report.

One of the main benefits of Submit It! from a B2B perspective is that it includes a vast range of industry-specific search engines. As with Web Position Gold, another advantage is that it saves time. Companies only have to enter their keywords, description and other relevant information once in a master form.

For sites with a larger budget, it could be worth investing in a paid service such as Media DNA's eLuminator (www.mediadna.com). This is an intelligent submission system with several unique features that help sites to achieve maximum visibility. Once a Web site has been submitted to the search engines, eLuminator verifies that they have indexed the site content. If they have, full text searching of the content is enabled, and Internet users are brought to publisher branded catalogue pages, from which they can proceed directly to the content itself.

Media DNA eLuminator also provides clients with detailed reports so that they can view for themselves the number of visitors eLuminator has directed to their content. As you might expect, the eLuminator service is aimed at sites that are very heavy in content (with over 1,000 articles or product listings) and that are already high in the search engines. As eLuminator puts it, the technology 'allows protected and/or deeply buried content to be submitted for indexing in a way that accounts for search engine requirements without revealing the original content'.

For business-to-business IT companies, Bit Pipe has also proved to be a useful service. It assists IT marketers to achieve very high IT searches.

Web positioning firms

For companies who really take search engine positioning seriously, Web positioning firms may present a valid option. Not only can they offer high rankings, but also constant monitoring of all the search engines. For instance, Jean-Pierre Eskenazi, chief executive of the Paris-based NetBooster, says his company is focused 100 per cent on manually registering a company's Web site on search engines. 'Our dedicated team keeps abreast of the many changes required by search engines for effective submission, and we guarantee our customers a high placement on search engines.'

However, although firms like NetBooster (which boasts such high profile clients as Intel and QXL) offer highly skilled, hand-tailored Web positioning services for sites such as Yahoo!, AltaVista, Google and MSN, there are many other companies which may not be able to live up to their promises. For instance, some companies that promote their services by sending mass e-mails promising to get companies into the top 10 rankings are only talking about the top 10 rankings for when your domain name is typed in.

In an interview with B2B MarketingBiz, Web positioning expert Anthony Muller (President of Web Mercs), expressed considerable scepticism towards some of the less scrupulous search engine consultancies. 'You have to be careful when you go to these guys,' he said. 'Some do mass e-mailings saying they'll get you into the Top 10 rankings guaranteed... There are people out there who will offer services but don't have a lot of knowledge,' he claims. 'For example, some Web designers offer to submit your site every month as part of their service. That actually hurts your site more than it helps.'

There are, however, a number of ways to check out the credentials of search positioning firms. For instance, NetBooster (along with other credible companies) is a member of the IPEA association, a circle of professional Web positioning companies that adhere to a common quality charter. As well as looking out for their logo, it is also important to check the client list of these companies (if they don't provide one, be wary). Once you know which companies use the service you will be able to judge for yourself how effective it is by checking their rankings in the major search engines.

The other thing to look out for are any untenable or extravagant claims. Owing to the ever-changing and subjective nature of search engines, any company making miraculous claims based on a certain keyword must be treated with caution.

Obviously, the cost of these firms varies according to the size of a Web site. The more pages that need indexing, the higher the price. There are two basic pricing models for search engine positioning firms. *Pay Per Click* is where companies pay a fee per click for visitors to their site. Obviously in this payment model the search engine has an incentive to make the ranking high. *Flat fee* costs several hundred to several thousand pounds/dollars for positioning of your pages. Also expect a monthly maintenance fee to keep the rankings from slipping. Some companies combine these payment models.

Yahoo! site submission
Submission page: www.yahoo.com/info/suggest/

For business and consumer users alike, as Yahoo! remains one of the most trusted search sites, it is arguably the most important place for your site to get listed. The main Yahoo! index is compiled by a staff of hundreds who assess each submission and decide whether it should be included in the directory, as well as a Yahoo! robot that trawls the Web. The staff can reject it if they personally do not feel the site is right for Yahoo!. As Yahoo! is the most famous search engine directory it has more site submissions than any other Web site. Owing to the competitive nature of its submission process and the fact that it is so important to get right, it is worth concentrating on the specifics of registering with Yahoo!. The other reason for focusing on Yahoo! is that it is generally considered to be the toughest submission process of all. Here are the steps you should take when submitting with Yahoo!:

- Visit Yahoo!'s home page.
- Locate the Yahoo! category you want to be listed under (commercial sites must be placed within a Business and Economy sub-category – under either Companies or Products and Services).
- Click on the 'Suggest a Site' hyperlink at the bottom of the screen. This will take you to the relevant 'Add URL' page.
- Write the name of your company and Web address.
- Add a description that is comparable to index headings or topics. It is important to note that Yahoo! does not allow you to suggest keywords in its submission form.
- Click on the 'Submit' button. If the form has been completed properly, Yahoo! will display a screen thanking you for the submission. If not, Yahoo! will display a screen informing you that the submission has failed. In this case, press the back key on your browser, make the necessary changes and resubmit.
- Resubmit your site into additional sub-categories. This is especially beneficial if you sell multiple products.
- Check your listing. Yahoo! submissions take between two and eight weeks to appear. If your site is not on the index within eight weeks you will probably need to register your site again.

Checking your rankings

If you are submitting your site to search engines in-house it is important to evaluate your search positions on a regular basis. As search engines change their index daily (even hourly), you simply cannot check your rankings enough. However, as the evaluation process can be extremely time-consuming it makes sense to use a search engine monitoring tool such as Web Site Rank (www.web siterank.com), which is available for free via its Web site. Not only does this service tell you where your site is ranked on all the main search engines, but it also provides a competitive analysis so that you can see where you are positioned against your opposition.

In addition Web Site Rank can be used to identify the top 10 pages in each search engine and the Web sites that have the best ranking. It then shows you how the top ranking pages are constructed.

As well as software, you may also be able to evaluate your search engine success through your Internet Service Provider (ISP). Most ISPs are able to provide Web sites with access logs (records of a site's activity based on file requests) that detail when a search engine robot has been to a site and whether they have subsequently included it in the listing.

Summary

Search engines cannot be ignored by companies if they are to fulfil all their marketing objectives, as they provide the main route to most B2B sites. The fact is that unlike many other marketing techniques, a high search engine position guarantees a regular stream of relevant visitors who have actively sought the site out. In the light of this, it is hardly surprising that search engine positioning ranks as the number one Web promotional method used by business-to-business sites, according to research published by ActivMedia. Ultimately, however, no matter how many submission techniques you adopt, the key to search engine success is providing a high quality Web site that appeals to its audience. Owing to the democratic nature of the Web, if your site is already proving popular with visitors and other Web sites, it won't be too long before the search engine robots are attracted there too.

ten

B2B advertising

Many B2B companies are now turning to online advertising in order to generate awareness among target audiences. However, just as B2B advertising is starting to take off, a new debate has emerged over the effectiveness of Internet advertising in general. This chapter therefore looks at the potential opportunities and pitfalls posed by Web advertising in the context of B2B e-commerce.

B2B banners

Banners can be static or interactive and can incorporate both text and images. Typically, they provide a hypertext link to the advertiser's home page, enabling users to *click through* the banner. Banner advertising remains the most popular, if also the most controversial, form of online advertising. The controversy derives from the sheer amount of money spent on banners, set against the fact that the success of a banner advertising campaign is often very difficult to quantify.

While Web banners were once considered a novelty by Internet users, nowadays they command less attention. Indeed, some users set their Web browsers to ignore banners altogether. According to some reports, click-through rates are now as low as 0.3 per cent and the conversion rates are even lower.

In a 2001 survey conducted in Britain by New World Commerce and *Marketing Week,* only 3 per cent of respondents said that Web banners were the most effective means of acquiring customers.

However, B2B companies have the advantage over their business-to-consumer counterparts when it comes to banner advertising, as business markets tend to be easier to target. Furthermore, some analysts believe that banner ads can prove very effective when used on the right sites. Analysts believe that instead of using banners to generate brand awareness among millions of Internet users, they should be used to target small numbers of relevant businesses. The most effective way of doing this is to concentrate on highly targeted vertical industry sites (eg industry-specific e-marketplaces).

Nevertheless, while many companies see the future of B2B banner advertising on these sites, few have actually tried it out for themselves. 'Advertising on verticals has not been widely tried yet,' states Jim Niall, senior analyst at Forrester Research, in NetB2B.com. 'We're finding that most B2B marketers have focused on building their site and e-mail marketing using their own internal customer list.' Even so, NetB2B.com reports that in the US, companies such as Engage Business Media and B2Bworks have targeted low traffic vertical industry sites via banner advertising.

B2B versus B2C advertising

According to findings from AdRelevance (www.adrelevance.com), the growth of online advertising by B2B companies has now overtaken all other industries. Furthermore, the AdRelevance 2000 survey found that the bulk of B2B online advertising centres on technology, with 62 per cent of all B2B ads promoting products and services such as e-commerce security, domain registration, Web design, network hardware, and affiliate network infrastructure.

Charles Buchwalter, the head of media research at AdRelevance, believes this shift represents a logical step. 'Now that so many companies in the B2B sector have a presence online, it makes sense for them to advertise there,' he says. 'It's the equivalent of putting up billboards across from the new industrial park: you reach your customers where they work, and in this case, they're working online.'

AdRelevance discovered that the site genres with the highest concentration of B2B advertising were Computing and Technology, Business and Finance, and General News. Those with the lowest concentration of B2B advertising were (predictably) Games, Children and Family, and Portal, Community and Search Engines. 'B2B companies are clearly targeting sites that cater to the work user,' says Buchwalter. 'Though the bulk of their advertising dollars are still spent at portals and search engines, they're much more likely to choose business-oriented sites than are advertisers in other industries.'

However, this is not the full story. Although B2B advertising is growing faster than B2C ad spend, it still only accounts for less than 10 per cent of online advertising spending. According to one leading figure in the anti-advertising camp, Hal Pawluck (www.pawluck.com), 'What's really happening with online advertising is that B2B companies are using their heads – they've figured out that they mostly don't need it. They know the Net is not a great ad medium for them, but is a terrific "business bazaar".' While this is a valid point, many advertisers are learning that their status in the 'business bazaars' (the B2B e-marketplaces) is enhanced through the brand awareness an advertising campaign can generate.

Harsh truths

Despite the fact that, according to Forrester Research, spending on Web advertising will climb dramatically to $33 billion in 2004, it is already being undermined by some harsh truths. Most people now appreciate that having your page turn up in the top 10 search engine finds is far more effective than Web advertising. If the role of advertising is to present the best possible face of a company, this is made redundant by the nature of the Web where the truth will always be outed. Consider the online reaction against Microsoft and AOL, for instance. The speed of word of mouth online is restricted only by how fast people can type, so it is worth remembering that any extravagant advertising claims must live up to their promises. As Rick Levine of Sun Microsystems has put it, 'Word of Web will trump word of hype every time.'

That is not to say that Web advertising should be ignored by B2B operators (as mentioned above, it can be a highly effective means of generating brand awareness). What it does mean, however, is that any advertising campaign must be based on objective information, not biased opinion.

Beyond banners

As a result of the decline in banner click-through rates, however, various other types of e-advertising have emerged. Here is an overview of the most common methods:

- *Interstitials*. Meaning 'in between', an interstitial is an advertisement that appears in a separate browser window while you wait for a Web page to load. Interstitials are more likely to contain large graphics, streaming presentations, and applets than conventional banner ads, and some studies have found that more users click on interstitials than on banner ads. Some users, however, have complained that interstitials slow access to destination pages.

  There is now a variant of an interstitial, called a superstitial. Superstitials are interstitials that only play once a Web page has been completely downloaded. Superstitials tend to be larger than interstitials (taking over the full screen) and have higher production values. The reason for this is that they need to be so attractive that the user will wait before clicking off the superstitial to see the already downloaded Web page behind. Due to their use of audio and video, they tend to be expensive to produce. Unsurprisingly, superstitials tend to be left untouched by B2B companies, and are favoured by the likes of Nike, AOL, Ford and other companies targeting consumer markets.
- *Sponsorship*. Sponsorships are increasing in popularity in the B2B sector. A sponsorship is when an advertiser pays to sponsor content, usually a section of Web site or an e-mail newsletter. The Internet market research company eMarketer has predicted that an increasing number of companies will opt for sponsorships in place of banner ad campaigns over the next few years.
- *Advertorial content*. Advertorial content refers to advertising designed to resemble editorial content. Advertorials are either integrated seamlessly into an existing Web site, or they are used as the basis of a completely new site altogether.
- *Opt-in lists*. These are lists of people or businesses who have subscribed to receive adverts. The main reason people sign up for these lists is because they are given incentives (competition entry, for instance). This means that a lot of business decision-makers receiving these e-mail ads have no interest whatsoever in their content.

Advertising rates

The main method of working out an advertising rate is by CPM. CPM stands for cost per thousand page impressions (the M being the Roman numeral for 1,000). This remains by far the most widely used pricing model, despite the fact that a page impression can mean different things. In terms of banner ads, it typically means that the banner is displayed on a page of a site 1,000 times. That does not mean, however, that the banner was actually seen 1,000 times (the person visiting the site may have set their browser not to display banners or, even if they haven't, may not look at or take notice of your ad). Advertising CPM rates are generally higher on B2B Web sites, because advertisers are willing to pay more to reach the highly-targeted audiences available on such sites, and because expenditures by businesses are usually much bigger than those by consumers.

As well as CPM methods there are also CPA or cost per action rates, which are often preferred by advertisers (although less popular among publishers). Many believe that CPA rates are more accurate than CPM measurements because they are based only on an Internet user's response to your ad. According to this arguably more sophisticated pricing model, you only pay for each time someone 'clicks through' a banner to link to your Web site. In addition, some Web publishers prefer to adopt a 'pay per day' method, which involves paying a set amount of money for a set amount of time.

Before spending money on Web advertising you should, therefore, be prepared to ask Webmasters (or their media sales representatives) questions relating to the advertising cost. In particular, potential advertisers need to bear the following factors in mind:

- *Method*. Obviously, the method of payment will influence the advertiser's decision.
- *Rate*. Banner advertising can certainly prove expensive. For instance, a standard CPM rate is about $10/£6. If you then consider the average click-through rate (0.4–0.6 per cent) in conjunction with the average click-to-sale conversion rate of 2 per cent you can see that you will have to pay for a lot of page impressions before you can guarantee a sale.

- *Flexibility*. Many vertical industry-specific sites are willing to negotiate the advertising rate and take on board the specific requirements of each advertiser.
- *Schedule*. Every site has a different payment schedule. For instance, sites adopting a 'pay per day' rate of advertising often require payment in advance, while sites following a CPM or CPA model (for obvious reasons) pay during or after the campaign has been conducted.

The main criterion, however, when deciding on where to place advertising is not the advertising rate, but audience relevance. Obviously, advertisers need to choose Web publishers that attract their target audience. According to Barry Silverstein (ClickZ columnist and B2B author), the principles are the same as for offline advertising: 'As with traditional print media and direct mail or telemarketing lists, you should work your way down in priority from most to least targeted Web sites.'

The reason why vertical industry portals (vortals) are an attractive proposition for B2B advertisers is because they eliminate much of the guesswork. Vertical sites enable advertisers to home in on a specific industry (eg automotive) and cut the chances of targeting irrelevant Internet users. Many advertisers also target the very same online B2B marketplaces within which they participate in order to maximize their exposure.

Advertising networks

Although it is possible for companies to plan and manage their own online advertising campaigns, many prefer to outsource to an Internet advertising network. These advertising networks can help companies set objectives, research audiences, establish a media schedule, design and create the advertising (banners, interstitials etc), place the advertising and then evaluate the campaign's effectiveness. Here are some of the main international advertising networks:

DoubleClick (www.doubleclick.net)

DoubleClick refers to itself as 'the industry leader at leveraging technology, media and data expertise to create solutions that help advertisers and publishers unleash the power of the Web for branding, selling products and building relationships with customers'. The DoubleClick Network represents over 490 publishers across 15 countries. With sites such as AltaVista, Dilbert, US News, Macromedia, MTV Europe, ZDNet Australia, Excite Europe and CNET Spain, DoubleClick reaches over 80 million unique consumers globally every month.

DoubleClick has 22 targeting criteria, which are divided into four basic categories: Content Targeting, Behavioural Targeting, User Targeting, and Tech Targeting. It also has the ability to customize targeting capabilities based on advertisers' needs, supporting all rich media including 'sophisticated banners', sponsorships, interstitials, and other formats.

DoubleClick offers CPM (cost per thousand impressions) pricing structures. For more details regarding pricing, see: http://www.doubleclick.net/advertisers/ad_rates/

The company's ad-serving technology (DART) performs targeting, reporting and inventory management for client sites. According to DoubleClick, DART offers 'the most comprehensive and flexible reporting available on the Internet'. The site reports contain information such as Total Impressions/Click-Through,

Figure 10.1 DoubleClick: the leading advertising network

Click-Through By User, and Click Per Keyword. However, although DoubleClick is one of the most prominent advertising networks, it mainly (but not exclusively) represents high-profile business-to-consumer sites.

AdVenture (www.adventure.com)

The AdVenture network offers B2B advertisers the choice of targeting by site, niche group and network. The network has grown at a record rate and now includes more than 3,600 Web sites. The network recently upgraded its targeting capabilities, providing more options to both advertisers and publishers. They have also added new ad channels targeted both by demographics and by content.

The B2B demographic channels include: Automotive, Small Business Owners, Financiers and Corporate Decision-Makers. 'Many advertisers buy based on demographics rather than content,' says Richard Baumer, president of VentureDirect (which owns AdVenture). 'Our new demographic channels offer advertisers an effective way to reach the most eyeballs within their target demographic.'

According to AdVenture, its network, affinity, and site-specific advertising options, make it 'the premier solution for marketers who want to drive traffic, generate leads, make sales, and create brand loyalty, as well as for Web publishers looking to create additional revenue opportunities'.

Advertising.com (www.advertising.com)

Founded in 1998, Advertising.com is an advertising services company that works with traditional advertisers and agencies to increase the value and effectiveness of interactive marketing programmes across the Web, e-mail and wireless devices. In 2000, Dun and Bradstreet rated Advertising.com the fastest-growing Internet Advertising Services Company in the United States. The company's clients include numerous Fortune 100 companies and leading Internet sites.

AdSmart (www.adsmart.com)

AdSmart was one of the first advertising companies to establish a B2B advertising network. The network enables AdSmart to target segments like insurance, real estate and high technology, as well as financial services, agriculture, medical, and telecommunications.

Sites signed to the network include Emplawyernet, a legal jobs database; FindForms.com, a legal and business forms search engine; Lawguru.com, the site to find free answers to legal questions; and Patent Café, GoTo.com's business intellectual property portal.

Engage (www.engage.com)

Engage is another company that offers a B2B ad network – Engage Business Media. The network is aimed at major advertisers targeting the small office, home office (SOHO) market, as well as more specialized marketers seeking particular verticals. Engage Business Media concentrates on 12 verticals – automotive, agriculture, building and construction, chemical, food, health care, hospitality, information technology, legal, printing, SOHO, and telecommunications.

Besides selling space on Web sites, most of which get between 25,000 and 200,000 impressions a month, Engage Business Media also sells e-mail newsletters to these audiences. The network includes companies like e-Steel, BevNET.com, LawForum, and Dirtpile.com. The sites represented include industry exchanges and marketplaces, as well as content sites focused on particular industries.

24/7 Media (www.247media.com)

24/7 Media offers a wider range of services than a standard advertising network as it has positioned itself as a leading global provider of 'end-to-end interactive technology and marketing solutions and services' for Web publishers, online advertisers, advertising agencies, e-marketers and e-commerce companies. 24/7 Media provides a comprehensive suite of media and technology products and services that enable these client groups to attract and retain customers worldwide, and to reap the benefits of interactive and other electronic media.

The company's solutions include advertising and direct marketing sales, ad serving, promotions, e-mail list management, e-mail list brokerage, e-mail delivery, data analysis, loyalty marketing, wireless and convergence solutions, all delivered from its industry-leading data and technology platforms. The company's 24/7 Connect ad-serving technology solutions are designed specifically for the demands and needs of advertisers and agencies, Web publishers and e-commerce merchants.

In addition, 24/7 Media is also leading the way in B2B and B2C wireless advertising as it manages the only global wireless ad network, and deployed the world's first Wireless Application Protocol (WAP) ad server in February 2000. This incorporates ad-serving management and reporting capabilities and monitoring and control of WAP and SMS (Short Messaging Service) campaigns.

B2BWorks (www.b2bworks.net)

B2BWorks is the leading full-service online B2B advertising network that gives marketers one-stop access to a wide range of the

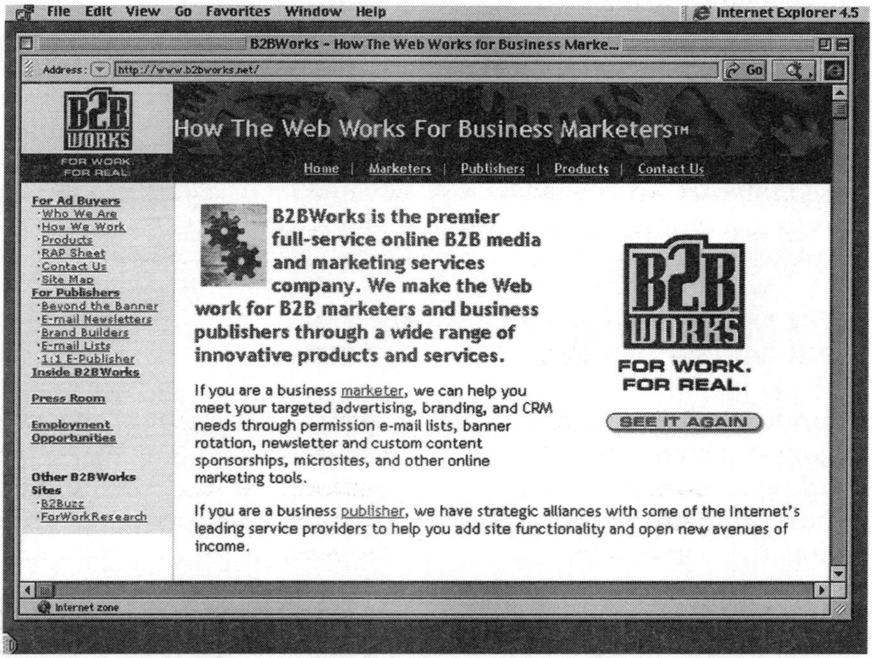

Figure 10.2 B2BWorks: the leading B2B advertising network

most popular business-content sites owned by leading trade publishers and associations. B2BWorks helps business marketers meet their targeted advertising and branding needs through focused banner campaigns, microsites, newsletter and custom content sponsorships, double-opt-in e-mail lists, rich media and other innovative marketing avenues.

B2BWorks now offers advertisers over 500 premium B2B Web sites spanning more than 60 vertical industry segments. Over the last two years, B2BWorks has increased its lead in offering the most diverse and robust brand name B2B portfolio available to Internet marketers.

OneMediaPlace (www.onemediaplace.com)

OneMediaPlace (formerly Adauction.com) is not a network as such, but a B2B e-marketplace devoted to advertising. The service brings media planners, buyers, and sellers together in a single, non-partisan marketplace. OneMediaPlace offers a convenient way to purchase across a variety of media and has a team of more than 11,000 media buyers worldwide.

Datacom (www.datais.com)

The Datacom Ad Network, a leading provider of click-through-based Internet advertising, was one of the first to offer a rich media services solution. Its technology gives advertisers the ability to display interactive banners across the vast Datacom network.

Real Media (www.realmedia.com)

Founded in 1995, Real Media is a worldwide provider of technology-enabled Internet advertising solutions. With an exclusive worldwide portfolio of over 1,400 premium sites, Real Media offers robust ad management technology, ad sales representation, and innovative services that help generate revenue for both Web publishers and advertisers.

While the networks mentioned above are great for large B2B operators, for those selling to small business owners, sites like OnVia.com, Office.com, and AllBusiness.com provide a good advertising environment that will target small business owners unlike anywhere else on the Web.

Niche networks

There is also a growing number of niche advertising networks emerging in the B2B sector in order to meet the increasing demand of advertisers. The construction industry, in particular, has benefited from this trend.

The Building Industry Media Network has captured an impressive 60 per cent market share by networking many independent, but content-related Web sites under a single advertising umbrella. The largest building industry Web sites can offer up to a million page views to one user base. The network of building industry Web sites offers tens of millions of page views to dozens of unique user bases. Marketers such as Sears and PSInet use such networks and find the resulting response to be of considerably higher quality than that obtained from similar Web-wide campaigns.

Richard Holden, CEO of construction firm RMC, now claims he 'will only advertise to Web sites that are used by builders and architects. I won't waste my money by advertising to non-building industry users.'

'Advertisers find that targeted-content Web sites offer more effective advertising than general interest portal sites by factors of five or more,' explains Chris Alarcon of AEC Media Network. He continues, 'The disorganized nature of the Internet and rapid proliferation of new sites makes the expertise of content niche networks a valuable resource to advertisers.'

By focusing on these content-related Web sites, advertisers have an excellent advertising opportunity. By pooling advertising space and outsourcing technical services, small and mid-size industry Web sites are now offering effective advertising opportunities and consequently niche advertising networks are developing quickly.

Case study: 24/7 Media and Tickets.com

Tickets.com, a leading business-to-business ticketing solutions provider for live events and the official ticketing supplier to the 2002 Olympic Winter Games, uses 24/7 Media as the exclusive seller of advertising for the Tickets.com Web site. Tickets.com provides the advertising company with the opportunity to work with private label and co-branded affiliate sites that use Tickets.com 'Ticketing Gateways' worldwide. For its part, 24/7 Media provides Tickets.com with a number of its technology-based services including 24/7 Mail, a targeted e-mail marketing solution; 24/7 Connect, an online advertising results measurement technology; and AwardTrack, a customer reward programme that develops customer affinity and loyalty.

'24/7 Media offers an impressive combination of cutting edge technology and world class customer service, which will help to expand our advertising capabilities,' says Kiliaen Van Rensselaer, vice-president of marketing for Tickets.com. 'This agreement enables us to maximize revenue from our own site, and offer our Ticketing Gateways clients the opportunity to generate an incremental revenue stream without jeopardizing customer experience.'

'We're pleased to be Tickets.com's exclusive advertising sales partner,' says Michael Rowsom, president of 24/7 Media Solutions. 'Our technology complements their ticketing solutions model and the range of venues and services they offer.'

Figure 10.3 Tickets.com: part of 24/7 Media's advertising network

Advertising exchange networks

The most cost-effective and arguably the most convenient way to advertise online is to participate in one of the many advertising exchange schemes on the Web. The way they work is simple. Advertisers go to one of the B2B advertising exchange sites and register for the service. They then submit a banner (usually 468 pixels wide by 60 pixels high). This banner will then be displayed in rotation at other sites that have also signed up for the exchange programme. As this is a reciprocal exchange, the advertisers then agree to save space on their site to display other ads within the exchange. There are, however, a few problems with these schemes:

- The advertisers' banners are usually only shown once for every two times that a visitor to their sites sees a banner from the exchange.
- They may have very limited control over where their banners will appear and, likewise, little say over which banners will appear on their site. (There are, however, a growing number of exchanges that allow you to specify.)
- Many exchanges force participating sites to incorporate a link back to the banner exchange's home page.

However, as these services are free, it may be worth trying one out for a set period. In addition, many advertising exchanges offer tailored statistics reports. These reports provide information on how often ads have been displayed on your site as well as how often your banner was put up on other sites. This information will be able to help you to measure the exchange's success.

In the UK

The largest UK-based banner exchange network is UK Banners (www.ukbanners.co.uk), which is used by over 23,000 Web sites around the country, and which serves in excess of 50 million banners per month. As mentioned above, most banner exchange programmes show a company's banner 50 per cent of the number of times that you show others'. With UK Banners, however, yours is shown 80 per cent of the time. UK Banners also provides comprehensive real-time hourly, daily and weekly graphs and statistics of page impressions, banner exposures, click-throughs and ratios.

Link Exchange is another well-respected free advertising network, enabling participants to target both US and European-based companies. Their banner network is an association of Web sites that trades free banner advertising space on over 400,000 Web sites, which follow a co-operative model. This means that (as with most major networks) for every two ads you show on your site, you earn a credit to have your banner shown on another member's site. The amount of free advertising you receive is directly proportional to the amount you give to others. In order to keep the service free, Link Exchange inevitably sells some of the network ad space to sponsors.

According to Link Exchange, its network is designed 'so that you can choose what type of site to advertise on to reach your prospective audience. And, since we are the largest advertising network on the Web, we can give you more exposure to increase your traffic.'

One of the main advantages of Link Exchange is that it tracks banner and site statistics by hour, day, week, and month in its 'Control Centre' (a 24-hour online reporting resource), which is accessible for every participant. This enables companies to analyse their current banner and site performance, as well as to compare these numbers with their account's past performance.

In addition, LinkShare offers B2B companies the opportunity to target by category. As everyone who joins categorizes their site in at least one of their 2,000-plus categories, participants can therefore target a banner ad to a specific audience or even by language in one of LinkShare's 32 language categories.

LinkShare also give participants control over the ads that appear on their own sites, enabling them to filter ads based on commercial status, category listing, and content rating.

Rich media advertising

Rich media advertising refers to adverts incorporating audio, moving graphics and interactivity. Rich media is becoming increasingly popular among advertisers seeking new ways to gain the attention of their target audience. Although it is used frequently by business-to-consumer companies, rich media is in many ways more suited to the business market. The main reason for this is the fact that home users generally have less powerful connections than business users.

Real Media, the global provider of marketing solutions to the digital advertising industry, is one of the companies to have helped advertisers see the benefits of rich media. For instance, it has integrated the rich media formats into its Open AdStream ad-serving technology for more accurate tracking. This will allow the company to count and measure the success of every rich media campaign, regardless of its format, and ensures advertisers will get accurate click-through counts and are able to assess the success of a rich media campaign regardless of the format.

One of the reasons for this tracking technology was to combat the lack of uncertainty advertisers feel towards rich media. As Real Media's vice-president of Media Services puts it: 'Rich media ads are proving to have higher click-through rates for most advertisers. But, the lack of standardization makes it hard for advertisers to determine if the additional cost of the ads is justified.'

One of the main developers of rich media advertising is Enliven, which provides advertisers with the opportunity to create interactive ads. Enliven uses streaming technology to enrich online advertising through the use of Flash and Java. Products like Enliven for Flash and Enliven Effect provide easy-to-use, cost-effective solutions that allow users to focus on getting the maximum return out of their advertising budget. Now, users can affordably and efficiently build brand awareness, capture leads, print coupons, promote click to their Web site, and fulfil information requests directly within their ad.

Selling advertising space

In order to generate additional revenues and to build relations with compatible companies, many B2B businesses sell advertising space on their Web sites and electronic newsletters.

Although portal sites remain the most popular for advertisers, virtually every type of B2B company has managed to attract advertising dollars. However, any site seeking advertisers should make sure they are willing to act with a degree of restraint. After all, by allowing an advertiser onto a site, a company is inevitably going to become *associated* with that site in the minds of its visitors. By being associated with an unpopular or disreputable advertiser, companies can often risk tarnishing their own brand identity.

If a site becomes cluttered with too many banner ads, sponsorships and affiliate schemes, it will ultimately distract attention away from the site's own marketing function. Furthermore, banners have a tendency to be garish and multi-coloured. The reason for this is because advertisers have to grab the attention of your site's visitors within a very limited amount of space. As well as garish colour schemes, banners often use animated graphics that can also damage the visual consistency of your site.

However, when handled intelligently, online advertising can actually enhance the value of a B2B Web site. If the advertisers are really relevant to the requirements of the business decision-makers visiting the site, then they will view the banners as useful links rather than as irritating distractions.

In order to make itself more attractive to potential advertisers, a B2B Web site should adhere to the following guidelines:

- *Adopt a simple rate system*. Advertisers are put off by highly complex rate systems, and it is therefore essential that any system adopted makes sense from the advertiser's perspective. Generally speaking, advertisers prefer systems based on a CPA (cost per action) model.
- *Create a Web page for advertisers*. Relevant information regarding the opportunity offered to advertisers should be incorporated within the Web site itself.
- *Provide an audience profile*. Advertisers require detailed information regarding who actually visits the site. Most Web hosting services are able to provide reasonably accurate site traffic statistics. However, it may be worth downloading free tracking software that can provide a more detailed visitor profile. For instance, the tracking software available from Extreme Tracking (www.extremetracking.com) provides information not only on how many people are visiting a site but also on how those people got there (search engines, links from other sites, e-mails etc). It even details keywords a visitor has typed in on a search engine to reach the site.
- *Incorporate a directory*. If a site incorporates a useful and relevant B2B directory, it will be used by visitors as a route to somewhere else. This inevitably renders it a more attractive proposition for potential advertisers.

If contacting companies direct seems like too much hard work, advertising networks (such as those mentioned in this chapter) are able to sell advertising on behalf of clients.

Summary

While there are still doubts over the effectiveness of online advertising in general, there is no denying that B2B Web advertising is growing at a rapid rate. If growth trends continue, the entire B2B online advertising spend could hit $3 billion by 2005, according to Jupiter Research. 'Due to its relative immaturity and smaller current base of ad impressions, we believe that the B2B market will maintain a faster growth rate in online advertising impressions than the overall industry for the next few years,' says Jupiter forecasting director Vipul Patel.

For those companies seeking to consolidate their online presence via a Web-based advertising campaign, there are, however, a number of serious issues to consider. Not only is budget an important factor, but issues relating to brand identity, IT capabilities, the target audience and marketing objectives also need to be thought through very carefully before embarking on any e-advertising campaign.

eleven

B2B affiliate marketing

Put simply, affiliate marketing involves the creation of a partnership between a host site and relevant affiliates in a joint revenue scheme. The most notable example of an affiliate scheme is probably Amazon's Associates Programme, which has almost half a million affiliated Web sites. Each affiliate earns commissions of up to 15 per cent on sales of products – just for enticing online shoppers to click over to Amazon.com's online superstore and buy something. However, as this chapter will show, it is not just business-to-consumer e-tailers who can benefit, as affiliate marketing is now a driving force behind many of the major B2B players.

Affiliate origins

The concept of affiliate marketing was first formulated in the mind of Jeff Bezos in 1996. He was at a cocktail party talking to another guest about his online venture, Amazon.com, when the guest told him that she wanted to sell specialized books on her Web site for divorcees. Bezos then decided that there must be a way to partner with niche sites in order to generate share revenue. Instead of just having sites linking to its home page, Bezos believed it would be a good idea to have other sites actually promoting and helping to sell its products. By offering sites a commission on products sold via this scheme, Amazon soon acquired a vast sales force of affiliates. Now Amazon has nearly half a million affiliates based across the globe.

Following Amazon's lead, big name B2C companies such as CDNow, eBay, Beyond.com, Outpost.com and Barnes and Noble soon got in on the act, gathering their own armies of online affiliates. Amazon's affiliate scheme remains, however, the archetypal and most influential model.

One of the secrets to Amazon's success has been ease of access. Any Web site (with suitable content) is able to act as an affiliate. It simply visits the affiliate page of the Amazon site and signs itself up. Once it has done this, the affiliate is able to send a customer from its site to Amazon and gain a commission on any purchases made. The affiliate site can link to Amazon.com either by incorporating a hyperlink to specific products or by placing a button or Amazon search box on their homepage.

Affiliate benefits

Many companies offer affiliate schemes as a way of generating traffic and sales for their businesses. These companies pay commissions based on the traffic they receive from links placed on affiliate sites. These commissions are worked out on either a pay-per-click, pay-per-lead or pay-per-sale basis. The reason why affiliate schemes have become so popular is because they benefit the host site and the subscribing affiliate equally. The advantages of affiliate marketing from the host site's perspective include:

- *Reach*. Affiliate schemes enable companies to reach new audiences and increase their number of potential customers. Furthermore, when promoting their own site, affiliates will indirectly be promoting the host site as well. Because affiliate programmes are almost always free to join, many sites ranging from one-person operations to mega-corporations promote affiliate programmes on their Web sites. 'When you go to your favourite Web site and see a banner for another site, it's usually an affiliate programme they are promoting,' says Associate-It.com's Riyaj Shaik.
- *Viral marketing*. By making it easy for sites to become affiliates, they are in effect making it simple for them to spread the word about their businesses.
- *Minimal risk*. Although affiliates get paid commission, they only make money if and when sales are made (this is only applicable on a pay-per-sale basis).

The benefits for the affiliate site are also apparent:

- *No expense*. Most affiliate schemes are free to subscribe to, and involve little management costs. Sites receive commission without the burden of taking orders or shipping products, both of which remain the responsibility of the site that sets up the scheme.

- *Extra revenue.* Although an affiliate scheme is unlikely to be able to sustain a site single-handedly, it can provide a substantial boost to revenue. Many affiliate programmes now pay affiliates 20 per cent or more of the price of the product sold.
- *Enhanced service.* By increasing the range of products or services a site offers, affiliate schemes can provide customers with an additional reason to return.
- *Convenience.* All the affiliate has to do is provide a link to the host site, and integrate this with its own site's content.

The growth of B2B affiliate marketing

In most discussions about affiliate marketing, the focus is on the initiatives taken by business-to-consumer companies – such as Amazon, CDNow, Art.com and GoTo.com – but it is in the B2B sector that affiliate schemes are really taking off. According to one of the most respected sources for Internet marketing information, eMarketer (www.emarketer.com), B2B affiliate marketing is 'widely regarded as the next evolutionary step in online advertising'. Furthermore, although in 1999 James Marciano (founder of affiliate directory Refer-it.com) could claim that 'B2B affiliate programmes have been an untapped resource in the e-commerce space so far', this is no longer the case.

As the case studies in this chapter will show, numerous B2B operators are now capitalizing on affiliate marketing to generate new leads and broaden their customer base. Since September 1999, the date when Refer-it.com set up a B2B category on its site, affiliate marketing has evolved to become a major force in the growth of B2B e-commerce per se. As e-commerce journalist Sean Collins puts it, 'Business-to-business affiliate schemes have emerged in all facets of e-commerce, from sports equipment to business machines, and the rapid growth of the industry dictates that B2B affiliates are here to stay, play and dominate.' Therefore, while the business-to-consumer affiliate concept may have been the first to win the market battle, the business-to-business affiliate model looks set to win the war for market share.

There is certainly no shortage of affiliate marketing advocates in the B2B sector. For instance, BeFree's executive vice-president Tom Gerace claims that 'today's leading online merchandisers have seen that affiliate networks result in increased sales at a fraction of the cost of Internet advertising'. Doug Wolford, in charge of marketing and sales at Network Solutions (the world leader in Web address registration) can also speak from first-hand experience: 'Word is out that our affiliate programme is a win for everyone involved,' he says. 'It gives members an opportunity to realize additional revenue without spending any money, and it really extends awareness of Network Solutions' domain name registration and other Internet identity services.'

Case study: BidCrawler.com

BidCrawler.com, an online auction and exchange aggregator, is one of the leading proponents of affiliate marketing in the B2B arena. It embarked on a B2B affiliate programme after its B2C affiliate scheme had already proven to be a success.

In conjunction with B2Bid Crawler.com (the company's B2B site), B2B affiliate partnerships are now a critical component of the company's business model. 'We have every confidence that our B2B affiliate programme will eventually surpass our B2C affiliate programme, which has already proven to be extremely successful,' says Greg Stone, BidCrawler.com's president. 'These programmes are an extremely cost-effective way to maximize a company's presence on the Internet – and we plan to leverage this model to its fullest extent.'

B2BidCrawler.com takes a more proactive approach than most, working with its affiliate partners to help enhance services for its target audience and increase its overall 'stickiness'. 'By partnering with BidCrawler.com, our affiliates are able to offer their targeted, business-oriented customers direct access to the Internet's top B2B auctions and exchanges, which is critical as e-marketplaces continue to redefine business commerce,' says BidCrawler.com senior marketing manager, Carolyn MacLeod. She also emphasizes the fact that the company understands the different requirements of affiliate members. 'We work with our affiliates to meet their sites' specific needs, and toward this end, have a variety of new banners available for them to always select from.'

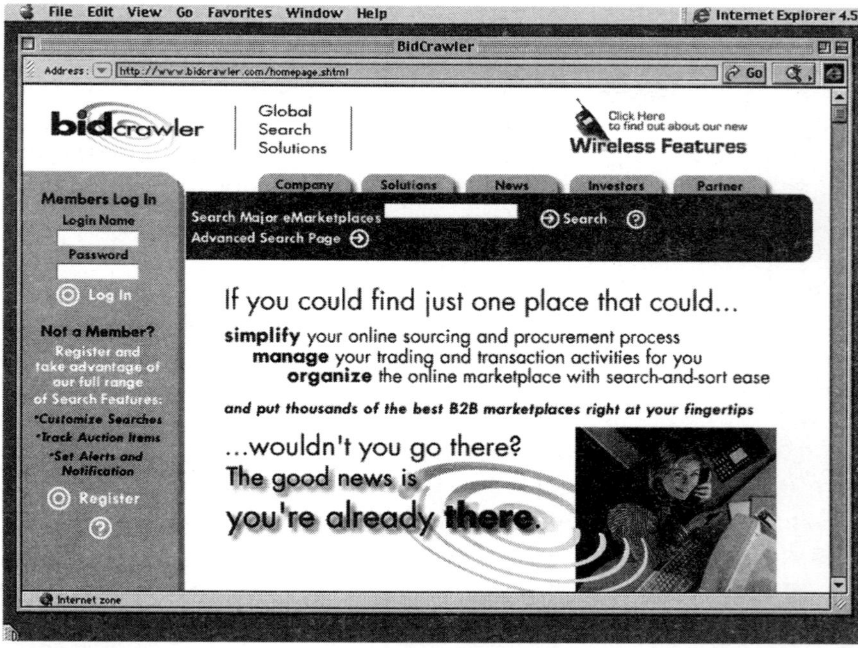

Figure 11.1 BidCrawler: an online auction and exchange aggregator

Case study: Yac.com

London-based Yac.com (You're Always Connected) boasts a wide variety of companies as part of its affiliate scheme, including professional bodies, recruitment companies, student unions, and travel commerce sites, all of which helped YAC subscribe 25,000 customers in its first quarter of operations.

YAC, which provides customers with a telephone number that can be programmed through its Web site to be freely redirected to any location, considers the affiliate programme as fundamental to the continuing growth of its online service. By entering an affiliate's Web site, users (typically mobile workers) are able to register for a unique YAC number and account, free of charge. Once activated, subscribers are able to manage their communications via telephone and e-mail, wherever they are.

Mike Feerick, CEO of YAC, says that their affiliates 'have been quick to realize that their communities are made up of modern individuals who travel, have an e-mail account and often a mobile phone'. YAC's high profile affiliate members include e-bookers, the Chartered Institute of Management, jobshark.com, taxi.com, netcom.net.uk, cableinet.co.uk and beenz.com.

Setting up an affiliate scheme

Furthermore, the emergence of cost-effective affiliate software solutions has made affiliate marketing an option for virtually every e-commerce business. Most affiliate software products enable companies to build their own pay-per-click, pay-per-lead or pay-per-sale affiliate scheme and use graphic or text advertisements to promote their products or services. Furthermore, software solutions provide online marketing sales statistics so that companies can track their clicks, impressions and sales. They can choose to use either graphic or text-based advertisements and have total control over the rate of commission paid for each click, sale or lead. Affiliates then join the scheme and display advertisements on their Web sites, sending customers and traffic back to the host site.

Some affiliate services, such as Clix Galore (www.clixgalore.com), also include each scheme on their database, which means that their affiliate members can locate and join them if they wish.

The most comprehensive products offer a fully automated process, where everything from signing up new affiliates to commission tracking happens automatically. More information on the various products and services can be found at Affiliate Zone (www.affiliatezone.com) and Click Travel (www.clicktravel.com). Here are some general guidelines companies need to consider if their affiliate scheme is to be successful:

- *Consider existing customers*. While many companies view an affiliate scheme as an effective way of reaching new business audiences, it is also important to consider existing site visitors and customers. After all, it is always preferable to get customers to shop at your own site direct rather than via an affiliate partner.
- *Don't be greedy*. The motto 'greed is good' may have suited Gordon Gecko in *Wall Street*, but it is not helpful in affiliate marketing. As most B2B affiliate schemes are free to join, so should yours be. Furthermore, it is important to consider the rate of commission very carefully. The reason Amazon has amassed such a huge number of affiliates is due, in part at least, to the fact that it pays affiliate partners a 15 per cent commission on each sale they make, while many of its rivals only offer a 5 to 10 per cent commission rate.

- *Provide information.* It is important not only to provide information before affiliate partners sign up, but also once the partnership is underway. Many affiliate networks (such as BeFree.com) enable host sites to offer real time information on the affiliate scheme and each partner site's success.
- *Take legal precautions.* As it is almost impossible to check out exactly how legitimate each partner is, it is important to cover your company from any legal pitfalls. By providing a comprehensive list of terms that partners have to agree to (including payment terms), companies can safeguard themselves from unscrupulous partners.
- *Partner with similar industry segments.* By partnering with affiliates that target similar industry segments, merchants can gain access to a relevant customer base that will increase traffic and drive online sales. Because affiliate partnerships are performance-based, most sites compensate affiliates only when the desired outcome, such as a click-through or a purchase, is obtained, making this channel highly cost-effective for merchants in even the most niche of industries.
- *Offer integration.* On its affiliate sites, VeriSign certificate services are integrated with other value-added services offered by the provider. Examples include an ISP that offers Web site digital certificates in conjunction with its Web site hosting services and a large e-commerce site that offers certificates to each member of its customer base to support secure user authentication and electronic messaging.
- *Be flexible.* To provide its affiliates with more flexibility in marketing, Network Solutions offers a selection of 10 banners in various sizes based on service offerings. Affiliate members can post the banners they select to their Web sites to let visitors know which Network Solutions services they offer. VeriSign (the world's leading provider of online trust services) also believes flexibility is important. Its affiliates can choose to offer digital certificate services to their customers either under their own brand, the VeriSign brand, or within a co-branded certificate hierarchy.

Case study: Lodging.com

Lodging.com is the fastest growing hotel affiliate programme online today. As Edward Silver, Lodging.com's vice-president of technology, puts it, 'This is the most aggressive, flexible affiliate programme in the hotel reservation market. We offer higher commissions, destination content and revenue tracking systems that make it easy for any size business to successfully offer hotel reservations to their customers.'

Lodging.com's deliberately aggressive programme is luring many travel Web sites away from traditional hotel suppliers that don't offer content and have strict and inflexible commission payment plans. By using Lodging.com, a travel Web site can easily build a customer-friendly Web site incorporating booking capabilities.

'We spent a lot of time speaking with companies that offer hotel reservations and most of them were frustrated with their current set of options,' says Mike Nadboy, Lodging.com's director of business development. 'This programme is a combination of everything people told us they wanted in an affiliate programme.' In addition to the benefits listed above, Lodging.com offers the ability to select specific hotel properties and provides a tiered system with access to more than 40,000 lodging properties.

The effort is already beginning to show results. According to Silver, 'The feedback has been overwhelmingly positive and we are getting enquiries from e-commerce companies every day.'

Pay-per-sale schemes

B2B affiliate schemes that pay commissions for actual sales generated by referrals remain popular and account for over half of all affiliate marketing. This method is certainly more cost-effective, at least from the affiliate host's perspective, than pay-per-click (based on click-through rates) and pay-per-lead models. However, this method means that affiliates must be up to the job. Of course, simply by incorporating goods that are directly related to their content, sites give their visitors the opportunity to make impulse purchases, and generate income for the host site.

In order to make considerable money from these schemes, however, affiliates are often tempted to subscribe to many at the same time. The approach has come under attack, by, among others, Forrester Research and the *E-commerce Times*. The *E-commerce Times* states that 'the proliferation of affiliate programmes may detract from the credibility of content sites, making them seem more like infomercials than information providers'. According to Forrester, the density of links on some sites is similar to the chaotic environment of Las Vegas. 'The affiliate sites are cluttered and there's no editorial voice,' one Forrester report claims. 'Neon lights may attract tourists on the [Las Vegas] Strip, but surfers want more substance. The power of affiliate marketing is not in the link, but in the context that creates the buying impulse.'

Case study: Peoplesound.com

The affiliate scheme set up by Peoplesound.com, Europe's largest music download Internet site, enables affiliates to link to its site and generate revenues through customer referrals and sales commissions. Although aimed solely at consumers, Peoplesound.com depends on its partnerships with other businesses to reach the consumer market.

Under the scheme, affiliate partners can link their Web sites to Peoplesound.com's 'value added' content, such as charts and search tools, free of charge. Affiliates receive payment for registrations and commission on sales of content. In addition, affiliates can access sophisticated real time reporting regarding their performance in the scheme and revenue due to them. The reporting service is offered through Commission Junction, one of the global leaders in affiliate programme services.

Ernesto Schmitt, president of Peoplesound.com, claims his company is 'constantly on the look out for innovative and compelling ways of distributing our content so that they can reach the widest possible audience. The affiliate programme allows us to do this and offers great benefits to all parties,' he says. 'Our affiliates not only gain access to some top quality traffic-generating content, but can also begin generating additional revenue as soon as they come on board. From our perspective, the affiliate programme allows us to enter into thousands of partnerships with sites in any locality, helping us to continue driving our growth as Europe's largest new music download Internet site.'

Figure 11.2 Peoplesound.com: linking with businesses to target consumers

Promoting an affiliate scheme

Once an affiliate scheme has been set up, relevant businesses need to know about it. Affiliate schemes, as mentioned above, can be a very useful means of generating awareness of a site within the B2B community, but in order to get to this level the scheme itself needs to be heavily promoted. Here are some of the most effective places to promote an affiliate network:

- *The host site*. The obvious place to promote an affiliate scheme is on the host site itself. It is here that potential affiliates expect to be able to access pages detailing the scheme, and how they can join. The information provided should include a description of the products sold via the scheme, the commission and payment terms, a privacy policy, and the general affiliate guidelines.
- *E-mail*. E-mail newsletters and other direct marketing material can be used to encourage companies to subscribe as affiliates.

They can also be used to get affiliates themselves to send businesses to the host site.

- *Affiliate directories*. Being indexed on relevant directories is vital for companies in order to attract potential affiliates, as they are likely to be their first port of call when looking for host sites. Indeed, affiliate directories are geared more towards site owners wanting to sign up for suitable schemes than any other audience (see the Affiliate directories sub-section).
- *Affiliates*. It is also important to engage in viral marketing tactics by explicitly encouraging affiliates to spread the word by mouth.
- *Affiliate networks*. If you belong to an affiliate network (such as Commission Junction or LinkShare) this also provides a valuable form of promotion, as it is often visited by potential affiliates.
- *Visit discussion groups*. According to ClickZ columnist Scott Wingo, 'If you really want to sign on those super affiliates, you should go where they go: affiliate marketing discussion boards. When you post well thought out messages to the discussion boards (with a signature that plugs your programme), you are posting a free ad for your programme, as well as exhibiting your active role in the education and success of affiliates.' Some of the more populated discussion boards are Associate Programs (www.associateprograms.com), Cash Pile (www.cashpile.com), iBoost (www.iboost.com) and Reve News (www.revenews.com).
- *Make direct contact*. One of the most effective ways of attracting new affiliates is to contact them directly. Concentrate on a few likely candidates and send a tailored e-mail explaining exactly why your scheme is relevant to their site(s), and what they can hope to get out of it.

Becoming an affiliate

Even if a company decides to set up its own affiliate network, it can still become affiliated to another scheme. Becoming an online affiliate is usually straightforward, often involving little more than copying a page of HTML from the host site. Most schemes are free to join and provide online statistics so that you can track commissions.

Once you have joined an affiliate scheme, companies are paid according to the scheme's payment method. A pay-per-click scheme pays each time an advertisement is clicked, a pay-per-lead scheme pays each time the affiliate forwards a lead to the host's site, while a pay-per-sale scheme pays commissions only when a purchase is made.

Some pay-per-sale commission schemes work on an ascending scale. That is to say, the more product units an affiliate site sells, the more favourable the rate of commission becomes.

It is important to remember that while affiliate schemes can and do make money for an affiliate partner, they are rarely able to financially support a site by themselves. However, by taking the role of affiliate partner seriously, companies are able to make considerable gains and enhance the value of the online experience offered to site visitors. Ultimately, the success (or otherwise) an affiliate partner achieves by subscribing to a scheme depends on the following factors:

- *Research*. Before deciding which affiliate scheme to join, companies need to conduct thorough research in order to know exactly what schemes are out there. Affiliate directories such as Associate It provide a useful overview of the variety of B2B affiliate schemes available.
- *Added value*. Affiliates are not offering their own, but another company's products or services. To get people to buy products from your site rather than the affiliate host itself, you need to make sure they have a reason.
- *Commission*. The rate of commission ranges between 5 and 20 per cent.
- *Relevance*. The more relevant the products you sell are to the content of the site, the easier it will be to convert site users into site customers.
- *Legitimacy*. The fact that you don't have to handle orders also means that you are putting the reputation of your site in another company's hands. It may even be worthwhile placing a few orders yourself before inviting your site users to do the same and, if possible, ask for references.
- *Evaluation*. Once the affiliate scheme has been incorporated on your site, it is important to evaluate its efficiency at regular intervals. It is important to set objectives and timescales for the scheme, in order to measure its success effectively.

Affiliate directories

Affiliate directories are searchable indexes, helping businesses find affiliate programmes that are relevant to their sites. If you run your own scheme, these directories will consider it for a free listing in their database. If a directory chooses to highlight a scheme as a recommendation in its newsletter then it can benefit from even more exposure. However, as affiliate schemes become ever more popular, directories are increasingly selective as to which schemes can qualify for a listing.

It's certainly worth noting that most directories won't accept submissions from affiliates themselves; submissions need to come from the programme owner. Furthermore, pay-per-click schemes are rejected by the majority of directories as they prefer a pay-per-sale scheme. In most instances, submissions are reviewed before being indexed in the directory. However, as well as being promotional tools, affiliate directories can also prove valuable for research purposes.

The directories enable companies to link to sites that already take part in schemes, for them to see how they work in practice. Some, such as the Associate Programs site (www.associateprograms.com), hold their own discussion forums where you can ask questions on any area of affiliate programs. Another directory, Site Cash (www.sitecash.com), rates sites on their ease of use, providing a comparative overview of different types of affiliate scheme. The three main directories, however, are Associate It, Refer-it and Affiliate Find:

Associate It (www.associate-it.com)

Associate It is arguably the most well known affiliate directory. As well as its categorized affiliate index, Associate It also incorporates a number of other facilities. These include:

- a top ten page to find out the top ranked associate programmes based on popularity and user rating;
- a discussion board that enables potential affiliates to get answers to any questions they may have, by posting questions to an affiliate manager;
- a newsletter to learn how to market an affiliate programme and generate additional revenue from a Web site;

- a 'Webmaster resources' section that includes excellent articles on Web design, promotion, marketing, e-commerce and other free resources to build and promote a site;
- a 'Webannouncer' that submits affiliate sites to major search engines for free.
- a promotional 'associate mall'.

'We don't list all the programmes submitted for inclusion in our directory,' says Associate It President and CEO Riyaj Shaik. 'We normally turn down a lot of programmes that look suspicious, we try to keep our directory as clean as possible and list only established programmes, companies that are selling their own products,' he says. 'Also we don't list adult pyramid and become rich fast programmes.'

How much does it cost to use Associate-it.com? 'Absolutely nothing,' says Shaik. 'We offer everything free to users and also it costs nothing to list an associate programme in our directory, we are trying to generate revenue through advertising and sponsorship.'

Refer-it (www.refer-it.com)

Launched in December 1997, Refer-it.com is the leading search engine for affiliate schemes. At the time of writing, Refer-it's database included descriptions and rating of 3,774 affiliate schemes, including many offered by B2B companies. Refer-it is part of Internet.com (www.Internet.com), the 'E-business and Internet Technology Network'.

Affiliate Find (www.affiliatefind.com)

This revenue-sharing resource offers a directory search engine of affiliate, associate, referral, commission, pay-per-click, and partner programmes.

Case study: Liquidation.com

The Liquidation.com affiliate scheme enables companies to get a share of the business surplus market by becoming a part of the Liquidation.com network of partners. The Liquidation.com surplus network has over 100,000 users in 107 countries. The scheme offers affiliated sites access to a broad range of facilities such as custom storefronts, to refer their users to transact on the Liquidation.com site. As with most B2B schemes, affiliates can then receive a percentage of the transaction revenue generated by their users.

Among the hundreds of affiliates signed up to the scheme are companies and organizations such as XSmartmaterials.com, Builder Depot, the Textile Rental Services Association and TrucksWholesale.com. According to Mark Johnson, president of XSmartmaterials, 'Displaying surplus listings on our site is a unique avenue for XSmartmaterials.com to directly provide our customers easy access to goods they want.'

Liquidation.com currently list millions of US corporate and government surplus on its exchange, including business jets, industrial metalworking machines and many more listings across 27 different categories. In a statement announcing the launch of the scheme, Bill Angrick, chairman and CEO, stated the benefits for both the host service and subscribing affiliate: 'The new affiliate programme is a unique opportunity for sites to offer surplus listings to their users and gain an additional revenue stream with little to no upfront costs. This programme is also a valuable resource for Liquidation.com to gain users, listings and increased liquidity on our surplus network.'

In addition, affiliates are able to track their referrals and commission through the exchange using special tracking software incorporated on the host site. Ultimately, Liquidation.com's affiliate scheme shows exactly how affiliate marketing can be a cost-effective method of acquiring new users and extending brand reach across the Web. The affiliate partners are able to realize increased revenues and have easy access to a Web-based reporting centre with areas to generate new promotional links for their sites and track the performance of the partnership.

Figure 11.3 Liquidation.com: offers its affiliates a broad range of facilities

Affiliate network services

Managing an affiliate scheme, even with the most comprehensive software solution, is a lot of hard work. That is why many B2B companies decide to sign up to an affiliate network that can manage the entire scheme on their behalf as well as provide the necessary information. As Jason Kelly (of *Neat Sheet* fame) puts it, this is 'a convenient way to bring more business to their sites without devoting an entire department to tracking commissions and writing cheques'. They also make it easier for affiliate sites to subscribe to several affiliate schemes simultaneously, as they can work within one single network. Here are some of the main affiliate networks that both host sites and their affiliates should consider:

Commission Junction (www.cj.com)

Founded in 1998, Commission Junction is the worldwide leader in affiliate marketing that 'matches online merchant products and services to online content at the consumer's point-of-interest'. Currently handling all aspects of the global network for more than 1,000 merchants and more than 250,000 content providers, Commission Junction audits e-commerce activity, manages all relationships and collects and pays commissions on sales generated, all at a cost that is lower than traditional online advertising programmes. Commission Junction's network includes heavyweight online merchants such as Excite@Home, Ticketmaster Online–Citysearch, A&E Television Networks and major content sites Road Runner and weather.com. Commission Junction is based in California but has offices in New York, London, Amsterdam and Hong Kong.

It should be noted that Commission Junction also offers a DIY software solution that costs approximately half the cost of its full network service. For the full service, Commission Junction charges a 15 per cent fee on all money owed to affiliates.

LinkShare (www.linkshare.com)

LinkShare was one of the first affiliate networks to acknowledge the significance of B2B affiliate marketing. In January 2000, it launched B2B LinkShare, an affiliate network that (as its name suggests) focuses exclusively on the business-to-business arena.

B2B LinkShare provides vertical portals ('vortals') and other sites devoted to business-to-business e-commerce, with a direct channel to the users of its products and services.

In addition to helping online B2B e-commerce players reach their customers efficiently, B2B LinkShare also helps companies offer significant cost savings through their corporate Intranets. By becoming an affiliate in B2B LinkShare, a company can provide its employees with links to all of their online suppliers in one place, getting a percentage of every sale back in the process. Moreover, using LinkShare, a company can track the actions of specific employees, giving it an easy way to monitor departmental purchases.

Be Free (www.befree.com)

Be Free calls itself 'the leader of performance marketing – the next generation of online marketing'. Be Free helps its customers build and manage affiliate schemes, enabling these sites to capture revenue by selling products in context throughout the Web. Collectively, Be Free's customers have more than 2 million affiliates in their sales channels and include some of the Internet's leading merchants such as America Online Inc, barnesandnoble.com, GoTo.com, Travelovity, Mercata, Reel.com, Cnet and Yahoo!. Affiliates can enrol in performance marketing programmes using Be Free's technology with a streamlined application form called Fast App, located at www.reporting.net/networks/affiliates.

Case study: OfficeMax.com

OfficeMax.com is a member of the affiliate network LinkShare and uses this service to reach new markets. For instance, the company claims its participation allows OfficeMax.com to acquire B2B-oriented vertical portal sites as online partners, including medical, legal and other industry specific sites.

'OfficeMax.com recognizes the importance of B2B affiliate relationships within our overall marketing strategy,' says Ryan Vero, OfficeMax's head of e-commerce. 'By participating in B2B LinkShare, OfficeMax.com has a powerful ally that will allow us to acquire thousands of small and medium-sized business customers.'

Vero also claims that through LinkShare's B2B service, OfficeMax.com gains further exposure through corporate Intranets. LinkShare's 'signature' technology allows companies to provide employees with links to OfficeMax.com, getting a percentage of sales back in the process while also tracking individual employees and departmental purchases.

In September 1998 OfficeMax.com, the online office superstore, launched one of the Internet's first business-to-business affiliate programmes. Since then, the site has developed thousands of online partnerships, including relationships with Office.com, Office Click.com and Work.com.

The OfficeMax Online Affiliate Programme creates sales opportunities for thousands of Web sites that provide content and services to the vast small business, home office and consumer markets. As with all pay-per-sale schemes following the Amazon model, affiliates earn commission on every delivered sales transaction generated through links from their sites.

Case study: About.com (www.about.com)

About.com, the leading network of niche vertical sites for consumers and businesses, set up an affiliate scheme using Be Free's network services. Be Free acts as an infrastructure partner and serves as an intermediary, tracking each click-through and reporting the results back to About.com. Through the affiliate programme, Web sites of any size can link directly to About.com's more than 650 targeted, topic-specific sites through text links, graphical banners and search boxes. Affiliate sites, from large special interest communities to home-grown personal hobby pages, provide visitors with links to relevant About.com content within their own content. These affiliate sites benefit financially, earning commissions when their visitors click-through to the About.com content.

'With Be Free's support, we've engineered an affiliate programme that works best for our unique business model – allowing us to extend our brand reach and drive qualified traffic to our hundreds of destination sites,' says John Caplan, senior vice-president of marketing for About.com. 'With an average click-through rate of 5 per cent, and some as high as 13 per cent, our affiliates can dramatically increase the amount of traffic to our network and offer an even greater return on investment for our advertisers and sponsors.'

Summary

Affiliate marketing can help practically any B2B e-commerce operator meet their marketing objectives. As it capitalizes on the so-called 'network effect' of the Internet, an affiliate scheme can help companies reach new audiences, increase market share and raise their revenues. It can also improve their relations among other businesses as it creates the kind of business Web (or 'b-Web') wherein every member can benefit.

twelve

B2B e-mail marketing

E-mail is one of the most powerful, but also most controversial, of online marketing tools. According to leading research organization Forrester Research, the use of e-mail marketing as a means of boosting long-term relations with customers is going to increase even further. It has predicted that marketers will send more than 200 billion B2B and B2C e-mails in 2004. Although e-mail can help to keep your company in the minds of existing customers, it can also cause annoyance if marketing messages are contributing to the problem of e-mail overload. This chapter looks at both the positive and negative aspects of e-mail marketing, in order to equip you with the knowledge needed to avoid pitfalls and maximize the opportunities e-mail brings with it.

The golden rules of B2B e-mail marketing

While every e-mail marketing campaign should be tailored to the requirements of the audience it is aimed at, there are some rules that remain consistent:

- *Remember your objectives*. In order for an e-mail marketing campaign to be a success, you need to be clear about the business objectives you want to achieve.
- *Gain permission*. Before you send any marketing material via e-mail, ensure that you have the recipient's permission. Make sure visitors to your site have to carry out an action such as ticking a box in order to opt in to your e-mailing list.

- *Use the Bcc: option.* When sending an e-mail to more than one company, use the Bcc: (Blind Carbon Copy) function in order to conceal each recipient's e-mail address.
- *Keep columns narrow.* Most e-mail software programs (including Microsoft Outlook) include a 'word wrap' function that enables you to set column widths to a certain size. By keeping columns narrow (under 80 characters) you will ensure that your e-mails are not broken up on each recipient's computer screen.
- *Be brief.* Keeping e-mails brief is even more important in the B2B sector than it is in the B2C sector as, generally speaking, e-mail overload is a bigger problem for business than it is for consumers. Business decision-makers generally have little time to read lengthy e-newsletters and similar material.
- *Avoid attachments.* Attached files not only lengthen e-mail download times, they are also more of a virus risk.
- *Enable recipients to 'opt out'.* Make sure every e-mail you send to your mailing list includes instructions on how recipients can opt out or unsubscribe. The simplest way to do this is to set up a separate 'unsubscribe' e-mail address such as optout@mycompany.com that can be clicked onto within the e-mail itself. This minimizes the effort required by each recipient and therefore ensures that every business on your e-mailing list remains willing to receive information from your company.
- *Measure results.* By keeping track of 'click-through' and response rates, as well as of the number of businesses choosing to opt out, you will be able to get a better idea of what works and what doesn't.
- *Break up your list.* Dividing your e-mailing list into different categories of business will help you to make your marketing messages more targeted.
- *Incorporate links.* Links to your Web site should be included in every e-mail you send in order to encourage repeat traffic. Also, make sure that the link takes people to the most relevant Web page.
- *Think of the 5Ws.* When sending a marketing e-mail, keep in mind what journalists and PR professionals refer to as the 5Ws (Who? What? When? Where? Why?). *Who* are you sending the message to? *What* objectives do you hope to achieve? *When* is the best time to send information? *Where* is your message going to be accessed? (Answering this question involves not only

locating where the businesses on your mailing list are based, but also finding out whether the message will be received via a desktop PC or other device.) *Why* are you sending the message and why should the recipient read it? This last question is, without doubt, the most important and should be at the back of your mind throughout every e-mail marketing campaign.

- *Make subject lines obvious*. The subject line determines whether an e-mail message is read. Subject lines should always indicate the content of the message. Vague subject lines such as 'Hello' or 'Urgent news flash' are likely to be seen as 'spam' messages and are unlikely to be opened. With the number of business e-mail messages increasing daily, the strength of a subject line becomes ever more significant.
- *Inform, don't advertise*. E-mail messages with informative content have more value for recipients than advertising messages.
- *Personalize*. Where possible, personalize e-mail messages in line with the needs of the recipient.
- *Be informal*. As e-mail is a more immediate means of communicating than sending a letter, the formalities of traditional business letter writing do not apply. For instance, there is no need to start an e-mail with 'Dear Sir' or to close with 'Yours faithfully'.
- *Be ready to respond*. Businesses expect to receive a response to their e-mail enquiries within a matter of hours. When your company sends out marketing material via e-mail you need to make sure that you will be able to handle the likely increase in incoming mail.

E-mail discussion lists

Although e-mail newsletters can be used to provoke responses from subscribers, they are based on a one-way mailing list structure. In other words, while recipients can contact the publisher, they cannot directly communicate with other subscribers.

If you want to make your mailing list more inclusive and interactive, you can set up a discussion list. A discussion list (often referred to as a 'two-way mailing list') not only enables subscribers to respond to messages, but also lets everyone else on the list see their responses.

There are two main types of e-mail discussion lists: moderated and unmoderated. In a moderated discussion list, the company that sets up the list retains some form of editorial control. The company is able to monitor and screen every message posted onto the list. This helps to keep the discussion on track, providing the editorial process is not so heavy-handed as to stifle the conversation entirely. In an unmoderated list, on the other hand, the individual or company that set up the discussion has no more nor less control over the list than every other subscriber. When a subscriber posts something, it goes to all the other list subscribers immediately. Clearly, an unmoderated discussion list involves a higher risk factor than moderated lists, particularly when it is set up in a company's name. To set up a list you can either use a freeware program (such as Pegasus Mail) or a more costly program (such as Listserv, one of the most popular mailing list software programs).

Contributing to discussion lists

As well as creating your own discussion list, you may decide to contribute to those of other companies and organizations. To find a mailing list relevant to your industry area you can visit the Liszt Web site (www.liszt.com), which has an index of over 100,000 mailing lists, searchable by subject. However, although finding relevant B2B mailing lists is not difficult, promoting your business within them requires considerable care. In order to maximize the chances of success within e-mail discussion groups it is necessary to adhere to the following advice:

- *Be a silent subscriber*. Before you send a message to the list you should become a silent subscriber for a while. This is necessary in order to see the type of messages that are posted and the responses they provoke. You will then be able to determine how the list reacts to messages of a commercial nature. If the group is moderated, you will also be able to get an idea of the type of message the moderator accepts. It's worth noting that a lot of moderated discussion lists post a set of guidelines to new members as soon as they have subscribed. This should be read very carefully before taking an active part in the discussion.
- *Create a signature line*. In groups where promotional messages are prohibited, it is still possible to generate awareness for your

Web site in your signature line. A signature line is a little block of text at the end of an e-mail that indicates who you are, where you are from, as well as a little bit about what your business does. You are also able to incorporate a relevant e-mail and Web address.

- *Answer questions.* One of the main reasons why people join a discussion list is to find answers to questions. If you are able to answer these questions you will be able to build up your status within the group. Furthermore, this may also enable you to promote your own services (at least in the signature line).
- *Ask questions.* As well as answering other people's enquiries you should also ask questions of your own. This will not only give the impression that you are a business willing to listen to what its target market has to say, but it will help you to calculate valuable market research. It will also enable you to keep a dialogue alive.
- *Keep messages in context.* If you are responding to a previous e-mail, place your posting in context by quoting the original message.
- *Avoid sales jargon.* Over-enthusiastic self-promotion is unwelcome in virtually every B2B discussion list. By writing a message inviting subscribers to check out 'THE BEST B2B SITE ON THE WEB!!!' you are likely to receive a lot of hostile (or 'flame') messages.
- *Don't over-post.* Only post when you have something of value to offer or have a genuine enquiry to make.
- *Never cross-post.* The cardinal sin of discussion list etiquette (or 'netiquette') is to post the same message into various lists simultaneously.
- *Be brief.* In a busy discussion list, subscribers may read lots of messages in one day. Brief messages are therefore preferred to lengthy ones.

Newsletters

B2B companies are increasingly using electronic newsletters in order to provide their customers with valuable and informative content. However, although e-newsletters are popular, they are often misused. The main problem is that companies often cannot resist the opportunity to push their products and services. While this may seem like a good way to promote what you have to offer, it will lead ultimately to a high rate of 'unsubscribe' messages. Although product promotion is an essential part of e-marketing, a newsletter is not the right place for sales literature.

Newsletter benefits

The fact that virtually every B2B sector you can think of has newsletters devoted to it indicates that newsletters must have considerable benefits for both publisher and subscriber. Indeed, the incentives for the subscriber are clear. E-mail newsletters provide a regular, relevant source of (usually free) information that does not have to be sought out through hours of Web surfing. And for the publisher? Well here are just some of the more obvious benefits:

- *Awareness*. By sending out a newsletter on a regular basis to your opt-in subscribers, you are making sure your core customer base remains aware of what you have to offer.
- *Mailing lists*. Research has shown that e-mail newsletters provide the greatest incentive to join an opt-in mailing list. The *New York Times* managed to add over one million names to its mailing list through its 'Today's Headline' e-newsletter. In the B2B arena, Wilson Web's Web Marketing Today newsletter now boasts a mailing list of over 100,000 subscribers. Edventure Holdings, ClickZ, Ziff-Davis and Peppers and Rogers are just some of the B2B companies that have also managed to build mailing lists of hundred of thousands of subscribers via their newsletters.
- *Viral marketing*. Newsletters are a good way to encourage 'word of mouse' publicity about your company within the business community. 'E-mail this to a colleague' and 'Spread the word' links can prompt business customers to market among themselves. You may soon find that, if you are providing useful content, the pass-along rate exceeds the number of direct subscribers.
- *Market research*. By using a newsletter as a feedback tool, companies can conduct valuable quantitative and qualitative market research.

- *Differentiation*. In an increasingly competitive environment, e-mail newsletters provide B2B companies with the opportunity to differentiate themselves from their rivals.
- *Customer retention*. Newsletters provide you with a way to retain first-time customers and increase loyalty to your company.
- *Information*. On the Internet, information itself becomes a product. In the B2B sector, companies are not only expected to provide effective services but also to offer valuable and, preferably, exclusive information. Newsletters are one of the best means to this end.
- *Revenue generation*. Although most B2B e-mail newsletters are made available for free, some (such as Esther Dyson's *Release 1.0*, www.edventureholdings.com) are distributed on a paid subscription basis. However, paid subscriptions are not the only way to make money from a newsletter. E-mail newsletters are becoming ever more popular among advertisers and sponsors as a means of carefully targeting new audiences. One of the reasons for this is the fact that click-through rates are higher for

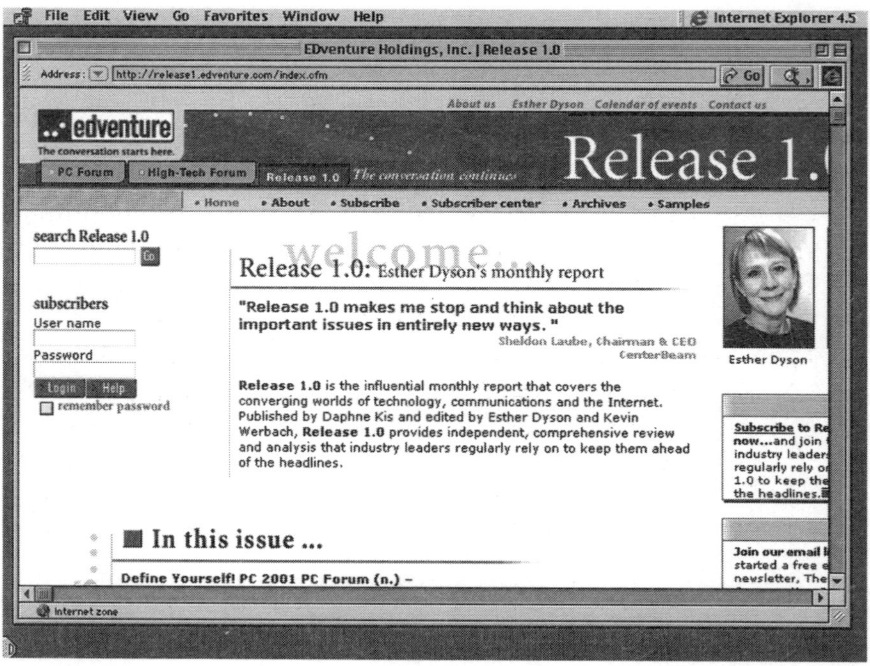

Figure 12.1 Esther Dyson's *Release 1.0* newsletter

e-mail advertising than they are for Web-based banners. The adverts in e-mail newsletters are either in plain text or HTML, depending on the newsletter format.

Newsletter guidelines

The main objective of a newsletter should be to build up long-term relations with your existing client or customer base. Information, rather than advertising, should therefore be the basis of the newsletter content. Here are some more guidelines to follow when creating a B2B e-newsletter:

- *Be relevant*. Although your newsletter does not have to be *about* your company (in fact it is often better if it is not), it should be relevant to your industry and the services you provide.
- *Avoid jargon*. One common flaw found in B2B newsletters is an over-abundance of business jargon and technical language. The aim, however, should be to inform rather than confuse your audience. You cannot assume that every member of your mailing list will be an industry insider.
- *Stick to plain text*. As mentioned elsewhere in this chapter, plain text is a safer, if more boring, means of sending marketing material than an HTML-based format.
- *Be realistic*. Once you have decided on the length and frequency of your newsletter you will have to stick to it. Therefore, you need to be realistic about what you will be able to manage. Obviously, producing a daily or weekly newsletter will be more demanding than sending it out on a fortnightly or monthly basis. The other factor you need to consider is how often will subscribers want to receive the newsletter. Some businesses will be reluctant to sign up to receive an extra e-mail every day or week, owing to the problems they already experience regarding e-mail overload.
- *Ask for feedback*. E-mail is a dialogic communications tool. In other words, it facilitates two-way communication or conversation. To get the most of the medium, you should embrace its dialogic nature by asking for feedback.

- *Archive your newsletters*. Most of the mailing list services (such as Lyris) enable you to incorporate your newsletters within a Web archive. By archiving newsletters on your Web site, you will be helping potential subscribers to make an informed choice over whether your newsletter is relevant to their business.
- *Type Web addresses in full*. In order to convert Web site references into a clickable link, remember to type Web addresses in full (including the http: part).
- *Use small paragraphs*. As e-mail newsletters tend to be longer than an average e-mail message, you should try to make text easy to read by breaking it up into small paragraphs. Also, include a line of space between each paragraph.
- *Indicate different sections*. If your newsletter includes more than one article or news announcement, you must clearly indicate when a section ends. You can do this by leaving two lines of space or by using the hyphen key to form a line of text (___).
- *Post to yourself*. Before you distribute a newsletter to your mailing list, send a copy to yourself to check that it looks correct.

Plain text versus HTML

Many companies use HTML (HyperText Mark-up Language) to format their electronic newsletters and other mass e-mails. As HTML is the coding used to create Web pages, it enables you to add colour and graphical elements to e-mail documents. However, although most e-mail software enables you to send HTML formatted material, it is not always preferable to plain text e-mail. Here are some of the main problems or drawbacks that can be encountered when creating and sending HTML e-mail:

- *Viruses*. 'Worm' viruses can attach themselves easily to HTML files without the sender's knowledge. Viruses are less common within plain text messages.
- *Compatibility*. Although most e-mail software is able to read HTML, HTML messages are often displayed differently.
- *Time*. Not only do HTML messages take longer to create, they also take longer to read. As ClickZ columnist Kim McPherson stated in an article on the subject, 'A business decision-maker's

time at work is limited, so messages should be quick to download and quick to read, with no fanfare whatsoever.'

If you do decide to use HTML in any of your e-mail campaigns it is always advisable to provide a plain text option as well.

Spam

Spam refers to unsolicited and indiscriminate bulk e-mail that is usually sent for commercial purposes. If you are guilty of sending spam messages you are likely to receive a hostile reaction from recipients. The antipathy towards unsolicited e-mail is evidenced by the number of organizations set up to combat the problem. For instance, the CAUCE (Coalition Against Unsolicited Commercial E-mail), which was founded in 1997, actively campaigns against the economic incentive to send junk e-mail. According to the CAUCE Web site (www.cauce.org) spam 'costs users and Web-based businesses millions every month'. CAUCE notes that it is rare to find a reputable company guilty of spamming and they have observed that most spam messages promote one of the following:

- chain letters;
- pyramid schemes (including Multi-Level Marketing, or MLM);
- Make Money Fast schemes;
- adult entertainment;
- offers of software for collecting e-mail addresses and sending unsolicited e-mail;
- offers of bulk e-mailing services for sending unsolicited e-mail;
- illegally pirated software;
- quack health products and remedies;
- stock offerings for unknown start-up companies.

Obviously these are not the sort of things a legitimate B2B company would want to associate itself with. The other reason unsolicited e-mails are so unwelcome is that they are often used to spread computer viruses ('the 'Melissa' and 'I love you' viruses were both sent in this way).

The main way to make sure that your company is never accused of spamming is to always make sure businesses have opted in to your mailing list. However, even believers in 'permission marketing' can sometimes be seen as endorsing spam. To make it 100 per cent clear that you oppose spam, it may be necessary to adhere to the following guidelines:

- *Publish a privacy policy on your site.* If you are intending to build a list of e-mail addresses via your site, you should include a privacy policy explaining how you intend to use these addresses (and any other personally identifiable information). This policy should also detail the security procedures that are in place to protect the loss, misuse or alteration of information under your company's control.
- *Do not sell e-mail addresses.* Many companies decide to make extra money by selling their e-mailing list to other businesses. This, however, is even worse than sending spam messages from your own address as it increases the chance that the e-mails will be irrelevant to the recipients.
- *Respond to spam accusations.* If you are wrongly accused of sending spam e-mails, it is advisable to respond by explaining that messages are only sent to businesses that opted in to receive them. If you have a record of when and how the e-mail address was obtained, you will be able to incorporate this information alongside details of how the recipient can opt out.
- *Confirm subscriptions.* If you have invested in an automated e-mail response program (such as EchoMail), you will be able to automatically contact businesses, confirming their decision to subscribe or unsubscribe to your e-mailing list. This combats the problem of 'spoof sign-ups', whereby an individual or business types in someone else's e-mail address.

Further information on what exactly constitutes spam can be found at the CAUCE site (www.cauce.org) as well as at Junkbusters (www.junkbusters.com). Incidentally, the term 'spam' originated as a reference to the Monty Python sketch where spam is served with everything.

Figure 12.2 The Web site of the Coalition Against Unsolicited Commercial E-mail

The B2C/B2B overlap

E-mail experts have traditionally viewed B2B e-mail marketing as a completely different discipline to its B2C equivalent. Indeed, there is no denying that B2B marketers need to take the problem of e-mail overload more seriously than their B2C counterparts. It is also true that while the emphasis in the consumer arena is on entertainment, in the business sector it tends to be on providing informative content. That said, it is no longer possible to view B2B and B2C e-mail marketing as mutually exclusive. Kim MacPherson from the ClickZ e-zine is just one of many commentators who now believe B2B e-mail marketers can use many of the incentives previously deployed in B2C campaigns. 'We've seen sweepstakes, free gift offers, contests, Palm give-aways, and, more typically, consumer-oriented offers work fabulously well in the B2B arena.'

Viral marketing

Viral marketing is the rather unfortunate term to describe word of mouth publicity on the Net. The word 'viral' refers to the infectious way word spreads about a company online.

According to Metcalfe's Law, the value of a network is the square of the number of users connected to it. As e-mail (potentially at least) places all users within the same network, a marketing message can spread far and wide in a very short space of time.

Viral marketing first became a significant topic when the free Web-based e-mail service Hotmail added the following message to the foot of every e-mail: 'Get your free Web-based e-mail at Hotmail'. This line of text incorporated a hyperlink to the Hotmail home page. Because this message was sent to people from their friends, colleagues or associates, it made more of an impact than if it was sent by Hotmail itself. As a result of this viral marketing tactic, Hotmail had 10 million registered users by Christmas 1996 (less than a year after its launch).

Although viral marketing originated in the B2C sector, it was not long before B2B companies followed suit. Indeed, in many ways viral marketing is more powerful among businesses than it is among consumers. After all, the volume of e-mail traffic travelling between companies is considerably larger than that moving between consumers.

Invitations to 'E-mail this to a friend' are now a common feature of many B2B Web sites (see www.venturedrome.com and www.clickz.com for two examples). Furthermore, the growing number of online business discussion forums provides further incentive for the would-be viral marketer. Here are some of the practical steps that can be taken in order to initiate a B2B viral marketing campaign:

- *Gain permission*. If you are planning to send an e-mail in order to initiate a viral marketing campaign, you will, of course, need to gain each recipient's express permission to receive material.
- *Have a good product*. According to Emanuel Rosen, author of *The Anatomy of Buzz*, 'One of the beautiful things about viral marketing is that all these mechanisms only work when you're talking about a good product.'

- *Focus on key influencers*. Some members of the online business community clearly have a wider reach and influence than others. By concentrating your viral marketing efforts on these key influencers, you will be able to make a maximum impact.
- *Encourage interaction at your site*. Web sites enabling visitors to interact with each other (via chatrooms, bulletin boards and other interactive forums) tend to have the advantage over static sites when it comes to viral marketing.
- *Make news*. Newsworthy information has much more value on the Web than any well considered marketing message.

Summary

As Jupiter Communications reports, more companies are turning to e-mail marketing as it offers high and faster response rates and substantially lower cost than postal mail and, as the most widely accepted and used application on the Web, reaches a greater number of consumers in a one-to-one fashion. However, although response to e-mail marketing campaigns tends to be a lot higher than other methods of direct marketing, in order to ensure that this response is not negative, you will need to make sure that information rather than advertising is the basis of each campaign.

thirteen

The future of B2B

Having survived the economic downturn relatively unscathed, the fact that B2B e-commerce has a future no longer seems in any doubt. What is less clear, however, is the exact direction it is headed.

Rather than make any wild predictions about the state of B2B online marketing in 10 years' time, this chapter focuses on some of the developments that are taking place right now, and which are likely to become even more significant. In particular, the potential impact of peer-to-peer (P2P) technology and the rise of the mobile Internet will be assessed in relation to B2B. A case study concentrating on a nascent B2B industry, Application Service Providers (ASPs), will also be included.

B2B on the move: the rise of the mobile Internet

While most Internet observers now accept that the mobile Internet will become increasingly popular as technology progresses, some remain sceptical over the long-term impact it will have for business. Beyond the obvious financial incentives for mobile operators, the slow m-commerce uptake suggests that many remain unsure as to how exactly it will benefit other members of the business community. However, when Bill Gates refers to 'third generation' mobile technology as 'the next big growth area', and when Amazon's Jeff Bezos remarks that the mobile Internet 'is going to be the most fantastic thing that a time-starved world has ever seen', it's time to sit up and take notice.

Although there have undoubtedly been teething problems (particularly in relation to WAP technology), most B2B companies clearly believe that they cannot afford to miss out on the opportunities offered by m-business. In fact, a study by Forrester Research found that 90 per cent of European e-commerce operators expect to launch mobile Internet sites. The study also discovered that these companies believe customers will automatically expect mobile Internet services in the future.

Forrester is not the only research company making radical pronouncements about m-commerce. For instance, the Gartner Group predicts that 40 per cent of all e-commerce transactions will take place through a wireless device by 2004. Another research firm, Strategy Analytics, has predicted that by that same year, the worldwide market for mobile e-commerce will generate 14 billion transactions annually.

Durlacher, the investment bank, has estimated that the European m-commerce market will be worth £15 billion by 2003, while the research and consulting company Ovum estimates that end-user spend on m-commerce services will reach more than £125 billion in 2005. 'The point is that this is going to be a big market,' claims Ann Walsh, a consultant at Ovum. 'The ability to reach over 1 billion people on mobile devices in 2005 is incredibly compelling for people.' Furthermore, owing to the standardization of GSM (Global System for Mobile communications) technology and the high levels of users in the UK, British businesses are now uniquely positioned to lead the m-commerce revolution. To succeed, however, companies must now watch the progress of the early m-commerce players very carefully.

Case study: Amazon Anywhere

It is perhaps unsurprising to find that Amazon is pioneering the integration of m-commerce, and that both B2B and B2C operators are watching its lead very carefully. Jeff Bezos predicts almost all e-commerce transactions on Amazon will be via wireless devices within 5 to 10 years. The way his company is getting there, it seems, is through forming 'strategic alliances' with the major mobile operators on both sides of the Atlantic. Amazon has signed deals with Sprint, Motorola, Vodafone Airtouch, BellMobility and Nokia, to enable mobile book, CD and video buying. Also, as part of its Amazon Anywhere initiative, it's working with Palm to let users shop and check online auctions. Jeff Bezos, speaking at the Wireless 2001 trade show in the States, acknowledged that although 'today, our revenues from wireless are minimal. . . in a few years, they will be mostly from wireless'.

Amazon.co.uk Anywhere was the first European service allowing customers to complete their whole transaction from their handset without making a voice call when it was launched in February 2000. Amazon Anywhere also gives customers with mobile Internet devices the ability to search for new auction items, enter and monitor bids and track sales directly from a handset. Consumers can create their own custom alerts to be sent to their handsets, notifying them of the status of their auctions.

WAP weaknesses

Most e-commerce companies have, by and large, been reluctant so far to get in on the act, viewing the buzz surrounding m-commerce as little more than 'wishful thinking elevated to a business strategy', as *Observer* columnist John Naughton recently put it in a scathing attack on m-commerce. The slow uptake of m-commerce is also attributable to the evident shortcomings of WAP technology. The poor usability caused by the tiny interface and keypad incorporated on WAP-enabled handsets has certainly put many people off.

World-renowned Web design and usability expert, Jakob Nielsen, is one of the most high-profile figures to have joined the tide of opinion against WAP. In an article on his own useit.com site, Nielsen claims the lacklustre response to WAP is easy to explain. As well as the small screens and digit-only keypads, he cites slow bandwidth and the need to reconnect every time WAP is used, among the overriding weaknesses inherent in the technology. (Nielsen, among many others, believes that the future of the mobile Internet lies in larger screens and constant connections.) It is little wonder then that WAP-based services have drawn far fewer subscribers than Japan's I-mode, which offers permanently high-speed bandwidth. 'WAP has given us a glimpse of the mobile Internet opportunity but everyone would agree it is not the killer application,' says Compaq's new economy director Mike Johnson. WAP should therefore be seen as a transient technology, rather than as an end in itself.

According to WCL (Wireless Commerce Limited), one of the world's leading innovators of mobile commerce platforms, for m-commerce to really take off, the current mindset needs to change. The organization has seen a contrast between the 'm-commerce' lifestyle evident in its home country, Finland, and the scepticism elsewhere. According to Mike Franklin, managing director of WCL in the UK, 'organizations need to seize the initiative and develop content to embrace existing technologies such as SMS text messaging, which requires no additional investment from operators'.

In Finland, Franklin maintains, the mobile Internet has become an everyday part of life: 'The Finns have taken mobile commerce to the next level, where it is social behaviour that is driving the technology forward. For example, over in Finland, people think nothing of using their mobile phone to select and pay for a car wash or even to pay for their lunch at the local coffee shop.' According to Franklin and other European commentators, businesses need to really look at the way people and organizations are using mobile technology if they are to benefit from m-commerce.

The third generation

Although understandable, the 'wait and see' attitude among many in the B2B e-business community is not, however, a healthy one. According to Johnson, companies must not confine themselves to the sidelines: 'B2B businesses cannot afford to sit back and wait until the technology matures – by that stage it will be too late.'

At the moment, the technology certainly seems to be moving at a faster pace than most e-businesses. PricewaterhouseCoopers, for instance, says the transition from the PC to handheld devices and the rapid shift from wired communications to wireless will be the two big overriding themes in technology over the next three years.

The fact that mobile operators such as Orange and Vodafone are investing billions of pounds into broadband wireless networks means that 3G (third generation) mobile devices will make the mobile Internet considerably more user-friendly. It also means that Web-focused businesses must act soon in order to keep up with these big budget technological advances. Indeed, the impact of 3G is expected to be so huge that Jupiter Research predicts two-thirds of the UK population will have Net-enabled handsets by 2003.

Location, location, location

Then there's the imminent arrival of location-based services (LBS) to the mass market. BT, among other operators, is set to launch LBS (using cell ID data to locate subscribers to within 100 metres) within the next few months. The impact LBS could have on business should not be underestimated. The fact that merchants will be able to physically locate potential customers will lead to new products and services that would not be able to exist on the standard Internet. Therefore, while it is predicted (by research firm Strategy Analytics) that annual revenue for operators from location-based services in Western Europe will hit $9 billion by 2005, the consequent LBS-based m-commerce revenues may exceed that figure.

Mobile benefits for B2B

As with e-commerce generally, the main immediate benefits of the mobile Internet are likely to be brought to the B2B market. Aside from commercial transactions, companies with a mobile workforce of field staff could clearly benefit from having mobile access to tracking systems, e-mails, contacts and other company information. 'When you dismiss the idea of the mobile Internet,' says Microgen director, David Serif, 'and concentrate on the idea of mobile information, it suddenly becomes a lot clearer to see where the benefits could lie.' As 20 per cent of the UK and US workforce is classified as mobile, m-business will undoubtedly assist many companies in dealing with their employees, partners, suppliers and business customers by offering location-aware and potentially low-cost solutions.

Time sensitive sales

According to Johan Monteliuo, a WAP specialist at Jupiter Communications, the most suitable m-commerce applications include travel information, finance services, betting services and online auctions. The factor that all these services have in common is that they are time-sensitive.

Owing to the way mobile devices tend to be used, it is hardly surprising that services that can be accessed quickly, explained briefly and ordered with a few key strokes, are the most successful. 'Cellphone users are more impatient than Internet users,' says Cindy Dahm, European director for Phone.com. 'The paradigm here is not surfing; all services for the mass market have to be pitched at users in such a seamless way that they need not even be aware that they are accessing the Net.'

Customer service

According to research from Compaq, the greatest benefit m-commerce is seen to bring to an organization is better customer service. Mobile devices will help e-businesses to personalize their services and will also bring greater convenience for the customer. The fact that mobile operators are developing microbilling systems, that will enable small transactions to be added to a user's mobile account, will inevitably persuade more people to use their mobile devices for shopping as well as communication. As Orange CEO, Hans Snook, has put it, 'These devices will be your remote control for life services wherever you are in the world, and they'll also be your e-purse and e-wallet of the future.'

Of course, there are still obstacles to overcome. After all, the problems of steep communications costs, limited applications and carrier-imposed content restrictions haven't been completely eradicated. It is also important to acknowledge that the mobile Internet will not be perfectly suited to every company. Some online retailers will inevitably be better positioned to benefit from m-commerce than others, as the mobile Internet will be used in a different way to the 'fixed' Internet accessed via a PC. As mentioned above, companies within the B2B arena are likely to fare better than their B2C counterparts. Furthermore, B2B companies selling goods that only require a short amount of text to advertise their products are likely to fare better than those that require a lot of decision-making.

However, even if the multi-channel, multi-functional future of wireless technology only delivers half of what advocates such as Snook believe it will, most B2B companies willing to rise to the m-business challenge will be able to enhance their marketing efforts and add considerable value to the products and services they offer.

Everyone making optimistic predictions about the future of m-commerce, however, is more than willing to concede that there is a long way to go. 'We're at the embryonic stage of this curve,' says Richard Siber, a partner with Andersen Consulting's wireless consulting practice. '*Nascent* doesn't even do it justice.'

Ultimately, the success of the mobile Internet in the B2B marketing arena will depend on the ability to deliver accurately to the target audience, as well as the effectiveness and relevance of the marketing message. As a report from B2B Works has predicted, 'B2B marketers will likely use wireless to steer the audience to a Web connection (from offline, wireline and wireless), which underscores the role of the Web as the nexus where customers and prospects will be directed for deeper information.'

In the meantime, it is important for B2B companies not only to keep track of the technology but also to look at how the market is developing. The sceptics may take a while to change their minds, but ultimately the wider perspective m-commerce will bring to the world of e-business will prove irresistible.

Case study: AOL and Mviva

AOL Europe is another major Internet player to have announced a 'strategic alliance' in order to expand its m-business operation. The deal has led to AOL's partial acquisition of the Mviva mobile Internet portal. Mviva, powered by AOL, is installed on Internet-enabled mobile phones sold by Carphone Warehouse's European Network.

Again, AOL is clearly taking an integrated approach to its mobile strategy as Mviva is accessible via both mobile and fixed-line devices, including mobile phones, PCs, personal organizers (PDAs) and even interactive TV. Significantly, it is available to customers regardless of which access device or mobile phone network they use – something that is critical when mobile phone upgrades are expected as new technologies and functionality are introduced.

The m-commerce transactions available on Mviva include gaming, auctions, share trading, CDs and tickets. In addition, it also offers AOL-style content (news headlines, breaking news, sports, travel and weather information).

Mviva's multiple revenue streams include fees from advertisers, one-off payments for introducing transacting customers to content providers, carriage fees for tenancy on the Mviva platform and an outgoing share of the retail sales margin in relation to customers introduced by Mviva who buy goods or services from content providers.

Max Alexander, managing director of Mviva, believes the popularity of text messaging is an indication that the mobile Internet is ready to take off in Europe. 'The growth of mobile short message service (SMS) is already phenomenal,' he says. 'I see this as one of the stepping stones to mobile Internet e-mail and to much wider usage of mobile Internet service and m-commerce.'

Figure 13.1 The Mviva mobile Internet portal

The ASP industry

The fact that B2B e-commerce has completely changed the marketing game plan is illustrated by its ability to create entirely new markets. One of these blossoming new sectors is that relating to Application Service Providers, or ASPs, an industry that simply could not exist without the Internet.

The main underlying principle behind ASPs is simple: the cost of data processing can be cut if many business customers share software and software support. What many ASPs have already started to discover, however, is that the convenience for the customer can be extended further if they only have to deal with one ASP that can provide all their application requirements.

In a study published towards the end of last year by UK telecommunications consultancy Analysis, researcher Margaret Hopkins notes: 'Full-service and aggregator ASPs aim to provide a complete desktop to the business user, with a full range of applications so the customer need have no software running locally at all.' The ASP aggregator groups applications together from various vendors and puts them into a single, interoperable package. Typically, these aggregated services will then be sold to clients for a monthly fee.

In the US, the ASP model is already viewed as a realistic alternative to an internal IT department. Jamcracker, the leading ASP Stateside, is positioning itself as a portal for all e-business connections (hosted applications, commerce and supply chain software, marketplaces etc) as they converge together. Indeed, Jamcracker co-founder K.B.Chandrasekhar (known simply as 'Chandra') has predicted that 'in five years, nobody will talk about applications anymore'. When that happens, he says, 'you get the kind of returns that will make hosted services the next revolutionary change in the computer era, in line with the development of PCs, ISPs, and data centres'.

Whether such enthusiastic claims are tainted with hyperbole remains to be seen. One thing, however, has already been made clear. The battle between ASP aggregators and single-service, niche ASPs seems, in the US at least, to be balanced in favour of aggregation. In fact, in an attempt to enhance their viability, many single-service ASPs are making the move towards offering aggregated services.

Ron Reed, CEO of ASP Fullscope, explains the aggregator's primary task: 'An aggregator's first role is to manage its customers' needs. It sells, implements, supports and leverages multiple products across multiple platforms and makes it good for everybody.' He adds that although 'aggregation is not a strategy for everyone, everyone should be part of a strategy of meeting the customer's needs. In niche markets, it makes a lot of sense [to partner] with an ASP aggregator.'

According to Feisal Mosleh, CEO of US-based ASP Agiliti, customers will ultimately reject the idea of a single service ASP altogether: 'If customers are renting multiple applications from multiple, one-off App providers, they're going to face multiple contracts and multiple risks, and as IT managers, they're having to test and qualify multiple times.'

However, aggregation in itself may not be sufficient, as end users will not only want an aggregated solution, but also ongoing support. Aggregated ASPs will need the resources available to add technical support if and when it is needed, and they should also be willing to provide their clients with a Service Level Agreement.

Then there is the issue of service delivery itself. When the ASP model first emerged, the industry pundits were proclaiming that the Internet provided the perfect delivery channel to the desktop. Now, ASPs are looking at other delivery channels to supplement their Web-focused activity. It is important to remember, however, that vendor experience of client requirements is limited by the lack of awareness within the market. Charles Thompson, communications director for Cable and Wireless' ASP, launched last summer, is one of those willing to concede that as this is currently an embryonic stage, suppliers rather than customers are shaping the market. 'It is an entirely new concept and the market has to be educated. At the moment, it is certainly supplier-driven rather than market-led.'

Owing, at least in part, to this supplier-driven situation, analysts predict that 80 per cent of first entrants into the ASP market will fail between the current date to 2002. However, Clive Longbottom, head of research at the independent IT and business analysts, Quocircal, believes that although 80 per cent of new ASP businesses in the UK may fail to have a long-term future, potential clients equipped with the right knowledge should be able to navigate the ASP minefield with relative ease. Because of such volatility, Longbottom claims that 'you must be able to transfer your data to a new ASP easily. You need a Plan B to have a warm ASP ready in case your first ASP goes down.' Clearly, this is especially important if a company is looking for an aggregated service that will be in charge of the entire e-infrastructure.

Analysts maintain that clients should also be making sure that the ASP initially chosen is able to move at their pace and meet their changing needs. The service needs to be scalable as well as reliable. An attention to security is, needless to say, also important.

The consensus opinion, as far as it exists, is that the ASP aggregator is certainly likely to be an attractive proposition to companies lacking certain IT skills in-house or those that need to set up their infrastructure in a short space of time. However, a multi-service ASP is going to be of less use to companies with an already established and highly complex internal system in place.

According to Karl Roe, founder of the UK-based ASP aggregator 7, 'The ASPs that succeed are the ASPs that will focus vertical software as a service-delivering applications to vertical market places.' Proclaiming itself to be a 'business services aggregator', 7 (so named because it takes responsibility for all seven layers defined in the OSI network infrastructure standard) provides a range of applications at guaranteed service levels to medium and large-sized businesses. Although partnering with existing systems integrators to implement services for end user enterprises, 7 does not simply offer a background wholesale role.

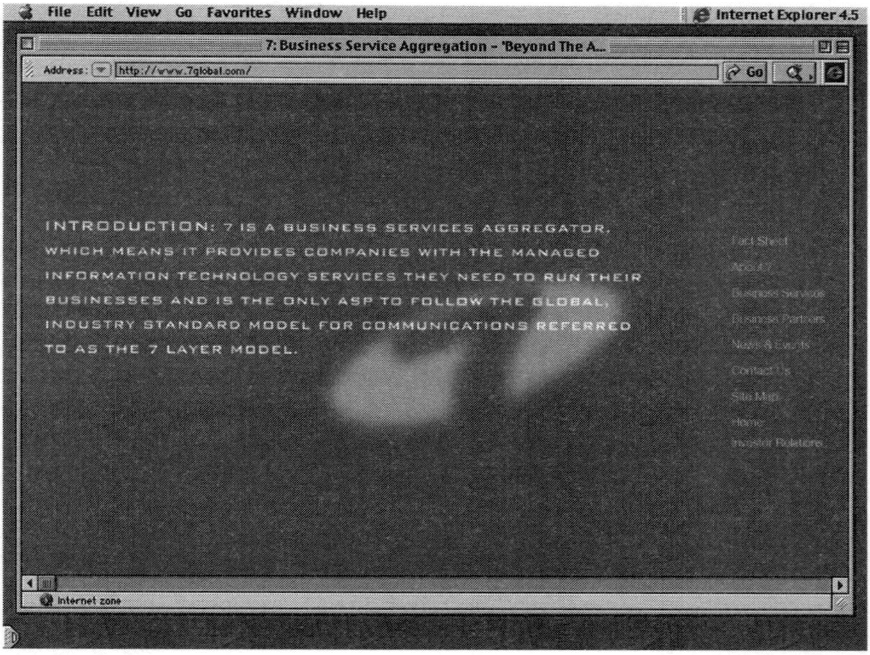

Figure 13.2 7: the ASP aggregator

It directly handles network links right through to the end user's desktop, providing a point of accountability for service levels and raising a single, itemized services bill.

However, 7 does not support traditional client-server applications; instead it concentrates on fully Web-based applications that can be delivered to a standard browser. 'That's the only way we believe scalability can be delivered,' justifies Roe. Understanding that one of the main reasons companies are attracted to ASPs is the simplicity they offer, 7 has made its pricing model as simple as possible. In fact, the separate charges for connection, a monthly standing charge, and then metered, pay-as-you-go charges resemble the billing model for electricity and telephone providers. 'For customers to buy,' says Roe, 'the pricing has to be coherent.'

The fact that customers are willing to buy, providing pricing and other factors are 'coherent', is illustrated by the handful of companies who have already embraced the ASP idea in practice as well as theory. Leading travel Web site CheapFlights.com was one of the first UK dot.com companies to benefit from the aggregated ASP model, having outsourced its Web and e-commerce infrastructure to UK ASP AppTap since August 2000. According to CheapFlights.com chief executive David Sookin, the aggregated model 'allows us to focus all of our resources on our core customer needs without having to recruit lots of IT staff and send them out shopping for tens of thousands of pounds worth of short-lived computers, software and security products'.

While ASPs such as AppTap and 7 are therefore already able to offer a fully aggregated service for their customers, most other ASPs apparently offering 'full service' solutions fall short when it comes to meeting a client's long-term requirements. End users should therefore not only be demanding a fully aggregated service, but should also make sure the ASP can provide ongoing support when the system is in place. Users should also ensure that, as with the ASPs mentioned above, the ASP they choose backs up their claim of support with a coherent, comprehensive Service Level Agreement. Furthermore, it is important that the ASP chosen does not conform to a 'one-size-fits-all' model, and is able to meet the specific network and application needs of each individual client. The other general point that needs to be considered concerns the market's volatility. Until the ASP market settles, it remains in the client's best interests to look at the future prospects of each specific ASP itself. After all, no ASP will be able to offer ongoing support if it has been squeezed out of the market altogether.

P2P

One of the main factors that will influence the future of B2B e-marketing is the development of 'peer-to-peer' (P2P) technology that harnesses the combined power of computers within a network. Although the media spotlight has remained focused on music file swapping, the scope of P2P technology has already moved beyond the entertainment industry. For instance, the open source Gnutella enables people to make practically any kind of files on their computer available to others.

While most media attention has been paid to the issue of Napster-induced intellectual property theft, the fact that peer-to-peer technology is used to exchange information between companies has largely been ignored. As US Internet guru Esther Dyson claims, 'The real value of P2P will be in handling and validating exceptional transactions between companies.' Already in the technology sector companies such as IBM, Microsoft and Oracle are endorsing the development of a new programming language, called DSML (Directory Service Mark-up Language), which will enable companies to take full advantage of P2P information sharing.

According to interactive technology expert David Kirkpatrick, P2P takes the capabilities of the Internet to a whole new level. 'Now a vast universe beyond the Web suddenly appears within our reach. Not only can big, Web-designated servers be searched, but every bit of digitized data everywhere will be fair game.' This therefore raises concerns that go way beyond the issue of copyright infringement.

Privacy issues

One of these new concerns relates to the question of privacy or, more precisely, anonymity. While the 'pure' P2P service Gnutella avoids the legal problems of Napster by working on a decentralized network (Napster used a central server), it does not protect or conceal the identity of its users. Everything put on the centralized network can be traced back to the computer that first uploaded the data. Therefore, although Gnutella is copyright proof, it becomes vulnerable to censorship.

Ian Clarke's Freenet project (another decentralized service) has got round this problem by encrypting information, so the person who originally put it on the network cannot be identified. This means that while networks based on the centralized model are working toward legitimacy through corporate alliances and fee-based systems, this decentralized P2P network not only promotes free music but also protects free speech. This leads to what John Perry Barlow has called 'the real Internet', a place where everyone has an equal right to download and upload information, and where copyright may no longer even be an issue due to the 'relationship between familiarity and value', bred by the technology itself.

A decentralized network's ability to, in Esther Dyson's words, 'democratize the Internet by undermining its hierarchical architecture', is expected (by Dyson among others) to revolutionize the ways in which businesses give and receive information. For this to happen, however, experts agree there is one final hurdle to overcome.

When computers become servers in their own right, the amount of information available for access becomes virtually unlimited. As most of this information (which mainly consists of e-mail messages) is irrelevant to the average user, keyword searches and other Web-oriented methods prove largely insufficient.

While an effective solution may yet be some way off, advances are being made toward improving navigation within P2P networks. Autonomy, the British software company, has already developed a navigation system designed around the P2P model; rather than relying on keywords, it analyses data for key concepts. According to Autonomy's chief executive, Michael Lynch, 'It shouldn't matter where the data comes from and it shouldn't matter what format it's in.' While such software can help users prioritize information within a network, it cannot discriminate between data that users want to put on the network and that which they would prefer to keep from public view. Although, it is clear that users are willing to distribute free music over P2P networks, it remains to be seen whether businesses will be willing to put everything else (including data they have generated themselves) up for grabs too.

Summary

The technological developments touched upon in this chapter are by no means the only factors affecting the future of B2B e-marketing. For instance, advances in broadband technology look set to have a significant impact on online advertising, as they may effectively turn the Internet into a broadcast medium by enhancing its audio-visual capacities. However, P2P and the mobile Internet together represent the ultimate forces e-marketing practitioners will have to respond to. Both these developments are enabling the Internet to overcome former constraints (confinement to the desktop, centralized servers etc) in order to facilitate the freeflow of information within and between organizations. Furthermore, although the full impact of these developments has yet to be felt, the B2B sector looks likely to be the first to benefit. Indeed, for those companies willing to pioneer the use of these technologies, the perceived 'future' is already here.

appendix 1

B2B e-commerce directory

Advertising

Advertising agencies

Adforce
www.adforce.com
An online advertising agency.

Ad Hunter
www.adhunter.com
This UK-based service offers a cheaper alternative to other media placement services.

Advalue
www.advalue.co.uk
A media planning agency.

Adventure Network
www.ad-venture.com
This New York-based service provides advertisers with 'targeting by site, affinity group, and network'. The network includes more than 3,600 Web sites.

Advertising
www.advertising.com
Advertising.com's clients include numerous Fortune 100 companies and leading Internet sites.

Agency
www.agency.com
A media planning agency.

B2B Works
www.b2bworks.net
A leading full service B2B advertising network.

Blubirds
www.blubirds.co.uk
List of agencies.

2CanMedia
www.2canmedia.com
2CanMedia provides advertisers with a site-matching service aimed at creating 'synergy' between publishers and advertisers.

DoubleClick
www.doubleclick.com, www.doubleclick.net
A media planning agency that can place ads for you across a network of 65 UK-focused sites (including Freeserve and Loot). DoubleClick has attracted a string of high-profile international clients, due to its insistence on CPA (cost-per-action) rates. The company uses its wide network of sites to place banner advertising that companies only pay for if and when a user acts upon (that is, clicks through) the banner.

Engage
www.engage.com
A B2B advertising network.

Eye Company
www.eyecompany.com
An online media planning and buying agency.

Flycast
ww.flycast.com
Flycast enables companies to conduct local online advertising, as it uses tracking software that can discover the geographic location of a user's computer.

One Media Place
www.onemediaplace.com
A B2B e-marketplace devoted to advertising.

Profero
www.profero.com
A media planning agency.

Value Click
www.valueclick.com/uk
Value Click will create and manage your ad space.

24/7 Media
www.247media.com
An international advertising agency network.

Web Promotion
www.Webpromotion.co.uk
A list of agencies is available from this site.

Advertising general

ABCe
www.abce.org.uk
ABCe was established in 1996 to audit the buying and selling of advertising space on UK and Ireland-based Internet sites.

Ad Value
www.advalue.co.uk
Covers all areas of online advertising.

Advert Express
www.advertexpress.com
An advertising exchange designed for SMEs in the UK. It provides a free searchable UK media database with information provided by BRAD.

AOL UK
www.aol.co.uk
Offers auditing of individual ad campaigns under a deal with ABC//electronic.

ASA The Advertising Standards Authority
www.admark.org.uk
The Advertising Standards Authority has introduced a kite mark approval scheme for online ads.

IAB (Internet Advertising Bureau)
www.iab.net
Includes ad statistics, articles, ad standards and a list of banner ad sizes.

World Advertising Research Centre
www.ware.com
A leading source of online knowledge for advertisers, advertising agencies, media buyers, media corporations and market research organizations.

Banners

Smartage
www.smartage.com
Download a program that helps you design animated banners.

UK Banners
www.ukbanners.com
A banner exchange.

Web Review
www.Webreview.com
Web Review includes reviews of the latest banner ad design tools.

Affiliate programs

Affiliate Zone
www.affiliatezone.com
Information on the various products and services can be found at Affiliate Zone.

Associate It
www.associate-it.com
An affiliate program directory.

Associate Programs
www.associateprograms.com
Information on Associate Programs can be found at this site.

LinkShare

www.linkshare.com

Affiliate program information can be found at this site.

The Net Affiliate Scheme

www.netaffiliate.com

The Net Affiliate Scheme provides a directory along with advice on how to choose the right program for your business.

Site Cash

www.sitecash.com

An affiliate directory that rates sites on their ease of use, providing a broad, comparative overview of all the different types of affiliate schemes.

UK Affiliates

www.ukaffiliates.com

UK Affiliates acts as middleman and sets up affiliate programs on your behalf. Affiliates can join at no cost through an online order form.

Banner exchanges

Link Exchange

www.linkexchange.com

The Link Exchange is the most widely used free banner exchange. Set up by the same subsidiary of Microsoft that manages ListBot, the Link Exchange covers a staggering 500,000 sites that collectively reach nearly half of the Web's traffic. As with many other similar exchanges, for every two times that you display a banner on your Web site, you automatically receive a credit that entitles you to have your ad displayed once on another site. Although the degree of control you have over where your banner appears is limited, the Link Exchange provides you with daily reports detailing traffic figures.

Mark Welch's Banner List

www.markwelch.com

A vast directory of banner exchange programs both in Europe and the US.

UK Banners

www.ukbanners.com

UK Banners is one of the most popular UK-based exchanges. It also works on a much more symmetrical ratio than the majority of other sites. For every 10 times a banner is displayed on your site, your banner ad appears eight times elsewhere within the exchange.

Business information

Business advice

Business Advice Online

www.businessadviceonline.org.uk

This Business Advice Online site is provided by the UK's Small Business Service. Features include: business topics, regulations/taxes, e-commerce/e-business, key contacts and business news. The site has useful links.

Business Link

www.businesslink.co.uk

Find your local business link at this site.

Companies House

www.companieshouse.org.uk

Search to see if your company name has been registered at this site.

Department of Trade and Industry

www.dti.gov.uk

This site offers a range of information including regulation and business support. There are links to all the key government and DTI sites.

Hoovers

www.hoovers.co.uk

Hoovers has key information on tens of thousands of companies. This site includes a news centre, competitor analysis, company profiles and free newsletters.

ICANN

www.icann.net

The Internet Corporation for Assigned Names and Numbers is a not-for-profit corporation. It manages domain names, root server systems and the allocation of IP address space.

Inland Revenue

www.inlandrevenue.gov.uk

The Inland Revenue Web site features news and information on tax and national insurance matters in the UK.

Shop

www.shop.org

An industry trade association for online retailers. The Internet industry and e-commerce statistics section provides useful research overviews.

UK online for business

www.ukonlineforbusiness.gov.uk

The DTI's UK online for business site provides small businesses with impartial advice on using Information and Communication Technologies.

Business portals

Altodigital.com

www.altodigital.com

A business community portal that includes a trading zone (with local and national links and deals), a business zone (over 70 business market summaries) and a focus zone (issues that affect your business).

The Biz (Business Information Zone)

www.thebiz.com

The Biz portal provides high quality data and is dedicated to services that every busy office needs. This B2B information site offers a popular bulletin board section where business opportunities can be posted. There is also an event zone and training zone.

Biz Travel Club

www.biztravelclub.com

The Biz Travel Club site includes everything from an exclusive members' club lounge to car-rental discount vouchers.

B2B Yellow Pages

www.b2byellowpages.com

This online business-to-business network and directory provides easy access to B2B Web sites, cost-effective ways to promote your site and organized marketplaces to facilitate B2B e-commerce.

E-business Europe

www.e-businesseurope.com

E-business Europe is a free Internet news and e-commerce consultancy. The site includes e-business resources such as Web promotion and advertising and marketing. The e-business newsletter is published weekly and contains news analysis and e-business hints and tips.

Success 4 business

www.success4business.com

This small business portal is produced by Lloyds TSB bank and includes business news, a traffic watch section, a route planner and a weather watch.

Work 24

www.work24.co.uk

Work 24 is a Web site for small businesses. It is powered by the Royal Bank of Scotland and Scottish Power. The site offers a unique range of products, services and information for small UK businesses. There are tools available to set up online meetings and build an e-commerce store. You can also shop for stationery, computer and IT supplies.

Business search

Ask Alex

www.askalex.com

Ask Alex is an online directory of over 1 million UK companies enabling you to search by keyword, name or town.

Big Yellow

www.bigyellow.com

Big Yellow World is a compilation of most of the Yellow Pages directories around the world.

The Biz

www.thebiz.co.uk

Biz stands for 'Business Information Zone' and The Biz Web site conducts searches based on industry, location and the alphabet.

British Companies

www.britishcompanies.co.uk

The British Companies site includes links to governing bodies, institutions, and associations.

City Pages

www.citypages.co.uk

City Pages is a UK-based directory of commercial links that categorizes information by postal code areas.

Click4itlocal

www.click4itlocal.co.uk

This directory is aimed to help people locate local businesses.

County Web

www.countyWeb.co.uk

A searchable database of UK businesses, which, as you might expect, are divided into separate counties.

Dun and Bradstreet

www.dunandbrad.co.uk

This site claims to have the most up-to-date definite database of company information in the world. It includes a global directory of over 500 million businesses in 230 countries. The company information includes business name, address, nature of business, number of employees and annual turnover. Even more usefully, it can provide you with a list of all the companies within a particular location, in a specific industry or of a certain size. Furthermore, each list includes the relevant contact names. However, only certain aspects of this service are free.

Infoseek

www.infoseek.co.uk

Although Infoseek is a general search engine, it also includes a very useful business directory. Thousands of company Web sites are classified under areas such as advertising, banking, employment, manufacturing, marketing, e-commerce, media and telecoms.

The Internet Pages

www.the-Internet-pages.co.uk

The UK's A to Z of businesses and services (as well as sales, repairs, hire and entertainment).

Kelly's

www.kellys.co.uk

Kelly's is a long-established directory of over 14,000 UK companies, providing contact details. Registration (which is free) is required before you can access the site.

Scoot

www.scoot.co.uk

Scoot's vast database incorporates 2 million records, over 3,000 business categories and 27,000 locations. The site enables you to search for companies either by name, location or business sector.

UK Business Net

www.ukbusinessnet.com

UK Business Net is a business-to-business information resource that includes a financial index, a business data file, and events diary and industry reports.

UK Pages

www.ukpages.co.uk

UK Pages is an extensive database of UK businesses with direct links to company Web sites.

UK Plus

www.ukplus.co.uk

UK Plus is a directory and search engine owned by the *Daily Mail*, and indexes a wide variety of UK Web sites.

Yahoo! Business and Economy

www.yahoo.co.uk

Yahoo!'s Business and Economy listing is probably the most popular UK business directory. The section has links to business libraries, business opportunities, classifieds, courses, electronic commerce, finance, marketing, Web directories and, perhaps most significantly, employment.

Yell

www.yell.com

The Yellow Pages site is an easy to use, comprehensive guide to thousands of UK Web sites. Each one has been reviewed by a team of researchers.

Business supplies

Buy

www.buy.co.uk

A portal for the UK SME business market that covers office supplies, equipment, insurance, finance and staff. Users can get quotes, advice and compare costs online.

Euroffice

www.euroffice.co.uk

One of the cheapest stationery suppliers on the Net. The site sells office supplies, computer equipment, toner and cartridges, business machines, furniture and services at a fraction of their retail price. Euroffice will also send you their special offers via e-mail.

Farnell

www.farnell.co.uk

Farnell is a UK electronic and industrial distributor. The site provides access to over 100,000 business products and services.

Mondus

www.mondus.com

A site for SMEs to request goods and services over the Net and then await quotes from suppliers. The site covers computer equipment, computer services, corporate hospitality, couriers, human resource services, Internet services, legal services, marketing services, office equipment, printing and related services, professional services, promotional items, telecom and communications and training services.

Royal Mail

www.royalmail.com

The Royal Mail site includes general information for marketing strategies.

Viking Direct

www.viking-direct.co.uk

Viking Direct sells office supplies and stationery. You can order online and the company offers free same-day delivery, one-year guarantee on all products and a 30-day home trial.

Vistaprint

www.vistaprint.co.uk

Design your own business cards and have them printed at a fraction of the cost at this site. You must have cookies enabled to view this site.

Weblaw

www.weblaw.org

Weblaw is an online intellectual property and digital law advice service. This site has links to a lot of interesting law-related Web sites.

Communication

Audio point

www.myaudiopoint.com

Audiopoint is a voice portal service that allows you to deliver and access content over the phone.

Band-x

www.band-x.com

Band-x is an independent exchange for international wholesale telecom capacity; in other words, Band-x trades voice and data bandwidth. Band-x provides bandwidth capacity exchange for phone operators. It targets the $20-billion market for spot telecom capacity and already has most telecom companies as customers.

Be Vocal

www.bevocal.com

Be Vocal provides voice portal solutions.

CellPoint

www.cellpt.com

CellPoint develops Internet applications using GSM cellular networks to locate cell phones. CellPoint recently partnered with Yahoo! Europe on mobile locator services.

Click to Call

www.clicktocall.co.uk

This company offers an instant response service called 'Click to Call'. The company says it has the lowest global freephone rates in the world.

Digia

www.digia.com

This company develops new software and business concepts for the wireless Internet application market.

Ericsson

www.ericsson.com

Ericsson provides services for all types of businesses including contact centres, mobility solutions, and communication systems. The company also offers Internet consulting.

Hey Anita

www.heyanita.com

Hey Anita provides software, hosting and services for beginners.

Internet Speech

www.Internetspeech.com

Internet Speech offers a product called netECHO that allows users to give simple voice commands like 'Google' to get to the related Web site. There is a business demo available at this site.

IoBox

www.iobox.com

IoBox provides Short Message Service (SMS) and WAP services over mobile phones.

It already has over 400,000 European subscribers.

More Magic Software

www.moremagic.com

More Magic connects phone operators, portals, Internet service providers, credit card firms and banks for real-time integration of user authentication, billing and payment. The firm's technology makes the process of content-based billing possible.

NetCall Telecom

www.netcall800.com

NetCall is a unique service that has the ability to capture e-mail addresses, phone numbers, the time of the call and the Web page that was clicked.

Phone Me

www.phoneme.co.uk

Information on the Phone Me service is provided at this site. A 'phone me' button allows vital customer communication. Clients include Compaq, Dell, Abbey National and the Halifax.

Red Message

www.redmessage.com

Red Message helps Internet businesses reach mobile customers.

12snap

www.12snap.com

12snap is one of Europe's leading portals for the mobile e-commerce market.

Space2Go

www.space2go.com

Space2Go helps people access personal information and files anywhere, anytime – from any device. Using Space2Go's electronic desktop, subscribers can access their own data, e-mail, addresses, telephone numbers, schedule and Internet bookmarks from any computer with Internet access.

Symbian
www.symbian.com
Symbian develops technology for mobile computing devices.

Teamphone
www.teamphone.com
Its communications system unifies businesses' existing systems and enables employees to work and be contacted anywhere and anytime via one number.

Tell Me
www.tellme.com
This is a voice application network that helps companies achieve interactive solutions.

Delivery

Business Express
www.businessexpress.co.uk
Business Express is a delivery and courier specialist. The site offers parcel tracking and distribution information.

DHL
www.dhl.co.uk
DHL specializes in business-to-business delivery of high value items such as hi-tech and consumer goods. The site includes a tariff and transit calculator, a speed booking service and tracking information.

Fedex
www.fedex.com
Fedex offers a range of online services such as shipment preparation, package tracking and shipment rates and tools tailored to the need of international shippers.

Now Now Now
www.nownownow.co.uk
Now Now Now is a same day Internet delivery service. This company promises delivery within hours (but it only operates within the M25).

Parcel Force

www.parcelforce.co.uk

Parcel Force is the parcel distribution arm of the Post Office. The Web site covers parcel pricing and parcel tracking.

Securicor Omega Express

www.securicor.co.uk/omegaexpress/index.htm

The Securicor site includes a weather update, parcel tracking, courier booking, home delivery and Euro express.

TNT

www.tnt.co.uk

TNT's Internet services include: track 'n' trace, online ordering, customized services, callback services, a quick shipper, TNT locations, a service bulletin and 'securEdoc' (the multi-security level transmission service that sends documents of any size electronically to multiple recipients).

UPS

www.ups.com

UPS's Web site has a number of interactive functions from tracking by e-mail to a time-in-transit calculator. There are also UPS wireless solutions available.

E-mail resources

Brightware

www.brightware.com

Response software is available at this site.

Echo Mail

www.echomail.com

Echo Mail offers you a way to respond to infinite incoming e-mails as they arrive in your mailbox. A computer response may not be ideal, but it is better than no response at all.

Eudora

www.eudora.com

The first e-mail client on the market was Eudora. As well as making sure your e-mail messages are sent and received on time, Eudora also offers mail filters enabling you to set up different mail boxes for different e-mail addresses, a spell check and automatic response tools. There is a free version of the program called Eudora Light that can be downloaded from the site. However, the best version of Eudora for business purposes is Eudora Pro.

FloNetwork
www.flonetwork.com
Browse a list of customers and read about the company's permission-based direct e-mail marketing services.

Listbot
www.listbot.com
A useful service that will help you manage your e-mailing list. The service offers free mailing list management and enables you to archive the messages you send. It also finds out demographic information about your subscribers.

List Proc
www.cren.net/listproc
Information on how to create filters in your e-mail program is available here.

Listserv
www.listserv.com
Can help you create an active mailing list (in which subscribers can post messages to each other).

Majordomo
www.majordomo.com
A special program that helps you create mailing lists.

Netscape Messenger
www.netscape.com
Netscape Messenger is Netscape Communicator's e-mail program. To access the program you click on the Communicator menu on the Netscape Web browser and select Messenger. Information about the program can be found at this site.

Outlook Express
www.microsoft.com
Outlook is Microsoft's e-mail client and its main advantage is that it fits perfectly with other Microsoft software such as Word, Office and Internet Explorer. If you have a computer running Microsoft Windows or Office, you will probably already have Outlook Express (a similar version of Outlook intended for personal and small business use.) Information about the program can be found at this site.

Pegasus Mail
www.pegasus.com
Pegasus Mail is freeware that offers the option of downloading just your e-mail headers and deleting irrelevant messages on the server.

PermissionDirect.com
www.permissiondirect.com
Businesses can use this service to distribute press releases and advertisements.

Powermail
www.powermail.com
Powermail is one of the few e-mail programs aimed solely at Mac users. It provides a comprehensive and powerful service.

TargitMail.com
www.targitmail.com
This company delivers permission-based e-mail database marketing products. Learn about the services at this site.

TKL Interactive
www.tklinteractive.com
This company provides permission-based marketing services including e-mail lists and campaign management assistance.

yesmail.com
www.yesmail.com
A permission-based e-mail network. See the client list and find out how the service works at this site.

Spam

The Coalition Against Unsolicited Commercial E-mail
www.cauce.org
The Coalition's Web site.

Junkbusters
www.junkbusters.com
A company that specializes in stopping spam.

Spam Abuse
www.spamabuse.net
A useful spam information Web site.

SpamCop

spamcop.net

SpamCop will help you eradicate spam. SpamCop analyses your spam and notifies the spammer's ISP. Registration is free.

StopSpam

www.stopspam.oreilly.com

Find articles and ideas about stopping spam at this site.

E-marketplaces

ECeurope.com

www.eceurope.com

A bulletin board that helps small and medium-sized businesses access a broader trading base.

ICommerce

www.icommerce.com

A business-to-business marketplace based in Ireland.

VerticalNet

www.verticalnet.com

The Internet's leading creator and operator of vertical trade markets. VerticalNet covers all industry sectors.

E-PR resources

Audit Bureau of Circulation

www.abc.org.uk

The Audit Bureau of Circulation site is particularly useful when you are researching a media campaign as it provides circulation figures and other relevant information for around 4,000 UK publications, both online and offline.

Brad

www.brad.co.uk

Brad provides full listings for national and local media, including both the business and consumer press. As with the print version, however, Brad online is a paid-for service. Prices vary according to your media requirements.

Business Wire

www.businesswire.com

One of the main international PR newswire services.

Copywriter

www.copywriter.com

The direct e-mail list source that includes information on e-mail advertising. It provides a list of companies with subscription-based e-mail lists, e-newsletters that carry ads, and even sponsorable newsgroups.

Internet Wire

www.internetwire.com

Internet Wire is a press release service that uses e-mail.

Liszt

www.liszt.com

A mailing list directory.

Media Finder

www.mediafinder.com

Media Finder provides a comprehensive database of international publications, with a variety of search options.

Media UK

www.mediauk.com

This UK-based directory offers free and fee-based listings. You can research papers, magazines and other media at this site.

NeoSoft

www.neosoft.com

A comprehensive index of mailing lists can be found at NeoSoft.

New Jour

://gort.ucsd.edu/newjour

Arguably the most comprehensive e-media directory, New Jour indexes Web sites, new and archived newsletters, e-zines and journals, many of which are not listed anywhere else. Its user-friendly search facility enables you to search by alphabetical category or keyword search.

PRCA

www.prca.co.uk

The Public Relations Consultants Association site includes links to various sites within the PR industry.

PR2

www.pr2.com

The PR2 site offers a free e-mail-based course on how to gain publicity for Web sites. As the home page boldly declares: 'Find out what works and what doesn't, and why you don't need to spend a lot of money to get a whole heap of traffic.'

Press Box

www.pressbox.co.uk

Press Box is a UK online press centre that offers press release writing and distribution.

PR Newswire

www.prnewswire.com

An electronic PR service that provides a customized service.

PR Web.com

Offers a free PR service.

Sourcewire

www.sourcewire.com

A vast database of technology-based PR firms can be found at this site.

Sponsor Me

www.sponsor-me.co.uk

A service aimed at matching sponsors with companies seeking sponsorship.

Evaluation

Access Watch

www.accesswatch.com

A fee-based media tracking service.

Click Sure

www.clicksure.com

A provider of quality assessments for online business.

Cyber Alert

www.cyberalert.com

Cyber Alert draws on both technology and human resources to conduct searches on 'feeder sites' (any searchable Web-based resource). Once you have provided sets of keywords to search for, the service collects, sorts and edits its search findings before saving them in an 'in box' that can be accessed by logging on to the Web site. The difference with Cyber Alert is that, unlike many other online clipping services, it doesn't limit its searches to Web sites. It can even search Web-based newsgroups for relevant messages as well.

Cyber Check

www.cybercheck.com

Cyber Check collects newsgroup postings. Basically, you can choose either to pay for the Web Check service (which only monitors Web sites) or the Forum Check service (which monitors over 150,000 online forums), or to have both services run at the same time.

Durrants

www.durrants.co.uk

Durrants is one of the UK's largest press cuttings agencies, and a firm favourite among PR consultancies. Alongside its print and broadcast services, it now also offers electronic monitoring.

Engage Online

www.engage.com

Online marketing analysts. This company measures and analyses your online marketing efforts.

EWatch

www.ewatch.com

EWatch is a service of PR Newswire that is particularly popular among companies wishing to keep track of any negative or libellous comments made on the Net. The main draw for CEOs suffering corporate paranoia is the Cyber Sleuth program that aims not only to uncover negative newsgroup postings, but also to find out who posted them.

Extreme Tracking

www.extremetracking.co.uk

Extreme Tracking is a UK-based company that provides free tracking software available for download from the Internet. As well as monitoring hit counts, the Extreme Tracking software can tell you how people are getting to your site (whether via an e-mail or newsletter link, other Web pages, search engines, direct from their browser and so on). If someone reaches your site via a search engine, Extreme Tracking will not only be able to tell you which one but will also be able to tell you the exact keywords or phrases the visitor typed in to reach your site. Therefore, this can not only help you get a better idea of who your online audience is, but can also help you improve your search engine rankings by revealing which keywords (and indeed, which search engines) prove most popular.

Hitbox
www.hitbox.com
Hitbox is a tracking service and search engine in one. The search engine indexes sites that use the Hitbox tracking service and ranks them according to how many hits they receive. Therefore, as well as providing you with comprehensive tracking information, this free service also includes your site on its widely used (especially in the business-to-business sector) search engine. The only drawback is that to use the tracking software you must be willing to incorporate a Hitbox banner ad on your site.

Link Popularity
www.linkpopularity.com
This site can tell you how many sites are linking to yours.

Mark Welch's Web site
www.markwelch.com
Full indexes of fee-based tracking and log analysis programs and services can be found here.

My Rank
www.myrank.com
A free search engine ranking tool.

Net Gen/Net Analysis
www.netgen.com
A fee-based media tracking service.

Net Mind
www.netmind.com
A free automated search tracking service. This service monitors any changes made to any of the major search engines and (once you have provided it with the keywords or phrases you want to cover) e-mails you every time a relevant new addition occurs.

News Tracker
www.excite.com
News Tracker is a clipping service offered by the major search engine, Excite. Although it is limited to the Web, News Tracker is a reliable and cost-effective service that is proving increasingly popular.

Rank This
www.rankthis.com
A free search engine ranking tool.

Super Stats
www.superstats.com
Super Stats software helps you identify which search engines and keywords visitors are using to get to your site. In addition, Super Stats can also tell you various other personalized facts and figures, such as how long each of your Web pages takes to load on each visitor's Web browser. The free service is supplemented by a more sophisticated fee-based service.

Web Manage
www.Webmanage.com
A fee-based media tracking service.

Web Position
www.webposition.com
Downloadable rank checking software is available at this site.

Web Trends
www.Webtrends.com
A fee-based media tracking service.

Financial

Bloomberg
www.bloomberg.co.uk
This financial site includes up-to-date business, stocks and bonds news. There is also an entrepreneur network and free newsletter to sign up for.

Durlacher
www.durlacher.co.uk
Find reports and market analyses at this site. There are some free reports available.

London Stock Exchange
www.londonstockex.co.uk
The official site of the London Stock Exchange. The site includes a technical library, a news and press area and, naturally, share prices.

NASDAQ

www.nasdaq.com

The NASDAQ exchange on the Web. NASDAQ was the world's first electronic market. Investors can log on to nasdaq.com and see how NASDAQ and Dow Jones and the S+P 500 are performing, scan the latest news and fund information and get quotes for stocks and mutual funds.

The Street

www.thestreet.com

This site covers everything from stock market investing to personal and business finance. This site is updated throughout the day.

Funding

Funding information

British Venture Capital Association

www.bvca.co.uk

This site includes key facts about venture capital in the UK, a BVCA members directory, research and press releases. It is the most comprehensive source of information in the UK venture capital industry on the Internet.

E-business

www.e-business.com

This site provides e-business resources including news, how-to's, networking and education, building your e-business, e-marketing, e-consultants, research, customers and partners.

E-cradle

www.e-cradle.co.uk

E-cradle helps develop new Internet business ideas. It includes hundreds of useful resources and links. The company is divided into three main areas: e-cradle.co.uk (the Web site with services, information and links to some of the best resources on the Net); the e-cradle network (an association of professional companies who work on a contingent basis) and the e-cradle nursery (where fully developed business ideas gain exposure to the UK's leading VCs). There is an e-cradle newsletter available at the site.

EVCA

www.evca.com

EVCA is the European Private Equity and Venture Capital Association. The EVCA site includes EVCA publications such as statistics, directories, newsletters and press summaries.

Tagmanet

www.tagmanet.com

Tagmanet is an e-fulfilment portal that has been designed to help retailers define, source and manage order fulfilment throughout Europe. The site covers news, views, events and industry reports as well as supplier listings across 15 fulfilment and related service sectors.

UK Business Incubation

www.ukbi.co.uk

The UKBI is the leading representative body for the business incubation industry in the UK. The site provides services, expertise, and is an excellent source of information on business incubators and accelerators in the UK.

Venture Site

www.venturesite.co.uk

The Venture Site is a not-for-profit matchmaking service for small companies seeking equity finance and business angel investors.

Venture capital and incubator companies

Advent International

www.adventinternational.com

Advent International specializes mostly in B2B and Internet-enabling technology. The company invests in both early stage venture capital and later stage private equity opportunities. The industries that Advent International works with include telecommunications, media, software, business services, health care and life sciences.

Amadeus Capital Partners

www.amadeuscapital.com

Amadeus has provided funding for Entropic (sold to Microsoft), Lastminute.com and Orchestream. It focuses on technology companies.

Apax Partners
www.apax.co.uk
Apax specializes in Internet-enabling technology, B2B and B2C.

Atom Wireless
www.atomwireless.com
A wireless commerce accelerator, specifically established to invest in m-commerce start-ups.

Brainspark
www.brainspark.com
An incubator that offers funding and help to UK and European start-up companies. The company provides seed capital and a physical infrastructure.

Business-Incubator
www.business-incubator.com
Get full technical support for your start-up company from this site. The site is affiliated with four Internet industry leaders: Cisco, Sun Microsystems, Oracle and Exodus, which together offer technology packages to ensure secure starts for e-commerce-based ideas.

Cube8
www.cube8.com
An Internet incubation and investment company.

Dawnay Day Lander
www.dawnaydaylander.com
An investor that helps start-ups and early stage Internet companies in the UK, Europe and Middle East. This company invests in companies that are too small or too young for traditional investors.

Equity Capital
www.equitycapital.com
Equity Capital specializes in B2B.

European Digital Partners
www.european-digital-partners.com
European Digital Partners focuses on early stage growth companies in the European Internet and wireless sectors. The company has provided funding for the gapyear.com.

Gorilla Park

www.gorillapark.com

Gorilla Park is a business accelerator that helps 'baby gorillas' become international companies. Gorilla Park accelerates B2B, B2C, wireless and Internet infrastructure companies throughout Europe.

3i

www.3i.com

3i provides capital for Internet start-ups.

Ideashub

www.ideashub.com

Ideashub provides investment and Internet start-up services such as legal advice, technology expertise, marketing services and recruitment.

Internet Partners

www.thli.com

A Net-friendly venture capitalist.

Ismartlab

www.ismartlab.com

A UK incubator that offers a comprehensive package of benefits for entrepreneurs.

Matchco

www.matchco.co.uk

A VC facilitator. This service helps you produce a business plan in a VC-friendly format.

MTI Partners

www.mtifirms.com

Specializes only in enabling technologies.

New Media Spark

www.newmediaspark.com

A technology and Internet investment company, listed on the London Stock Exchange's Alternative Investment Market.

Schroder Ventures

www.schroderventures.com

A venture capitalist specializing in B2B.

Top Technology

www.toptechnology.co.uk

Top Technology offers early stage venture capital for British technology companies.

Host servers

Web Fusion
www.webfusion.co.uk
If your site becomes very popular, you should look at host servers such as Web Fusion.

Internet news and information

Internet information

Ask a librarian
www.earl.org.uk/ask
Earl brings the resources of UK public libraries to your desktop. Simply e-mail a question about any subject and get a response within 48 hours at this site.

Ask Me
www.askme.com
The Ask Me Business Solutions section provides customized solutions to B2B marketplaces. Get questions answered by experts for free at this site. You must register for the service.

Britannica
www.britannica.com
This site lets you search the Britannica encyclopedia, expert reviews of Web sites, articles from leading magazines and related books.

Dictionary
www.dictionary.com
This is an online dictionary. Other resources at this site include a Roget's Thesaurus, grammar tools and a translator.

Information Channel
www.informationchannel.co.uk
This site is geared towards beginners and is simple and easy to use. The areas that are covered include news, weather, sport, property, jobs and leisure.

Info Please

www.infoplease.com

Information Please is the world's largest free reference site. You can find facts on thousands of subjects including business and technology.

Quick Advice

www.quick-advice.com

Get advice from other Net users at this site. Simply post your question and let the world advise you.

Spark Online

www.spark-online.com

This site covers contemporary technological issues. This publication describes itself as 'about the self and its relationship with e-society'.

Web Reference

www.webreference.com

Easy to understand Web reference guide, updated daily. Part of the Internet.com Web site, Web Reference is one of the oldest and most respected Web development sites. Articles and features cover areas such as authoring, HTML, browsing and advanced site design.

Internet news

Business Week

ebiz.businessweek.com

This is the online version of *Business Week* magazine. The e-business section includes features, company close-ups, movers and shakers and Web site makeovers. There is also an e biz Q+A section. The Business Week technology forums cover trends and issues, products, people and companies.

European Technology Forum

www.euro-techforum.com

The European Technology Forum is a pan-European network of the technology industries' key executives. The site includes news section, events information and a directory.

Hottest Internet sites

www.hot100.com

The hottest Internet sites in the world are ranked and reviewed at this site. The ranking system is via Web site visits. The areas that are covered include business, international, technology and finance.

Internet Commerce

www.commerce.net

Commerce Net is a global non-profit organization that focuses on business-to-business e-commerce. The site is a good source of information, education, research and inspiration. Approximately 600 decision-makers are actively involved with Commerce Net.

Internet News

www.internetnews.com

Part of the Internet.com family of Web sites, this site provides real time Internet business news. The site covers general business news, ASP news, ISP news and finance. There are advertising and stock reports available at this site along with an Internet news radio station.

Internet Technology

www.businesstech.com

Business Tech is a Web resource for Internet business, emerging technology, strategy and trends. There is an annual fee for the subscription news and analysis service.

Links and Web rings

Linkomatic

www.linkomatic.com

A 'Free-for-All' link service. This site provides link lists that anyone can join for no fee whatsoever. You can submit your site to hundreds of free link pages at once.

Loop Link

www.looplink.com

A Web ring service.

RainFrog

www.rainfrog.com

A Web ring service is available at this site.

Sadiq's Web Ring Directory
www.users.dircon.co.uk
Another Web ring directory.

Web Ring
www.webring.org
This is the most popular Web ring service. It is US-based but it does have an international focus. Web Ring manages around 70,000 rings with approximately 500,000 sites altogether taking part.

What Next
www.what-next.com
What Next includes templates for making reciprocal link requests.

Marketing information

B2BMarketingBiz.com
www.b2bmarketingbiz.com
This B2B marketing Internet site offers practical news and case studies for B2B advertisers and marketers on reaching medium–large businesses effectively online.

B2BOnline.com
www.netb2b.com
B2B Online provides overviews of the top 'B2B 100' advertisers (by spending or by medium). It also includes strategy profiles of the best media buyers in the business and the site provides the 'NetMarketing 200', a ranking of the best B2B Web sites.

Click Z
www.clickz.com
A very popular e-zine with articles on branding, advertising and marketing from a US perspective.

Cluetrain
www.cluetrain.com
The Cluetrain Web site offers a provocative and intelligent look at the way the Internet changes the nature of business, brands

and marketing.

EMarketeer

www.emarketeer.com

This long-established site not only provides useful information on all aspects of Internet marketing, but also a discussion forum populated by e-marketing experts. This could therefore be a useful place to seek personal and professional advice on your online brands.

Guerrilla Marketing

www.gmarketing.com

Offering information on a wide range of guerrilla marketing tactics.

JV Marketer

www.jvmarketer.com

Greg Schliesmann's JV Marketer site enables you to subscribe to a weekly free e-mail newsletter called Breakthrough Internet Marketing. As it centres on cost-effective and free marketing techniques, there is a lot of information on e-media relations. The most useful part of JV Marketer, however, is the discussion forum that enables you to ask any question relating to your publicity efforts.

The Marketeer

www.themarketeer.co.uk

This online magazine features the latest news and reviews about advertising, marketing and design in England. The feature section includes Web site reviews by industry insiders.

Marketing Online

www.marketing.haynet.com

Marketing Online is produced by *Marketing* magazine. The site includes features, plus regular news updates and a New Media 'What's New' section.

Marketing Sherpa

www.marketingsherpa.com

Marketing Sherpa is a media publishing company. The site includes useful news, case studies, and best practices data about Internet and integrated marketing for advertising, marketing and PR professionals. Marketing Sherpa also covers tactics, advice and results in its newsletters and special reports. The articles are written exclusively by the company, with a focus on what's working for advertising, marketing and PR professionals who work for medium–large companies and for the agencies that serve them. It covers both traditional companies as well as dot.coms.

Marketing Tips

www.marketingtips.com

The Marketing Tips site provides tips on practically every aspect of marketing, including market research. The Marketing Tips site has a particularly useful PR section, with advice provided by public relations consultants and marketing reporters. The emphasis is on providing advice for small businesses with an online presence.

Marketing Today

www.marketingtoday.com

The Marketing Today site includes a free direct-mail / e-mail campaign ROI (Return on Investment) Calculator. Simply enter your campaign costs and projected results and the calculator instantly produces an estimated ROI.

Marketing UK

www.marketinguk.co.uk

This site provides public relations advice, contact databases, and links to other marketing and publicity sites.

Net B2B

www.netb2b.com

The Net B2B site provides PR advice for business-to-business Web sites.

Promotion World

www.promotionworld.com

Promotion World provides online promotion techniques, tutorials, articles, reviews and resources.

Web Site promote

www.websitepromote.com

Meta-tag services and advice can be found at this site.

Web Site Promotion

www.web-sitepromotion.com

A diverse range of tips and techniques for promoting online is offered at this user-friendly site. Web Promotion is a free resource covering advertising, marketing and promotion.

Wilson Web

www.wilsonweb.com

As one of the best marketing Web sites around, Wilson Web provides a mine of information relating to online brand building. It could also be worthwhile signing up for the Web Marketing Today fortnightly newsletter that occasionally provides practical advice on Internet branding.

Media

Online industry magazines

ClickZ

www.clickz.com

ClickZ is an online marketing magazine providing regular features on market research methods from marketing consultants and journalists.

E-Business

www.e-business.uk.com

The online version of *e-business UK* magazine includes a free newsletter, Web development directory, glossary of common e-business language, e-business reports and book reviews.

E-commerce Times

www.e-commercetimes.com

All aspects of Internet news are covered at this site.

Ecompany

www.ecompany.com

This Internet resource provides access to over 10,000 articles from eCompany Now and *Fortune* magazine. The site includes an eCompany Guide that has more than 7,000 topics and access to nearly 26,000 sites and is a rich resource for learning about business online. The Talent Pool section is an online meeting area where you can promote your skills and expertise.

European Business News

www.ebn.co.uk

This site provides comprehensive and up-to-date market news with a European slant.

The Industry Standard magazine
www.thestandard.com / europe
The online version of the *Industry Standard Europe* magazine.

The Internet Works
www.iwks.com
The Internet Works Web site provides a comprehensive list of Web design firms as well as freelance design consultants.

Mad
www.mad.co.uk
This is an online community for the media, marketing, advertising and design industry.

.net Magazine Online
www.netmag.co.uk
The online home of *.net magazine* includes a 'Web Builder' section full of Web design tips for the amateur and professional.

The New Statesman
www.newstatesman.co.uk
Looks at domestic and world affairs.

Wired
www.wired.com
Find skills or suitable experts for your own business.

Online newspapers

The Economist
www.economist.co.uk
The Economist online.

The Express
www.express.co.uk
The *Daily Express* online.

The Financial Times
www.ft.com
Excellent financial resource with share indexes, industry news and personal organizer.

The Guardian

www.guardianunlimited.co.uk

This site includes all the daily news stories from the UK and around the world plus e-mail bulletins, film, sport and job information. The content is free to use on your Web site – just follow the links to find out how to incorporate it.

Telegraph

www.telegraph.co.uk

The online version of the *Telegraph*.

Online newsfeeds

Ananova

www.ananova.com

This virtual newscaster displays all the latest stories and also reads the headlines directly. The articles are often brief. UK-based Ananova enables you to create your own customized newspaper that can then be sent to your e-mail address. Once you specify the information you are interested in, and prioritize that information, the service will provide you with updates as and when relevant stories emerge.

BBC News

news.bbc.co.uk

The latest news from the BBC is available at this site.

Business Wire

www.businesswire.com

A fast and free news-based service.

Infobeat

www.infobeat.com

An online news service.

Moreover

www.moreover.com

A newsfeed service with over 1,500 sources worldwide.

News Now

www.newsnow.co.uk

News from the UK and US news sites.

Newswatch UK

www.newswatch.co.uk

A service that provides news from the UK.

UK Internet
www.uk.internet.com / uk-news
A round-up of news and events in the financial and Internet world.

Newsgroups and chat

Software

ChatWare
www.eware.com
Special software that helps you set up chat rooms is available at this site.

E-ware
www.eware.com
Special conference / chat software is available from this company. When the software is installed, you can conduct a conference at any time.

Freecode
www.freecode.com
A vast and diverse range of bulletin board software is available for free at this freeware site.

I-chat
www.ichat.com
This company provides chat software.

Proxicom
www.proxicom.com
Another company specializing in conference and chat software.

Payment

Catalog
www.actinic.co.uk
An e-commerce site-building system.

Click and Build

www.clickandbuild.com

An 'off the shelf' building tool that is very straightforward. It enables you to cut and paste a workable order form directly onto your site. It can also help you to build an e-commerce site straight from scratch, although packages such as these don't offer a great deal of sophistication in terms of Web design elements. Click and Build has a reputation for being one of the simplest and most user-friendly shop building products. No programming experience is necessary as Click and Build enables you to design, build and manage an online shop within minutes by simply answering a series of questions. Using pre-designed templates and forms, the shopping-cart system can take you through the whole Web design procedure if required. Click and Build caters for businesses of all sizes as it allows storage of thousands of products within its inventory. The only drawback is, as it relies on pre-designed templates and does all the work for you, the degree to which you can tailor the e-shopping procedure to the specific needs of your site is somewhat limited.

Datacash

www.datacash.com

Datacash enables merchants to receive credit card and debit card payments via its Web site. You can quickly set up a merchant account at the site.

Get a Result

www.getaresult.co.uk

Get a Result is an online service that eases small businesses' late payment problems. It is managed by the CPA (Credit Protection Association).

ibill

www.ibill.com

Ibill is an Internet billing company. The company provides secure transaction services that enable Web merchants to accept and process real time payments over the Internet. It also offers back-office functions.

Intershop

www.intershop.com

Intershop is a widely used e-commerce software product, targeted at businesses that are willing to offer template-based services to their clients. The Intershop product is available at three different levels of sophistication: ePages, Hosting and Merchant. The highest level package, Merchant, can cater for just about any site, no matter how much traffic it receives. Furthermore, as well as incorporating a broad range of different templates that can be tagged on to an existing site, it can be used in conjunction with standard Web design products (such as Front Page or Dreamweaver) to create more personalized and individual e-shop designs. If you want your e-commerce site to show off a versatile range of multimedia elements, Merchant also lets you integrate audio, video and JavaScript (the Web-building code that enables dynamic and animated graphics to appear on a Web site). As well as enabling your site to process orders, it can also track customer accounts and control inventory. The Merchant package also offers various order, traffic and customer behaviour reports to help you understand your audience that little bit better. Intershop also covers your security concerns, as all payment details are encrypted using a coding system called Secure Socket Layer (SSL) and each customer's details are encrypted and stored within the Intershop database. The other advantage of Intershop is that, at every level, it is easy to use, providing a simple point-and-click

Maestro Commerce

www.maestrocommerce.com

An e-commerce site-building system.

Netbanx

www.netbanx.com

Netbanx has several services and products that enable you to make transactions online.

Open Market

www.openmarket.com

Open Market is an advanced shop-building alternative to Click and Build.

Red Pay

www.redpay.com

This service enables British businesses to send invoices and receive payment electronically via EBPP (Electronic Bill Presentation and Payment). Sales information and a free trial account are available.

Secure Trading

www.securetrading.com

Secure Trading is a provider of 'plug+play' solutions for processing credit cards on your Web site in real time. Secure Trading offers the highest level of security and fraud control.

Shop Site

www.openmarket.com

Shop Site is a shop-building system aimed at the small to medium-sized business. Unlike Intershop, you do not have to install software onto your computer as it is a Web-based system run from the user-friendly Open Market site. Open Market takes you gently through the steps involved in setting up your own online shop. This includes filling in a few forms and choosing graphics to upload, but nothing too strenuous. The only drawback is that as you have to work with the design templates provided by Open Market, the visual design of your site can become slightly compromised. Having said that, it is possible to modify each template and edit individual pages, although this can be rather time-consuming. Unlike other 'shop in a box' solutions, orders are not held on your Web server but on that of the Open Market site. When an order is processed, an order notification message is sent to your e-mail address. As with all the other 'shop in a box' options, Shop Site supports credit card payments, although it can only handle two types of currency. As an Internet magazine reviewer concluded, 'Overall, this is a well-designed straightforward tool for building shop fronts that are functional but not too complex.'

Shop Zone Professional

www.btsw.com

An e-commerce site-building system.

Verifone

www.verifone.com

An e-commerce site-building system.

Web Sockets

www.websockets.com

An e-commerce site-building system.

World Pay

www.worldpay.com

World Pay has a service called Click and Build that enables you to set up a merchant account within a matter of hours.

Software

Actinic Software Ltd

www.actinic.co.uk

Actinic is an SME e-commerce specialist offering B2B products such as Actinic Business.

BT Webworld

www.btwebworld.co.uk

BT offers Web hosting services from entry level solutions to dedicated services.

Cossax

www.cossax.com

Cossax's product called Web Shop helps you get your business on the Web.

ec Builder Pro

www.multiactive.co.uk

Multiactive provides corporate solutions and small and medium business solutions.

EROL

www.erol.co.uk

Erol helps you build and maintain an online store.

Shop Creator

www.shopcreator.co.uk

Shop Creator provides secure e-commerce solutions.

Surf Net COWS

www.cows.co.uk

COWS Online Worldwide Shopping offers very easy solutions to help anyone sell online.

Protx

www.protx.com

A trusted third party system that holds credit card details offline for merchants signed up to its services. There is no need for online customers to input their credit card details more than once.

Research

Active Media

www.activemedia.com

Active Media is a company that aims to make your Web business a success by connecting your site to your target market and converting your prospects to loyal online customers. The company offers online media planning, media buying, usability testing and focus groups, analysis and reporting and creative services.

BMRB

www.bmrb.co.uk

BMRB is a UK Internet market research company. BMRB's research areas include stakeholder and market performance, consumer, global resources, financial, media and product. The Web site has a news section full of Internet facts and figures. The company offers a series of free training seminars through its Centre of Excellence programme.

Computer Economics

www.computereconomics.com

Computer Economics offers online advisory services and printed reports to give organizations the edge they need. Its services include IT cost management, e-business and e-business market forecasts. There are links to report overviews at the site (subscription is required for full site access).

CyberAtlas

www.cyberatlas.com

CyberAtlas is a guide to online facts. This site provides valuable statistics and Web marketing information to readers. Sign up to CyberAtlas's free newsletter, which takes a weekly look at one specific industry or market relevant to online marketers. Also, once a month, the newsletter includes a stat pack (a numerical look at what went on on the Internet in the past month). There is an online forum at this site.

Daily Internet Statistics

www.statmarket.com

Stat Market provides data on global Internet user trends. Its statistics are produced from the surfing patterns of more than 40 million surfers. Stat Market has a variety of subscription and access options. You can also sign up for a free Stat Market newsletter at the site.

Digitrends

www.digitrends.net

Digitrends provides reviews of interactive marketing solutions, including news, case studies, peer-to-peer exchange and strategic analysis of current marketing campaigns. Digitrends' information resources include a magazine and daily e-mail newsletter.

Emarketer

www.emarketer.com

EMarketer provides quick and easy access to the latest trends and statistics about the Internet and e-business. The site sells e-reports and also offers free daily eStats. Sign up for the Web site newsletter to receive statistics in your inbox.

Fletcher Research

www.fletch.co.uk

Fletcher Research focuses on the strategic and business implications of new media. Fletcher is affiliated with Forrester Research (see below). The Fletcher site includes a 'Today's news stories' section. The company can help you build and implement strategies for the Internet.

Forrester Research

www.forrester.com

Forrester Research is one of the largest and perhaps the most-respected Internet research firms. The Forrester Research site provides news, event information, reports and assessment tools.

Internet Advertising Bureau

www.iab.net

The Internet Advertising Bureau is devoted to maximizing the use and effectiveness of advertising on the Internet. The site includes information on IAB events, research, news and membership.

Jupiter
www.jup.com
Jupiter Research offers research and advisory services that assess challenges and define success in the global Internet economy. Jupiter also focuses on how the Internet and other technologies are changing consumer industries. Jupiter produces a wide range of forums and its research studies are available for purchase at the site.

Media Metrix
www.mediametrix.com
Media Metrix provides research on consumer behaviour and trends on the Internet and digital media.

Nielsen Media Research
www.netratings.com
The Net Rating site provides weekly top tens for sites, banners, advertisers and usage as well as including information on its research services. The Nielsen/Net Ratings Reporter service can be received by e-mail – simply sign up at the site.

Nop
www.nop.co.uk
Find news, survey results and Internet research information at this site. There is also a good links section.

NUA
www.nua.net
The NUA Internet Survey section is an excellent source to find out the latest Internet trends. You can also sign up for the NUA Internet Survey e-mail newsletter.

Web Trends
www.webtrends.com
Web Trends provides analysis and reports of e-Business and Internet-based systems.

Search engines

AltaVista
www.altavista.com
One of the longest running search engines on the Web and remains among the most popular. AltaVista enables you to narrow searches using specific commands and also allows you to conduct 'plain English' searches. In addition to its search box, the

AltaVista home page enables you to link to 'Current News Stories' and 'Frequently Used Links' sections.

Ask Jeeves

www.askjeeves.com

Ask Jeeves enables you to conduct searches in plain English. Ask Jeeves also breaks down its directory into various sections. These sections include 'Money', 'Travel', 'Health', 'Shopping' and 'Computers'.

Excite

www.excite.com

Excite is a popular search site, partly due to its Power Search option. The Power Search enables you to customize your search matchings to a greater extent than a standard keywords search allows. Another reason why Excite is popular among e-marketers is its NewsTracker service. NewsTracker tracks the news from hundreds of online publications and searches for specified keywords.

Google

www.google.com

Fast becoming the best general search engine.

HotBot

www.hotbot.com

HotBot provides a 'SuperSearch' option that again enables you to fine tune your search according to specific criteria.

Infoseek

www.infoseek.com

The Infoseek home page contains links to categories and sub-categories that you can access to find specific information about one topic.

Lycos

www.lycos.com

Lycos combines sophisticated technology with a more human approach in its Top 5 per cent Web sites link, where site reviewers pick their top sites within different categories.

Northern Light

www.northernlight.com

Alongside its main Web index, Northern Light includes a 'Special Collection' consisting of news articles and content from press wires (news services such as Reuters).

Yahoo!

www.yahoo.com

Yahoo! is a directory with a search engine (Google) attached. As a directory, sites are indexed by humans as opposed to search engine robots and information is organized into categories such as 'Computers', 'Business and Finance' and 'Media'.

Search engine information

Beaucoup

www.beaucoup.com

Beaucoup is a directory of over 1,000 specialist search engines.

Northern Webs

www.northernwebs.com

Meta-tag services and advice can be found at this site.

Search Engine Watch

www.searchenginewatch.com

This site provides tips on search engine positioning and links to hundreds of search engine articles. Search Engine Watch is full of useful advice on how to get the most out of search engines. It also provides search engine news, reviews and comparative analysis.

Site Up

www.siteup.com

Meta-tag services and advice can be found at this site.

Web Site Ranking Tips

danjay.com/subpages/ranking_tips.html

This site features tips on how to get to the top of the search engines.

Search engine positioning

Agent Web Ranking

www.aadsoft.com

A search engine positioning tool.

Sign Poster

www.signposter.com

Another search engine positioning tool.

Submit It!
www.submitit.com
A search engine submission site that will submit your Web site details for free.

Web Position Gold
www.webposition.com
A search engine positioning tool that is inexpensive and effective.

Security

Baltimore Technologies
www.baltimore.com
Baltimore Technologies offers online security packages.

Card Guard
www.card-guard.com
Card Guard records all e-tailers' dealings with customers, providing proof that the goods have been dispatched correctly.

Click for Cover
www.ecomrisks.co.uk
Offers protection against the many problems businesses connected to the Internet could experience.

Cybersource
www.cybersource.com
One of the biggest names in the e-commerce fraud detection markets is Cyber Source. The Cyber Source site has links to sites such as the 2000 Fraud Survey, White Papers and Global Tax Services.

F-Secure
www.fsecure.com
F-secure is a leading vendor in the security arena. It specializes in data security solutions. F-Secure protects laptops, personal digital assistants, enterprise workstations and servers against Web attack. It provides security solutions for mobile enterprise, including integrated anti-virus and file encryption.

iD2

www.id2.se

ID2 has developed public key infrastructure solutions that enable users to be identified securely across the Net. The company encryption and smart card support a range of devices, from PCs to mobile phones.

IORA

www.iora.co.uk

IORA is a UK mobile Intranet specialist. It enables all mobile professionals to access corporate Internet information.

Magex

www.magex.com

Magex is a digital rights management technology company. It allows companies to sell content securely on the Internet, while protecting copyright.

Security Focus

www.securityfocus.com

The Security Focus site provides commentary on all security issues. It is the Internet's largest and most comprehensive database of security knowledge and resources to the public. It also hosts a BUG TRAQ mailing list.

Security Space

www.securityspace.com

Security Space is a Web security portal that provides Internet security-related news, resources, tools and service. Security Space offers free security checks and it also has coverage of the latest security shows.

Zone Labs

www.zonelabs.com

Zone Labs is a software technology company that provides Internet security products.

Staff

Elance

www.elance.com

Elance is a professional services marketplace. Web-based projects can be posted at the site and freelancers/companies bid for the work. The site has a global reach and typical project areas include software development, Web design, creative services, research, translation, copywriting and more. There are online collaboration tools such as a global billing and payment system. Over 200,000 businesses and individuals from over 140 countries are registered at Elance.

Freelance work exchange
www.freelanceworkexchange.com
This site includes lots of links for those looking for skilled workers. The freelance work exchange provides job news, market reviews and information. You can post projects for free at this site. There is also a very useful news section.

Virtual malls and auctions

Auctions

Adauction
www.adauction.com
An auction site for B2B companies selling and buying media space. The site does offer a targeted service.

Business-auctions.com
www.business-auctions.com
Business-auctions was the UK's first online auction company and has become a market leader in the auctioning of surplus business assets over the Internet. It covers auctions on commercial vehicles, computing/IT, construction, engineering, marine, materials handling, medical, mining, office, paper, power generation, printing, retail surplus, telecoms and textiles.

Compare Net
www.comparenet.com
Promoted as an 'interactive buyer's guide', this site is a comparative shopping service. The site's database of products is over 40,000 items. The site also includes discussion groups.

E-Bay
www.ebay.com
E-bay is the 'world's personal trading community'.

Software

Instil
www.instil.com
An auction software product.

Open Site
www.opensite.com
An auction software product.

Web awards and assurance certificates

Award Sites
www.focusa.com/awardsites
A comprehensive list of Web awards is available at this site, which also gives you an idea as to how valid each scheme is and how relevant it would be to your site.

Awards Jungle submission service
www.awardsjungle.com
If you want to submit your site for lots of site awards simultaneously, take a look at the Awards Jungle submission service that does just that.

Clicksure Certified Merchant
www.clicksure.com
A reassuring logo that can build customer trust.

Net Announce
www.erspros.com/net-annoucnce
Net Announce enables you to provide a more detailed description of your site than most of the other services. It does, however, have strict submission criteria that can be (perhaps deliberately) off-putting.

Netscape What's New
www.netscape.com/netscape/new
Netscape offers a Yahoo!-style What's New service, updated on a daily basis.

Project Cool
www.projectcool.com
This was the first major Web award scheme.

Truste Scheme
www.truste.com
The Truste Scheme is a reassuring logo that can build customer trust.

UK Index
www.ukindex.co.uk
One of the main features of the UK index is its What's New directory, intended to announce new UK-based Internet companies.

VeriSign
www.verisign.com
A Webserver certificate from VeriSign proves you are a legal and trustworthy business (providing you are a legitimate business, the certificate is not very difficult to receive).

Which?
www.which.net/webtrader/
The Which? Web Trader logo inspires confidence in Web sites. To become a member of which.net, an e-commerce site must confirm that its shopping facilities are secure.

Yellow Pages What's New
www.yell.co.uk/ukyw/whats_new
The Yellow Pages' Yell Web site incorporates a What's New announcement section alongside its standard index. As with the main directory, the What's New section is broken into different indexes based on different regions and then again into different business areas.

Web design and Web usability

Content help

Good Keywords
www.goodkeywords.com
Good Keywords will help you find all the relevant keywords related to a primary keyword.

The Global Ideas Bank
www.globalideasbank.org
An online think-tank that contains over 3,000 social inventions from around the world.

HTML Validator Lite

www.htmlvalidator.com/lite

This is an HTML version of a grammar and spell-checker. Download the CSE HTML Validator for free from this site.

Ideas A Day

www.idea-a-day.com

A forum for sharing or stealing bright ideas. An original idea is published every day free from copyright to do with what you wish.

Ideatown

www.ideatown.com

Ideatown develops, launches and markets innovative ventures in entertainment, business and industry.

Jargon Scout

tbtf.com/jargon-scout.html

Jargon Scout provides a glossary of geek-speak. The site aims to give you advance warning of jargon that is about to be used in the Net's language. There is a 'Jargon du Jour' section that provides comments on new jargon terms.

Nameboy

www.nameboy.com

Domain name suggestions can be found at this site. The Nameboy site also lists names for sale and auction.

The netiquette guide

www.albion.com/netiquette/index.html

The site includes the core rules of netiquette, a complete online edition of netiquette by Virginia Shea (an exhaustive guide to netiquette), a netiquette quiz and a mailing list.

Quoteland

www.quoteland.com

Quoteland includes thousands of quotes on every topic imaginable.

Web Reference

www.webreference.com

This site includes articles covering subjects such as DHTML, Java Script and XML.

Content providers

BEA

www.bea.com

This company helps businesses develop and launch e-businesses. Clients include Nokia, Amazon.com and Fed Ex. BEA is one of the world's leading e-business infrastructure software companies.

Deymo

www.deymo.com

Deymo is an Internet software development company. You can edit your Web site content any time from anywhere in the world by using the software available at this site.

Documentum

www.documentum.com

Documentum provides content management services such as creation, personalization and delivery.

Epic Realm

www.epicrealm.com

Epic Realm is a content delivery network dedicated to enabling business over the Internet.

Framfab

www.framfab.com

Framfab is a strategic consulting and digital services company. It has expertise in wireless Internet and broadband services.

IBM

www.ibm.com

The IBM home page is an entry point to information about IBM products and services.

Icon Medialab

www.iconmedialab.com

Icon Medialab is a Web site design and consulting company that works with many multinationals.

Multi-link

www.multi-link.com

Multi-link is the leading provider of conferencing solutions. Its software enables Web-based conference management.

Place Ware
www.placeware.com
Place Ware offers Web conferencing solutions. There are links to headlines, seminars and live events at this site.

Reef
www.reef.com
The firm's Internetware enables non-techies to manage e-commerce, online publishing, content brokering and more.

Spaceworks
www.spaceworks.com
Spaceworks offers everything from real-time ordering to interactive marketing for B2B e-commerce companies. The site includes articles, seminars, upcoming events and a 'Spaceworks Navigator'. The 'Spaceworks Navigator' analyses your ROI potential for free.

Sterling Commerce
www.sterlingcommerce.com
Sterling Commerce provides complete e-business solutions for companies of all sizes.

TIBCO
www.tibco.com
Tibco provides complete e-business solutions. Its clients have included Cisco, Yahoo!, Sun and mySAP.com.

Design help

Alpha Project
www.alpha-project.net
This site provides free online Web design tutorials.

Builder
www.builder.com.
Billed as 'The Site for Site Builders', Builder provides features and workshops on successful site design as well as links to helpful design tools.

Colour Picker
www.chunting.com
You can find the RGB Hex code of any colour at this site.

Developer
www.developer.com.
This is where you go to find out technical information, as its content includes advice on programming and HTML. Although the information is aimed at technophiles, a lot of the articles are very accessible.

Dynamic Drive
dynamicdrive.com
Dynamic Drive is a resource for DHTML featuring DHTML scripts, tutorials and components to enhance your Web site.

Eboz
www.eboz.com
Eboz includes features and tutorials that help you create a successful Web site. The site covers backend, Web design, domain names, graphics, programming, software and Web hosting.

Net B2B
www.netb2b.com
The Net B2B site is full of useful articles on Web design from a business-to-business perspective.

Smarter Work
www.smarterwork.com
Smarter Work is an online marketplace for Web designers, writers, programmers and the like. It is a managed site and all projects and experts have the Smarter Work 'Seal of Satisfaction'.

Tips and Tricks
www.tips-tricks.com
As its name suggests, this site provides plenty of 'tips and tricks' on designing Web sites. It also provides lots of useful links to other Web design sites.

User Interface Engineering
www.uie.com
Providing more advanced technical information on the principles and practice of Web site design.

Web Design
www.webdesign.about.com.
This site has done the hard work for you as it provides links to a wide variety of articles at different design sites.

Web Designers UK

www.ukwebdesigners.net

Links to hundreds of UK Web designers are on this site. This site is part of the Internet Works Magazine Site (www.iwks.com).

Web Developer's Virtual Library

www.stars.com / WDVL

A highly recommended resource for Web developers. WDVL is a free encyclopedia of Java, HTML, Javascript, CGI, DHTML, XML, Perl, Web design and domain name tutorials and resources.

Web Tools

www.webtools.com

Web Tools provides product reviews, how-to's and other features for Web site designers, developers, programmers and Webmasters. The site covers programming, design, software and browsing technologies and includes technology discussion boards, free e-mail newsletters and a technology Web site links section.

Software

Fantastic

www.fantastic.com

Fantastic offers broadband multimedia software.

Infineon Technologies

www.infineon.com

Infineon Technologies makes memory products and semiconductor solutions.

Imediation

www.imediation.com

This company provides software and services for managing Internet selling relationships.

Lernout & Hauspie

www.lhs.com

LHS offers speech recognition technology.

TietoEnator

www.tietoenator.com

TietoEnator develops software applications for business and helps implement and run the solutions.

update.com
www.update.com
This company makes customer relationship management software.

ZoomON
www.zoomon.com
ZoomON offers B2B applications in Web and wireless environments.

Usability

Click Sure
www.clicksure.com
Click Sure assesses e-commerce sites. The company has listed the top ten mistakes made by online businesses. They include: bad Web design and navigation; unintelligible content; slow or crash prone sites; no company information; sketchy product information and hidden costs; vague delivery information; no privacy policy for customers' details; poor security; no returns policy or customer care policy; no quality marks from third-party organizations.

Link Prover
www.tafweb.com/linkprover.html
This freeware program scans your Web files for image links that lead to non-existent sources. It can also check links to http: or ftp: files.

My Helpdesk
www.myhelpdesk.com
This site provides technical information on software and hardware products. Navigation is simple and there are hundreds of links.

Siteowner
www.siteowner.com
Web site analysis is available at this site.

Tag Reference
www.tagreference.com
Tag Reference enables you to look up tags as well as their browser compatibility. This site is not for beginners who want to learn HTML. However, it does provide links to beginners' Web sites.

Usable Web

www.usableweb.com

Usable Web is a collection of links about Web usability. The site is frequently updated with hundreds of links to relevant articles about methods, design tips, strategy issues and technology.

Use It

www.useit.com

Use It is Jakob Nielsen's Web site, and contains more than five years' worth of articles about site usability. The site is updated bi-weekly.

Web Site Garage

websitegarage.netscape.com

A free service that checks your HTML, browser, load times, links and spelling. There is also an automatic tune-up service and you can receive e-mail notifications of possible troubles. Analyse your own meta-tags at Web Site Garage.

appendix 2

B2B e-commerce dictionary

access provider A company that provides connections to the Internet.

address book A directory in a Web browser where you can store and manage e-mail addresses.

ADSL Asymmetric Digital Subscriber Line. A high speed, high 'bandwidth' (see below) telephone line.

advertorial content Advertorial content refers to advertising designed to resemble editorial content. Advertorials are either integrated seamlessly into an existing Web site, or they are used as the basis of a completely new site altogether.

affiliate directory Affiliate directories are searchable indexes, helping businesses find affiliate programmes that are relevant to their sites. If you run your own scheme, these directories will consider it for a free listing in their database. If a directory editor chooses to highlight a scheme as a recommendation in their newsletter then it can benefit from even more exposure.

affiliate marketing Affiliate marketing involves the creation of a partnership between a host site and relevant affiliates in a joint revenue scheme.

agent Intelligent software that can be used in an exchange or auction to monitor prices and conditions on behalf of buyers and supplier.

angel investor An individual or group of individuals willing to invest in e-business ideas.

anti-sites These sites are sometimes referred to as suck sites or hate sites. They are Web sites that are devoted to attacking a company or organization.

applet An application written in Java and used in an HTML program.

article The name given to a single message posted to a newsgroup.

ASCII American Standard Code for Information Interchange. A code that assigns a number to each key on the keyboard.

ASP A service that will host and maintain your site for a fee. Application Service Providers cut the cost of data processing by sharing software and software support.

attachment A file added to an e-mail to be sent via the e-mail system.

audience Refers to each individual section of your online public. Each business has various audiences (customers, investors, journalists etc).

authentication The way a computer on the Internet verifies your identity. For example, the mail server that stores your mail must verify your identity by using your name and password before it downloads your mail to you.

Autoresponders Autoresponders enable Internet users to send automated e-mails when they are not able to respond to incoming e-mail.

Back-end system Systems that handle order processing and inventory, for both buyers and suppliers.

Backlink checking A means of finding out which Web pages are linking to a specific Web site.

Back-up A copy of data saved on your computer's hard drive. By making back-ups of your computer's files and programs you can safeguard your data against the threat posed by viruses.

bandwidth The capacity of fibre optic cables that carry information. The higher the bandwidth, the faster information will pass through a cable.

banner A small advertising area on a Web site.

banner ad An electronic advertisement displayed as a band of text and graphics within an e-mail publication (such as a newsletter) or on a Web page. The fact that many Internet users can now set their browsers to ignore banner ads, has led to advertisers looking for other types of online advertising.

banner views Refers to the number of times a banner has been viewed.

B2B Business-to-business.

B2B aggregators Companies that aggregate the services or products of others.

B2B auction B2B auctions are Web marketplaces that provide a mechanism to negotiate prices and bids for services.

B2B infomediary A site that serves to provide essential information. It is a variation of the portal. It provides specific information for an individual industry. Its aim is to bring together as much customizable business information as possible, in order to facilitate B2B activity. Although they have a long way to go, infomediaries are already providing useful and wide-ranging services.

BBS A bulletin board system.

B2C Business-to-consumer.

Bps Bits per second. The speed by which modems are measured.

BRC Business Reply Card.

Beta Version A test version of an application or program that is made available prior to the official release.

Tim Berners Lee Conceived the Web in 1989 as a tool for sharing information via his invention of HTML. Now he is the director of the World Wide Web Consortium (W3C)

b-Web Business Web. The term 'b-Web' was first coined by the US Internet journalist and consultant Don Tapscott to refer to the information age's 'primary business unit, in which groups of firms come together over the Internet. While each company retains its identity, the companies function together, creating more wealth than they could ever hope to create individually'.

Jeff Bezos Founder and CEO of Amazon.com.

binaries Files attached to newsgroup articles, usually in the form of images of zip files.

biometrics Voice and fingerprint recognition.

blind carbon copy (BCC) A way to send a copy of a message to a person without their name or address appearing in the recipient list.

bookmark A bookmark is a software tool that automatically loads the page it refers to.

boolean search A search allowing the inclusion or exclusion of documents containing certain words through the use of operators such as AND, NOT and OR.

bricks and clicks Refers to an integrated offline/online approach.

bricks and mortar A phrase used to evoke the 'real world'.

bricolage Claude Levi-Strauss, the French anthropologist, refers to bricolage as the act of creating things from whatever is lying about. Many people use the term to describe the opportunistic way in which the Web is put together.

broadband High bandwidth technology that is revolutionizing the way the Internet is used by businesses and consumers.

brochureware a derogatory term used to describe commercial e-mail and Web content that resembles a company brochure. Brochureware e-mails depend (like their printed counterparts) on one-way, not two-way, communication.

browser Software that allows you to access the Internet and World Wide Web. Internet Explorer and Netscape Navigator are the most commonly used browsers.

bulletin board Software that provides an e-mail database where people can access and leave messages.

cache A small memory bank inside an Internet user's computer. Each time you visit Web sites on the Internet, the cache stores all the images and text from those sites. This speeds up the download time when users revisit a site.

cancel option Useful in mail and newsgroup systems. Allows you to delete a message before or just after posting an e-mail message or newsgroup article.

Steve Case CEO for AOL.

C2C Consumer-to-consumer.

central processing unit (CPU) The main silicon chip that runs a computer's operating system and application software. It performs a computer's mathematical functions and controls essential operations.

CGI Common Gateway Interface. Used to enable interactive forms.

channel marketing Marketing done through channels such as retailers, distributors and resellers.

chat system Enables users to have an interactive, typed conversation. Chat systems therefore build an online network of people who interact not just with the Web page but with other users as well.

churn The cycle of acquiring new customers and losing others that characterizes consumer e-commerce and reduces lifetime customer value because switching is so easy.

clicks and mortar See *bricks and clicks*.

click through This refers to the act of clicking on a link to be transported to another site. The phrase is most commonly used in the context of banner advertising.

click through rate (CTR) The percentage of click throughs to banner views.

clipboard A holding area that temporarily stores information copied or cut from a document.

closed loop system A lead generation and fulfilment process.

community A group of Internet users with a shared interest or concept who interact with each other in newsgroups, mailing-list discussion groups and other online interactive forums.

concept search A search for documents related conceptually to a word, rather than specifically containing the word itself.

conference area Conference areas are the business-to-business equivalent of chat rooms. They enable companies to conduct business meetings, live seminars and press conferences from their Web site.

content services Sites dedicated to a particular topic.

conversion rate The percentage of shoppers in an online store who actually make a purchase.

cookie Cookies are small files that recognize repeat users of a Web site.

corporate portals Web sites for employees.

CPA Cost-per-action. A pricing model for online advertising based on the number of times an Internet user clicks on a banner ad that is linked to your Web site.

CPM Cost per thousand impressions. Another pricing model for online advertising (the M stands for the Roman numeral for 1,000).

crawler A type of search engine 'robot'

cross-posting The act of posting the same messages into several different news or discussion groups simultaneously.

customer relationship management (CRM) The strategy and process that supports customer relationships.

cyberspace Term originally coined in the sci-fi novels of William Gibson, referring to the online world and its communication networks and evoking its intangible sense of space.

database marketing The practice of using databases to improve the marketing process.

digital ink Changeable electronically charged ink particles.

discussion list A list of people who share the same interest and wish to correspond publicly online. Correspondence is made not only by sending messages to each other, but also by contacting the distribution list moderator, who then passes each message on to all the other list members. Distribution lists now number in the hundreds of thousands, covering every topic imaginable.

disintermediation Refers to the fact that the Internet enables companies to bypass intermediaries such as journalists and editors to communicate directly with their audience.

distribution channel The way a manufacturer or software developer delivers its goods to customers and receives payment in return. A direct channel (catalogue sales, direct mail, or telemarketing) is common in business-to-business commerce. Indirect channels use any variety of distributors, resellers, retailers, agents, or other intermediaries.

distribution list A list of e-mail addresses given one collective title. You can send a message to all the addresses simultaneously by referring to the list title.

domain name The officially registered Web site address of your site.

dot.bam Dot 'bricks and mortar'. A real world business with a strong Web presence.

dot.com Used to refer to a company based exclusively online.

download The term used to describe the transfer of a computer file from a server to a PC.

drownloading The act of simultaneously downloading so many files that a computer crashes.

DSL/cable modem High-speed computer modems for use with a cable or phone network.

e-business The catch-all term referring to the business world online. It also signifies an individual online business or company.

ECML Electronic Commerce Modelling Language. A standard for universal acceptance of online payments.

e-commerce Refers to business transactions over the Internet.

EDI Electronic Data Interchange. The transfer of data between businesses and organizations via established security standards.

E2E E2E stands for exchange-to-exchange e-commerce, where buyers and sellers conduct transactions not only within exchanges, but also between them. Although exchange-to-exchange e-commerce initially seems to complicate the B2B environment, it does have some obvious advantages. The main benefit is that sellers can get higher prices for their services by putting them on various sites simultaneously.

e-mail Electronic mail. A message sent across the Internet, or the act of transferring messages between computers, mobile phones or other communications attached to the Internet.

e-mail address Your electronic 'address' on the Internet or an Intranet. An e-mail address is commonly formed by joining your user name and the mail server name, separating the two with an @ symbol.

e-mail marketing The act of marketing via e-mail. E-mail can help to keep your company in the minds of existing customers; it can also cause annoyance if marketing messages are contributing to the problem of e-mail overload.

e-mail system The collective e-mail software systems that allow you to create, send, receive e-mail messages.

e-marketplace Consists of many companies gathering together in Web-based exchanges or auctions in order to buy and sell products or services in a highly competitive environment.

e-media relations The practice of building relations with editors and journalists via the Internet, especially when they work for the e-media.

e-media release An online, interactive press release sent via the e-mail system.

encoding A method of sending binary (non-text files) with e-mail messages. Common encoding options include: Mime, BinHex, UUencode, etc. Sender and receiver must both use the same method.

encryption The process of converting data into a coded form.

e-procurement The way B2B e-commerce affects the way companies buy products and services. It is a more convenient, timesaving and cost-effective means of purchasing products.

enterprise resource planning (ERP) Complex applications used by large enterprises to manage inventory and integrate business processes across multiple divisions and organizational boundaries.

exchange Exchanges are the main type of business-to-business marketplace. The B2B exchange enables suppliers, buyers and intermediaries to come together and offer products to each other according to set criteria. B2B Web exchanges provide constant price adjustments in line with fluctuations of supply and demand.

Extranet An Internet-enabled network designed primarily for a company's internal use, but that allows access to selected external customers, clients etc.

e-zines Online interactive magazines that only exist on the Internet.

filter Software that can discriminate between types of incoming and outgoing e-mail messages.

firewall A software/hardware combination that separates an internal local area network from the external Internet.

flame A 'heated' and hostile message posted in a newsgroup, usually in response to 'spam'; also, the act of posting such a message.

form A means of collecting data on Web pages, using text boxes, radio buttons and other facilities. Forms are used as a way of making sites more interactive as well as for sales and marketing purposes.

forums Newsgroups, mailing list discussion groups, chat rooms and other online areas that allow you to read, post and respond to messages.

fragmentation A market condition where many buyers are chasing many suppliers, often inefficiently.

freeware Free software programs.

FTP File Transfer Protocol. This is the standard method of uploading content from your computer to your server.

full-text index An index consisting of every single word of every document catalogued.

fuzzy search A search that will find matches even when words are only partially spelled or misspelled.

Bill Gates Microsoft Chairman. Although slow to appreciate the importance of the Internet, Gates has converted Microsoft into a company aiming to write the code for the next generation of Net compatible devices.

GIF Short for graphic information file. Used on the Internet to display files that contain graphic images.

groupware A set of technology tools enabling businesses to share software.

Guerrilla marketing Refers to any extreme or outlandish attempt to generate publicity, either online or offline.

hard copy A physical document, usually text on paper.

header The part of e-mail messages that includes instructions on how to handle the message. This is similar to the information that you find on the envelope of a letter you send through the post. A header includes information such as the subject, date, sender and recipient.

history list A record of visited Web pages you can access through your browser. It can help you find sites you haven't been able to bookmark.

hit A hit is a transfer from a server to a browser. Each time a browser transfers a text page that has no graphics, that represents one hit. If the page has a graphic inside it, that's two hits. If it has two graphics, that's three hits and so on. Hits therefore do not provide an accurate measurement of the number of times your Web site has been visited.

hit counters Software that records hits.

home page The first and or main page on a Web site.

horizontal market A market that sells materials or services that any company needs.

host A company that holds your site on its server.

host computer This simply refers to a computer connected to the Internet.

HTML HyperText Mark-up Language. A computer code used to build and develop Web pages.

HTTP HyperText Transfer Protocol.

horizontal market Horizontal portals cut across industries and automate functional processes.

hub A neutral electronic marketplace where buyers and sellers aggregate and which mediates electronic transactions among businesses.

hyperlink See *hypertext links*.

hypertext link Generally found on Web pages (although they can be used in e-mail messages), hypertext links link onto HTML pages and documents.

hypertime Refers to the fast moving pace of the Internet, as well as the decentralized nature of online time.

icon A graphic, picture, or small graphic element.

ignition The point at which a market gains momentum.

IMAP Internet Message Access Protocol. A method to access and manipulate e-mail that is stored remotely on another computer. Messages do not get transferred to the user's computer, making it easier to manage e-mail when accessing from multiple computers.

impression The number of times a banner ad appears in an established period of time.

index The searchable catalogue of documents created by search engine software.

information overload The situation of having so much information on your site as to bore or intimidate your customer.

intermediary Aggregates data and facilitates transactions by bringing buyers and sellers together.

Internet The global network of computers accessed with the aid of a modem. The Internet includes Web sites, e-mail, newsgroups, and other forums. This is a public network, though many of the computers connected to it are also part of *Intranets*. It uses the Internet Protocol (IP) as a communication standard.

interstitial Meaning 'in between', an interstitial is an advertisement that appears in a separate browser window while you wait for a Web page to load. Interstitials are more likely to contain large graphics, streaming presentations and applets than conventional banner ads, and some studies have found that more users click on interstitials than on banner ads.

Intranet Internal, private computer networks using Internet technology to allow communication between individuals within organizations.

IRC Internet Relay Chat (see *chat system*).

ISP Internet Service Provider. A firm that provides Internet services such as e-mail and Web hosting facilities.

itchy finger syndrome A slang reference to the Internet user's hunger for interactivity.

Java Web programming language that works on any computing platform.

JPEG Joint Photographic Experts Group. A compressed graphical image format.

junk mail See *spam*.

keywords Words used by search engines to help find and register sites.

keyword search A search for documents containing one or more words that are specified by a search engine user.

kill file An instruction used in a newsgroup by your newsreader to skip particular articles, according to criteria you specify.

LAN Local Area Network. A computer network that operates and is located in one specific location.

LDAP (Lightweight Directory Access Protocol) LDAP is a protocol for accessing online directory services. These directory services let you search their databases to find the names and e-mail addresses of people or businesses.

lifetime value The amount a customer spends over time with a supplier minus the cost of acquiring the customer.

link Text or graphic icons that move you to different Web pages or sites. Links are activated by clicking them with a mouse.

liquidity Volume of transactions.

list server Software that runs a mailing list.

local folder Folders that are stored on your computer. If you have a POP server account, any folders you create are local folders.

log on/off To access/leave the Internet.

lower level domain The main part of the domain name. For most e-business sites this is usually the company or brand name.

lurk To read messages in newsgroups or mailing list discussion groups, but not post anything yourself.

m-commerce Mobile commerce. E-commerce via mobile phones using WAP and other technologies.

mail server A remote computer (usually your ISP) enabling you to send and receive e-emails.

mailer daemon A Unix program used in the management of e-mail messages. Not generally encountered by a user unless the user gets a bounced message.

mailing list A collection of e-mail addresses of people who have asked to receive regular mail discussions on a particular topic, and for which they can sometimes submit messages for disbursement to the entire group.

mailing list manager An automated program to handle the administrative functions of adding/removing subscribers, disseminating the message postings, sending topic-related and help files etc for the entire mailing list. Example MLMs include Majordomo, Listserv, ListProc, Mailbase, etc.

Scott McNealy Chairman and CEO, Sun Microsystems. Played an instrumental role in the shaping of the Internet.

meta-tag The keyword and description commands used in your Web page code used to help search engines index your Web site.

micropayment Internet transactions for very small amounts.

microsegmentation The process of dividing an audience into very small identifiable segments.

moderator Someone in charge of a newsgroup, mailing lists, discussion group or similar forum. The moderator censors any unwelcome messages.

modulator/demodulator This is an internal or external piece of hardware plugged into your PC or Mac. It links into a phone socket, enabling computer-based information to be transmitted over a phone network.

multi-phased medium A medium, such as the Internet, that can be used in different means for different ends.

navigation The way a visitor travels around, or is directed around a Web site, via links.

Net Shorthand for Internet.

net-head Internet-obsessed individual.

netiquette The etiquette of the Internet. It is used mainly in the context of e-mail and newsgroup communication.

newbie Slang term for a new newsgroup member.

news reader Software enabling you to search, read, post and arrange newsgroup messages.

newsgroup Collectively referred to as the 'Usenet', newsgroups are online discussion areas centred on a subject of common interest. People post messages to the groups that all the other members can read. There are over 40,000 active newsgroups on the Internet covering topics as diverse as Social Welfare Reform and *South Park*.

niche A narrow but unified market or audience segment. The Internet is particularly suited to niche markets and audiences.

NNTP Network News Transport Protocol. In newsgroups NNTP is the method by which newsreader software communicates with news servers across the Internet.

offline Used to denote any activity or situation that does not involve being connected to the Internet.

one-to-one marketing Personalization of marketing programmes.

online The state of being connected via a modem to the Internet.

online catalogue Online catalogues simply collect the catalogue data of every supplier in a particular industry and place it on one central Web resource. B2B catalogue sites are sometimes referred to as procurement portals.

ontology A hierarchy of relationships.

operating system Software stored in a computer, which controls hardware components and the processes that run on them.

opt-in lists These are lists of people or businesses who have subscribed to receive adverts.

patch A piece of computer code used to update software applications or to remove or repair a bug.

pay-per-click Affiliate scheme based on click-through rates.

pay-per-lead Affiliate scheme based on number of leads.

pay-per-sale Affiliate scheme that pays commissions for actual sales generated by referrals.

PDF Portable Document Format. Created by Adobe.

permission marketing The concept of sending e-mail or marketing only to individuals who give their permission to receive the marketing messages.

phrase search A search for documents containing an exact sentence or phrase specified by a search engine user.

plain text Text that is encoded and contains no layout information, non-HTML text.

POP Post Office Protocol. The most common Internet standard for e-mail. Once POP is in use, all new incoming messages are downloaded from the server as soon as the e-mail account is accessed. All POP e-mails are stored on the server until the user removes them.

portal As in the real world, a portal on the Internet grants you access to other places.

post The act of sending an article to a newsgroup.

PPP Point to Point Protocol. One of the protocols that allows computers to connect to the Internet using a telephone line and a modem.

P2P Peer-to-peer. Referring to technology that allows Internet users to download compressed files from other users. Can also stand for 'path to profitability', which investors look for in new Internet start-ups.

precision The degree to which a search engine lists documents matching a query. The more matching documents that are listed, the higher the precision.

price transparency When both buyer and seller know pricing structures. Net markets eliminate arbitrage situations when only a broker knows the price. Net markets result in sellers making more money and buyers paying a lower price, since broker margins are reduced.

private folder Folders on an IMAP server whose contents can only be read by its creator or a selected group.

procurement hub A marketplace for routine purchases such as office supplies and travel services.

protocol The rules for information transferred over the Internet so that your computer will know what to do when it receives the information.

proxy server A program added to a network to provide one-way (outward) access to the Internet for users of the network. As well as providing Internet access for those within the Intranet, the Proxy Server creates a firewall to prevent external users (in other words, the Internet population at large) from accessing the private network.

pull technology The Internet is essentially a 'pull' technology. This means that users seek out, then pull information towards them, rather than having it pushed in their way. Understanding the 'pull' nature of the Internet is often considered to be one of the key factors in determining a Web site's success.

pure brands E-brands are often referred to as pure brands because they are unburdened by real world constraints (such as their geographic location).

push technology Interactive medium that pushes facts to the user, such as outbound e-mail.

RAM Random Access Memory. RAM is a computer's temporary working storage area. More RAM means faster performance, and increased productivity.

rank A search engine position.

real world Everything outside the Internet.

recall Related to precision, this is the degree to which a search engine returns all the matching documents in a collection.

refresh The act of reloading a Web site page or site.

relationship marketing Marketing that is intended to build an ongoing relationship over time.

RFP Request for Proposals. Invitation to suppliers to bid on supplying products or services.

RFQ Request for Quotation. Invitation to suppliers to bid on supplying easily described products or services.

rich media Media that incorporate multimedia, sound, motion, interactivity or e-commerce.

robot A tool used by search engines to find and examine Web sites.

ROS (run of site) Refers to displaying a banner ad throughout a Web site or a banner network with no targeting by keyword or site category.

ROT13 Rotate 13. A method of scrambling the contents of a message. Each letter in a word is rotated alphabetically 13 letters to the right.

scalability The ability of a Web site to grow to support thousands of users without sacrificing performance or losing the ability to display and still execute transactions.

search engine A site that enables you to conduct a keyword search of indexed information on its database. Also refers to the software used in this process.

secure server Hardware and software that secures e-commerce credit card transactions so there is no risk of people gaining access to credit card details online.

segmentation The process of dividing an audience into identifiable segments.

signature (file) Information appended to the end of a message that identifies the sender's details. You only need to write a signature file once and you can then attach it to your e-mails as often as you like.

signature line A set of four to eight lines of text placed at the end of a mail message to provide the reader with the author's contact information, favourite quote, special of the month, autoresponder/ Web site address, etc. The signature line is composed and placed into the e-mail software's signature file for automatic appending.

SMTP Simple Mail Transfer Protocol. An e-mail protocol used to help pass messages along their route. SMTP is understood both by the e-mail software you use and the server computers each e-mail message passes through on its way to the recipient's computer.

snail mail Net-head term for the 'real world' postal service.

snooze news Company 'news' that will not interest journalists or editors.

spam Junk mail on the Internet, normally in the form of unsolicited and unwelcome e-mail messages. The term is used most frequently in the context of newsgroups, referring to the same article being posted repeatedly to different newsgroups. The term is a reference to the famous Monty Python 'spam, spam, spam' sketch where spam is served with everything.

spider A type of search engine 'robot'.

sponsorship A sponsorship is when an advertiser pays to sponsor content, usually a section of a Web site or an e-mail newsletter.

SSL Secure Sockets Layer. The main type of secure server used to take orders online and to transfer sensitive information.

stemming The ability of a search to include the 'stem' of words.

stickiness Sticky sites use techniques to get visitors to stay.

superstitial A variant of an interstitial. Superstitials are interstitials that only play once a Web page has been completely downloaded. Superstitials tend to be larger than interstitials (taking over the full screen) and have higher production values. The reason for this is that they need to be so attractive that the user will wait before clicking off the superstitial to see the already downloaded Web page behind. Due to their use of audio and video, they tend to be expensive to produce.

supply chain A network of facilities and distribution options that performs the procurement of materials, transformation of materials into intermediate and finished products, and the distribution of finished products to customers.

system administrator Someone responsible for the management of an e-mail system.

sysop Systems operator. See *moderator*.

TCP Transmission Control Protocol enables computers linked to the Intranet to connect and communicate with each other.

thread An ongoing newsgroup topic.

toolbar The row of buttons on the top of each window in your e-mail software program that you can click to perform common tasks.

top level domain The concluding part of a domain name, such as the .com or .co.uk suffixes.

traffic The number of people visiting your site.

trolling The act of posting a newsgroup article with the deliberate intent of provoking a heated or 'flamed' response.

UCE Unsolicited Commercial E-mail. See *spam*.

upload To send a file to a network.

URL Uniform Resource Locator. A full Web address, for example: http//www.yac.com

usenet The system that distributes newsgroups. Also the collective term for newsgroups.

VAN Value Added Network.

VAR Value Added Reseller.

vertical markets Vertical e-markets are Web sites where buyers and sellers can come together to communicate, share ideas, advertise, bid in auctions, conduct transactions, and coordinate inventory and fulfilment.

viral marketing Viral marketing refers to word of mouth publicity on the Internet.

virtual event An event that occurs online.

virus A piece of computer code written to damage systems.

visitors The people who come to your Web site.

VPN Virtual Private Network allows an organization to extend its network service to branch offices and remote users, creating a wide area network (WAN).

WAN Wide Area Network is a company located in various geographical areas connected electronically into an Intranet.

WAP Wireless Application Protocol. The mobile equivalent of HTML.

Webmaster Someone in charge of a Web site.

Web page A single document stored at a Web site. A single Web browser window displays a single Web page at a time.

Web ring Collections or communities of different Web sites and pages.

Web site A collection of Web pages.

word wrap function This function enables you to set column widths to a certain size.

World Wide Web The World Wide Web does not mean the Internet. The World Wide Web is, in fact, a software system running across the Internet. It consists of (literally) billions of Web pages, usually containing text, images and HTML links.

Yahoo! The world's most popular search engine.

XML Extensible Mark-up Language.

appendix 3

Recommended reading

Aldrich D (2000) *Mastering the Digital Marketplace: Practical Strategies for Competitiveness in the New Economy,* John Wiley

Armstrong S (2001) *Advertising on the Internet,* Kogan Page

Berners Lee T (2000) *Weaving the Web: the Past, Present and Future of the World Wide Web by its Inventor,* Texere

Bloor R (2000) *The Electronic Bazaar,* Nicholas Brealey

Cunningham, M J (2000) *B2B: How to build a profitable e-commerce strategy,* FT.com

Cunningham M J (2001) *Smart Things to Know about E-commerce,* Capstone

Davis J (2000) *Guide to Web Marketing,* Kogan Page

Downes L and Mui C (1998) *Unleashing the Killer App: Digital Strategies for Market Dominance,* Harvard Business School Press

Easton J (1999) *Striking it Rich.com,* McGraw-Hill

Fischer J G (2001) *E-Business for the Small Business,* Kogan Page

Gladwell M (2000) *The Tipping Point,* Little, Brown and Company

Godin S (1999) *Permission Marketing,* Simon and Schuster

Hagel J and Armstrong A G (1997) *Net Gain,* Harvard Business School Press

Hagel J and Singer M (1999) *Net Worth,* Harvard Business School Press

Hamel G (2000) *Leading the Revolution,* Harvard Business School Press

Hartman A, Sifonis J and Kador J, *Net Ready,* McGraw-Hill

Haylock C F and Muscarella L (1999) *NetSuccess: 24 Leaders on Web Commerce Show You How to Put the Web to Work For Your Business,* Adams Media Corporation

Jensen B (2000) *Simplicity,* Harper Collins

Judson B and Kelly K (2000) *Hyperwars: Eleven Essential Strategies for Survival and Profit in the Era of Online Business,* Touchstone Books

Kalakota R and Robinson M (2000) *e-Business – Roadmap for Success,* Addison Wesley

Kim A J (2000) *Community Building on the Web,* Peachpit Press

Kosiur D R (1997) *Understanding Electronic Commerce,* Microsoft Press

Lindstrom M and Andersen T F (2001) *Brand Building on the Internet,* Kogan Page

Lindstrom M (2001) *Click, Brick and Brands,* Kogan Page

Locke C, Levine R *et al* (2000), *The Cluetrain Manifesto,* Financial Times – Prentice Hall

Lynch D C and Lundquist L (1996) *Digital Money: The New Era of Internet Commerce,* John Wiley and Sons

Meyer C and Davis S (1998) *Blur: The Speed of Change in the Connected Economy,* Capstone

Peppers D and Rogers M (1997) *Enterprise One to One: Tools for Competing in the Interactive Age,* Currency

Reichheld F F (1996) *The Loyalty Effect: The Hidden Force Behind Growth, Profits and Lasting Value,* Harvard Business School Press

Ridderstrale J and Nordstrom K (2000) *Funky Business,* Financial Times – Prentice Hall

Rosen E (2000) *The Anatomy of Buzz,* HarperCollins

Siebel T (1999) *Cyber Rules: Strategies for Excelling at E-Business,* Doubleday

Siegel D (1999) *Futurize your Enterprise,* John Wiley and Sons

Schwartz E (1999) *Digital Darwinism,* Penguin

Timmers P (1999) *Electronic Commerce – Strategies and Models for Business to Business Trading,* John Wiley and Sons

Treleaven P (2000) *E-business Start-up Guide,* Kogan Page

Index